THE WOMAN'S PAGE:
JOURNALISM AND RHETORIC IN EARLY CANADA

In the late nineteenth and early twentieth centuries, journalism, politics, and social advocacy were largely male preserves. Six women, however, did manage to come to prominence through their writing and public performance: Agnes Maule Machar, Sara Jeannette Duncan, E. Pauline Johnson, Kathleen Blake Coleman, Flora MacDonald Denison, and Nellie L. McClung. *The Woman's Page* is a detailed study of these six women and their respective works.

Focusing on the diverse sources of their rhetorical power, Janice Fiamengo assesses how popular poetry, journalism, essays, and public speeches enabled these women to play major roles in the central debates of their day. A few of their names, particularly those of McClung and Johnson, are still well known today, although studies of their writings and speeches are limited. Others are almost entirely unknown, an unfortunate fact given the wit, intelligence, and passion of their writing and self-presentation. Seeking to return their words to public attention, *The Woman's Page* demonstrates how these women influenced readers and listeners regarding their society's most controversial issues.

JANICE FIAMENGO is an associate professor in the Department of English at the University of Ottawa.

JANICE FIAMENGO

The Woman's Page

Journalism and Rhetoric in Early Canada

UNIVERSITY OF TORONTO PRESS
Toronto Buffalo London

© University of Toronto Press Incorporated 2008
   Toronto Buffalo London
   www.utppublishing.com
   Printed in Canada

   978-0-8020-9782-8 (cloth)
   978-0-8020-9537-4 (paper)

   Printed on acid-free paper

Library and Archives Canada Cataloguing in Publication

Fiamengo, Janice Anne, 1964–
   The woman's page : journalism and rhetoric in early Canada / Janice Fiamengo.

   Includes bibliographical references and index.
   ISBN 978-0-8020-9782-8 (bound) ISBN 978-0-8020-9537-4 (pbk.)

   1. Women in journalism – Canada – History – 19th century. 2. Women in journalism – Canada – History – 20th century. 3. Women journalists – Canada –
   History. I. Title.

   PN4914.W58F43 2008   070'.0820971   C2008-901259-3

University of Toronto Press acknowledges the financial assistance to its
publishing program of the Canada Council for the Arts and the Ontario
Arts Council.

This book has been published with the help of a grant from the Canadian
Federation for the Humanities and Social Sciences, through the Aid to
Scholarly Publications Programme, using funds provided by the Social
Sciences and Humanities Research Council of Canada.

University of Toronto Press acknowledges the financial support for its
publishing activities of the Government of Canada through the Book
Publishing Industry Development Program (BPIDP).

For my parents, Vince and Helen Fiamengo

Contents

Acknowledgments

This book has been a long time coming and has accrued many more debts than I can name here. First and foremost, it would never have been written without the untiring encouragement and advice of my former supervisor at the University of British Columbia, Eva-Marie Kröller. From the days of struggle with my doctoral dissertation well over a decade ago through perennial small crises of confidence and energy since then, she has always been a superb mentor and friend. I have also benefited greatly from the ideas and intellectual energy of teachers and colleagues past and present who have read my work and shared theirs with me, including Susanna Egan and Laurie Ricou at UBC; Carole Gerson at Simon Fraser University; Paul Denham, Susan Gingell, Dianne Hallman, Peggy Martin, Carol Morrell, and Gail Osachoff at the University of Saskatchewan; and Tom Allen, Ian Dennis, Peggy Kelly, Seymour Mayne, Anne Raine, Robert Stacey, and Cynthia Sugars at the University of Ottawa. Their intellectual companionship has been a great boon and comfort. Special thanks for warm friendship, mental enrichment, and much laughter are due to Francis Zichy and Gerald Lynch, wonderful friends whose wise criticisms and wit are a blessing. The infectious high spirits and love of literature of my aunt, Marya Hardman, have had a profound impact on me. And no one has listened to my complaints more patiently or read my work so thoroughly and generously as Lisa Vargo, to whom I owe a special debt of gratitude (KBO!!!). I am also very thankful for the prayers, witness, good conversation, and firm confidence of Hannah Chukwu.

I first saw this project whole at the 'ReCalling Early Canada' conference and workshop at McMaster University in June 2003, a generative gathering of scholars made possible by the selflessness and vision of

Daniel Coleman and co-organized by Jennifer Blair, Kate Higginson, and Lorraine York. I thank them for putting together such a wonderful conference. The roots of the project go back almost a decade earlier, when I met for two years with my writing group partners Noel Currie, Gabriele Helms, and Joel Martineau, whose collegiality and enthusiasm were unparalleled. It is a deep sadness that our great friend Gabi, who so supported and stimulated us all, is not alive to receive my thanks. Warm thanks are also due to Jenny Lawn, Liz McCausland, and Peter Wilkins for many wonderful evenings of good talk and constructive criticism.

Many individuals have provided practical aid, material assistance, and useful advice over the life of this project. In particular, I would like to thank my research assistants: Tom Hodd, for patient work photo-copying the journalism of Sara Jeannette Duncan, as well as for many rewarding conversations; Kathleen Patchell, for her meticulous check-ing of quotations from Kit Coleman's columns and for tracking down the images in this volume; and Tobi Kozakewich for her extremely help-ful and astute proofreading of the manuscript. Siobhan McMenemy, my editor at the University of Toronto Press, shepherded me through the process in a very professional manner and provided excellent advice and useful queries. Janet Shorten and Elizabeth Hulse helped me pre-pare the manuscript for publication. I am also very grateful to the two anonymous readers for their suggestions and corrections. All of the er-rors that remain are, of course, entirely my responsibility.

Research for the book has been supported by a Standard Research Grant from the Social Sciences and Humanities Research Council of Canada. David Rampton, chair of the Department of English at the University of Ottawa, made coming to work a pleasure and helped me to believe in this project.

And finally, I thank Clare Hauer, who knows how crucial she was and is.

THE WOMAN'S PAGE:
JOURNALISM AND RHETORIC IN EARLY CANADA

Introduction:
Strong Statement, Trenchant Ideas, Promising Plans

In 1879 Agnes Maule Machar (1837–1927) published 'The New Ideal of Womanhood' in *Rose-Belford's Canadian Monthly and National Review,* Canada's most prestigious cultural periodical. Part of a series by the author on the changing status of women, the article claimed for them a significantly expanded public role. Where once a woman's duties and responsibilities were severely limited, Machar argued, she was now conceded 'a right to her share in the world's work, whether in what has been rightly considered her more especial sphere, or in any other for which she is fitted.'[1] As so often in Machar, alongside the acknowledgment of women's 'especial sphere' is a far-reaching claim on the world. She dismissed neither women's particular duties as wives and mothers (though, as an unmarried woman, she regarded such duties at a respectful distance) nor the feminine qualities that made the home their special place. But her stress on a woman's 'right to her share in the world's work' is a forthright, even rather aggressively phrased, claim to a larger life at a time when women were barred from most Canadian universities, as well as from the professions of medicine, politics, and law, and would not achieve the federal right to vote for nearly forty years.

Machar went further in the essay to indict those who linked work and higher learning with unwomanliness. Addressing the social prejudice against female doctors, she denounced the decadence of a society that not only encouraged complicity in wrong but also persecuted right endeavour:

> It is worthy, indeed, of an age which never stigmatised as 'unwomanly' the presence of ladies at the slaughters of innocent animals, termed *battues,*

or their adorning themselves in the plumage of beautiful birds, sacrificed
by thousands to gratify an idle vanity and a barbarous taste, or their wearing tissues and flowers, the dyes of which are a slow poison to the women
who make, and even occasionally to the women who wear them; but
reserved the misplaced stigma for the noble women, who, obeying the
God-given impulse within them, have sought to qualify themselves, by a
laborious training, for fighting disease and death, and alleviating the
physical miseries of their own sex![2]

In contrasting unjust condemnation with dangerous laxity, as well as
frivolous complicity with high-minded commitment, and in insisting
on the relationship between seemingly trivial indulgence and larger
systems of abuse and degradation, the passage is characteristic of
Machar's rhetoric: impassioned, rigorously logical, full of moral conviction, and designed to change minds. The reference to a woman's
'God-given impulse' is no mere flourish for Machar, a committed
Christian for whom personal fulfilment and duty to God were inseparable. Always interested in the relationship between individual conduct and social structures – and moved throughout her life by the
innocent suffering of poor women and animals – she here emphasizes
how seemingly neutral consumer choices, such as the wearing of birds'
feathers or pretty fabrics, were embedded in systems of exploitation. A
society that encouraged such exploitation while scorning the women
who sought to better themselves and their sex had, in her opinion, lost
its moral foundation.

Machar's arguments reflected her awareness of debates in the
United States and Britain about women's rights and social justice, and
her analysis was not unprecedented in Canada, where Emily Howard
Stowe had recently formed the Toronto Women's Literary Club to discuss suffrage and other reforms. I begin with Machar's words because
they are in many respects exemplary of the intellectual ferment, quest-
ing spirit, rhetorical assertiveness, and moral confidence that marked
women's reformist writing in the last two decades of the nineteenth
century and the first two decades of the twentieth, when a significant
number of Canadian women began to speak publicly on questions
affecting the nation. Machar's article launched a sweeping criticism of
her conservative Victorian society; it was a rather bold undertaking for
a forty-two-year-old spinster, daughter of a Presbyterian clergyman in a
well-connected Kingston family, who, according to contemporary commentator Ethelwyn Wetherald, had 'so strong a distaste for everything

approaching publicity'[3] that she for a time cloaked her identity as a writer in a variety of pseudonyms. Yet trenchant criticism and probing analysis were typical of the many articles Machar published in *Rose-Belford's Canadian Monthly* and the other major periodicals of her day. These publications included insightful review essays, reflections on contemporary social issues, and learned analyses of current theological controversies. Willing to enter debate in print on the most serious subjects of the day, including the prohibition of alcohol, the Labour Question, and the relationship between religion and morality, she earned a name for herself as a formidable social critic and intellectual. How was it that the rather quaint, mild, and retiring woman her contemporaries described came to write with such conceptual reach and vigour? By what rhetorical means did she claim her right to speak on such a range of public issues?

Looking specifically at their 'arts of language,'[4] this study explores answers to these questions about Machar and five other Canadian women who made a name for themselves through writing and public speech at a time when their chosen spheres of journalism, politics, and social advocacy were largely – though by no means exclusively – male preserves. Machar, Sara Jeannette Duncan (1861–1922), Pauline Johnson (1861–1913), Kathleen Blake Coleman (1856–1915), Flora MacDonald Denison (1867–1921), and Nellie L. McClung (1873–1951) were well-known public figures whose pungent analyses of their society found a ready audience. Over the course of their careers, each of them gained the respect and willing assent of a significant portion of her readers and listeners, and each is important to an understanding of the strategies of self-presentation claimed by writing women in the period 1875–1915. Relying loosely on rhetorical theory to understand how speakers and writers use language for persuasive ends, I focus on their creation of credibility or ethos as well as their techniques of argument, patterns of arrangement, and use of tropes such as metaphor, personification, and irony to intervene in social debates.

Each of these women, working in different media and to different ends, established a significant public – in many cases, international – presence. Machar was for at least three decades one of the most respected advocates of social reform in the country, an essayist so widely admired that her work was sought by Goldwin Smith, pre-eminent man of letters, when he founded *The Week* in the1880s.[5] There and in other journals of public opinion, hers was often the lone female voice and was accorded serious consideration by such adversaries as W.D.

LeSueur, well-known Canadian rationalist and sceptic. The much younger Sara Jeannette Duncan, best known today for her novel *The Imperialist* (1904), was a precocious young journalist in the 1880s, the first woman to work full-time in a Canadian newspaper office, that of the *Globe*, after holding the position of literary editor of the *Washington Post*; a contemporary critic, Thomas O'Hagan, called her 'one of the cleverest women Canada has yet produced,' a writer who 'flashed across the literary sky of her native land with a splendour almost dazzling in its brightness and strength,'[6] and according to Marjory Lang, she was so widely known for her witty newspaper work that other journalists reported on her activities.[7] Pauline Johnson was a celebrated poet and by far the most famous travelling performer and recitalist of her day, considered a 'great personage' by a young Nellie McClung, who wrote in her autobiography *The Stream Runs Fast* (1945) about putting on 'white gloves and polished shoes'[8] to meet the Mohawk poet when she toured McClung's home town of Manitou, Manitoba. Johnson not only travelled across Canada but made two much-publicized journeys to England and several trips to the United States. An American interviewer wrote in an article for the Vancouver *World* in 1908, 'There are surely few more interesting women in Canada with whom to spend an hour than Tekahionwake.'[9]

Both Kathleen Coleman ('Kit' of the *Mail*) and Flora MacDonald Denison were widely read columnists who wrote for mass-circulation Toronto newspapers; Coleman was famous, through syndication, across Canada and in the United States for her witty narratives and advice to the lovelorn; and Denison, perhaps Canada's most radical feminist, propagandized on behalf of woman suffrage in the Toronto Sunday *World* and defended the English militants, led by Emmeline Pankhurst, at a time when their tactics of public confrontation were considered extreme and unwomanly by most Canadians. Each was employed by a popular paper seeking to attract a large female audience. As for McClung, she became a celebrity during the Manitoba election campaign of 1914, when she was credited with bringing the provincial Conservative government to its knees, and her collection of essays *In Times Like These* (1915) has been called 'the best feminist writing Canada has yet produced.'[10] During her years in the suffrage movement after 1914, McClung toured the western Canadian provinces, Ontario, and significant portions of the United States.

Considering the widespread appeal of these six authors, I am concerned with basic questions about their sense of purpose, relationship to their audience, and self-presentation. What did it signify, for each of these women, to speak as a woman in the public arena? By what rhetorical means did they claim audience attention and authorize their public interventions? What kinds of self-image did they project, and how did they use the tools of logic, metaphor, and emotionally charged language for persuasive ends? Looking carefully at their argumentative strategies, sentimental appeals, and overtures to readers or listeners, I explore how each of them created a public voice.

My interest in such questions was first provoked by discussion, some years ago, of the significance of language around the turn of the century in Canada – part of the linguistic turn in historical scholarship that affected how historians worked and conceived of their discipline in the 1980s. Mariana Valverde's *The Age of Light, Soap, and Water: Moral Reform in English Canada, 1885–1925* (1991) was one of the first sustained examinations by a Canadian social historian of the centrality of language in late nineteenth-century and early twentieth-century reform movements, and it continues to be widely cited. Relying on the Foucauldian idea of discourse as a specialized sub-language – terms, images, associations, and metaphors – that defines its subject in particular ways, Valverde proposed that what historians often dismissed as 'the flowery rhetoric of the time'[11] is deserving of careful consideration for the clues it provides about key assumptions, patterns of thought, and social relations. Analysing pamphlets and records of meetings of the National Council of Women, the Salvation Army, the Woman's Christian Temperance Union (WCTU), and a host of other reform organizations dedicated to cleaning up Canada's cities and purifying national life, she argues that reformers' language worked through compelling imagery and allegorical correspondence to shape the subjects under discussion. As she explains, such discourse was important not so much for the precise content it conveyed as for the way it produced, 'through inspiring imagery, the right type of consciousness,'[12] a consciousness inclined to recognize the struggle for spiritual salvation in mundane experiences and to invest certain people with moral authority, while viewing (racial and lower-class) others as inherently more vulnerable to depravity.

Valverde's specific examples – Niagara Falls as an allegory of souls plunging to perdition, dishwashing as a metaphor for spiritual purification – are illuminating, and the material she amassed from the archives of various evangelical and philanthropic organizations is fascinating. I have always hoped that further investigation into such material would be conducted, perhaps from a perspective more sympathetic to the Christian beliefs and world views that were so important to many of those involved. Particularly noteworthy, for my purposes, is Valverde's insistence that the language she examines was transparent to the speakers and hearers of the discourse, 'invisible precisely because it was familiar.'[13] By 'familiar,' she means not only that the patterns of language were widespread and generally accepted as true but also that they conformed to the structural relations of turn-of-the-century Anglo-Canadian and Protestant society; language and lived reality were, in other words, one. Putting aside the question of whether evangelical Protestantism was really the dominant and coherent structure of beliefs that Valverde seems to assume it was for all her reformers – and even putting aside whether any particular structure of beliefs could attain such an unchallenged and uniform status – her assessment is provocative for positing a perfect correspondence between metaphor and experience and a sublime unconsciousness of language use on the part of her speakers and listeners. As she explains it, 'the excessive metaphors we are about to dissect were neither rhetorical flourishes nor stumbling blocks in rational arguments, but were rather, to the audience, the *inconspicuous vehicles* in which truths about moral and social reform were conveyed to the public.'[14]

Valverde says no more about this aspect of her study's theoretical underpinnings, and the later chapters are more concerned with reform campaigns and various social concerns such as the white slavery panic and immigrant slums than with the question of language use per se. Perhaps the brevity with which she dispatches the subject speaks to its status as a conceptual given in her discipline at the time; or, conversely, perhaps it indicates its lack of clarity as an accepted but counter-intuitive theoretical position, the full implications of which are difficult to work out in practice. She never makes clear whether the writers or speakers who formulated a particular text were passive receivers of discourse to the same extent that their listeners and hearers were, though her statements suggest that they too accepted the discourse as truth. Her comments raised for me a provocative question about the extent to which activists and persuasive writers of the turn-of-the-century period were conscious of the linguistic horizons within which they operated. More recently, Valverde's argument has been taken up and extended by Jennifer Henderson in *Settler Feminism and Race Making in Canada* (2003), which argues that women writers of the period claimed authoritative speech by adopting a discourse that subjected them to its norms and constraints; they could speak only as the discourse of femininity allowed them,[15] and therefore their assumption of agency was always an unconscious acceptance of limitation that went to the very core of their identities as women.

I have mulled over this idea, which is also a key concept in Misao Dean's *Practising Femininity* (1998), for some time, considering its implications for the journalists, essayists, and performers I was reading. Were these witty, ironical, and astute women so entirely constrained by their discourse; were their arguments, world view, and self-construction so thoroughly shaped by it? A very different conception of the relationship between identity and language can be found in Ernest Forbes's 'The Ideas of Carol Bacchi and the Suffragists of Halifax.'[16] First published in 1985, the essay responds at some length to Bacchi's *Liberation Deferred? The Ideas of the English-Canadian Suffragists* (1983), considering her arguments in light of Halifax suffrage activity of the 1890s. Bacchi had been one of the first historians to question, rather than uncritically chronicle, the achievements of turn-of-the-century suffragists, paving the way for other revisionists such as Valverde, and Forbes takes her to task for her conclusions about suffrage language and arguments. Bacchi is critical of suffragists for, as her title suggests, failing to fully liberate themselves or launch a thoroughgoing challenge to traditional gender roles. Most of the suffragists, she argues, were part of a conservative elite determined to defend their social position. Alarmed by fundamental changes in Canadian society such as working-class resistance to industrialization and opportunities for sexual freedom in the city, middle-class suffrage women sought the vote to bring about favoured reforms, including the prohibition of alcohol (a cause that, for Bacchi, clearly bespoke their repressive moralism) and legislation regarding sexual conduct. Perhaps most damningly, they did not argue for gender equality, instead accepting and even reasserting the traditional associations between women, domesticity, and mothering. As Forbes summarizes Bacchi, 'by accepting and stressing the terminology of a separate "maternal" sphere for women and at most a "housekeeping" role in society, the social reformers undercut feminists who sought occupational and domestic equality.'[17]

Once again, 'terminology' is at issue, and here, as well as on other grounds, Forbes challenges Bacchi's conclusions. The fact that women relied on maternal language stressing women's natural affiliation with motherhood was not, he asserts, evidence that they believed such affiliation to be inevitable and unalterable. Rather, it indicated their justifiable political caution and savvy. Forbes points out that 'successful women leaders of necessity became experts at dissimulation and deference in a male-dominated society.'[18] He chronicles a number of legislative defeats for the suffragists in the 1890s and the resulting softening of their rhetoric; he notes, for example, that at a WCTU meeting in 1897, with nearly two decades of unsuccessful campaigning behind them, one of the suffrage leaders 'suggested that, since "women's rights" had been so criticized, they should talk more of the "rights of children."' Such talk, he argues, was not evidence of waning conviction, as one might conclude from reading only the public statements of suffragists, but 'a pragmatic shift of emphasis to goals which enjoyed some hope of achievement in the near future.'[19] Forbes goes further to note how the discourse of maternalism was used to reassure and even deceive opponents: 'Whenever possible the leaders avoided taking a confrontationist stance on feminist issues. For that purpose the maternalistic philosophy was very useful.'[20] Stressing usefulness and a tactical response to opposition, he argues that women's rhetoric in the public sphere was sophisticated and strategic, rather than unconscious and debilitating.

Underlining Forbes's and Valverde's arguments are two different understandings of the relationship between speaking subjects and their language. Forbes's is the more old-fashioned, humanist view; he understands the speaking subject as an autonomous and coherent agent of discourse, controlling and shaping language to her a priori ends; Valverde's position is closer to the post-structuralist view of the subject of discourse as one 'subjected' to and by it, formed by discourse rather than the other way around. In Forbes's understanding, suffragists used language cannily and strategically, manipulating the language available to them for persuasive purposes. In Valverde's account, subjectivity does not pre-exist discourse but is created in and through it; the suffragists' rhetorical position was itself determined by the language and ideology of their day. In the years since these two scholars articulated their opposing positions, Valverde's account has had the greater influence on the disciplines of feminist social history and literary criticism in Canada.

My own position on the issue is somewhere between these two, and the complex relationship between women writers and their chosen language is my primary subject in the chapters that follow. I recognize that speaking subjects are not entirely in control or aware of the operations of language; always there are taken-for-granted assumptions and associations dictated by the discourse within which we are formed as subjects. At the same time, however, it is difficult to see individuals as entirely subject to discourse, given the evidence of variety, recognizable contradictions, fundamental disagreements, and degrees of discursive self-consciousness exhibited by speakers and writers in any particular period. Not all thinkers use language in the same way or make the same assumptions and associations even within the same discourse. The operation of ironic and parodic modes, in particular, contradicts Valverde's assertion about the transparency of discourse and suggests that, in analysing the rhetoric of historical subjects, one needs to be careful neither to impose a false uniformity nor to underestimate speakers' and writers' sophistication and agility.

I was first struck by the difficulty of generalizing about such matters when reading the journalism of Sara Jeannette Duncan, a writer always intensely aware of language use, inclined to techniques of ironic distancing and parodic playfulness, with a preference for deliberately tangled metaphors, hyperbole, coy understatement, and mocking questions. She liked to ridicule stale or overblown patterns of speech and habits of association, even her own, and she very much disliked the rhetorically saccharine, ponderous, or predictable; certainly, it is difficult to imagine Duncan as the sort for whom metaphors could be 'the inconspicuous vehicles in which truths about moral and social reform were conveyed.'[21] I have written elsewhere about her ambivalent and often aggressive relationship to the rhetoric of feminism, a relationship characterized by a critical sensitivity to the standard metaphors and modes of address employed by her feminist contemporaries. As the following irritated comment in the *Globe* about women's habits of speech suggests, Duncan was, though a suffrage supporter and New Woman, far from a passive receiver of feminist truths:

I do not attend a suffrage convention for the exercise of my emotions, and I confess I should like to go to a temperance meeting without running the risk of being called a 'dear sister.' Upon sober reflection, you know, nobody wants to adopt the sisterly relation to a lot of damp females of possibly questionable orthodoxy and unreceipted millinery bills. And when you sit in your place and wait for strong statement or trenchant ideas or promising plans, and Mrs. A. opens the deliberations by asserting with tears in her eyes that she is convinced this is a good work and ordered of the Lord, you feel she has not speeded it towards its consummation, and when Mrs. B. continues them by affectionately stating that her heart went out to Mrs. A., whom she never saw before, what can you do but wish it would stay out, and shut the door.[22]

There is much to be said about this audacious and rather cruel passage, in which Duncan's virtuoso satirical skills and supreme sense of entitlement are vividly displayed; most important to my argument is that the passage demonstrates, *pace* Valverde, that the evangelical rhetoric of suffrage and temperance sisterhood – the tears, evocations of divine mission, maternal and sisterly diction, privileging of feminine intimacy – was a rhetoric far from invisible to an observer such as Duncan (it had its own dress code, tone of voice, and gestures as well, which she observed when she covered the Washington suffrage congress in 1886). She herself used the rhetoric on occasion (though cautiously, wary of sentimentalism), supported the goals of the women's movement, and continued to attend women's conventions and meetings; but she also stood outside the discourse and attended to its clichés with ironic wit. The passage suggests that the rhetoric of temperance sisterhood was a strategic discourse – a way of defining feminine subjectivity and organizing social relations – that could be assumed or questioned, more or less transparent as its context determined. One could don a feminist identity by consciously taking on its language and postures. This is not to say that Duncan or anyone else was perfectly free to assume any identity she wished – far from it. But neither was her identity predetermined.

Duncan's contemporary and rival Pauline Johnson, who recited her poems in Native garb, was also acutely aware of how identity was produced through representation, and she was perhaps more conscious than Duncan of the limited choices available to her and even more determined to resist, mimic, and strategically deploy a range of positions and poses. Such awareness is evident in 'A Strong Race Opinion,' a perceptive piece of literary criticism she wrote for the Toronto *Globe* in May 1892, the same year in which she launched her decade-and-a-half-long career as a stage recitalist. Perhaps emboldened by her new authority as a performer, Johnson satirized the composite 'Indian girl' created by non-Native writers, a stock character lacking individuality or tribal specificity and possessed of a propensity for unrequited love for a white man and an early death through suicide or self-sacrifice. Johnson's tone throughout the article is perfectly controlled, her comical weariness with predictable novelistic productions sweetening a serious condemnation of authorial ignorance. Referring to the practice by North American authors of recreating the same 'regulation Indian maiden' in every work of fiction, a maiden who 'never had a prototype in breathing flesh and blood existence!'[23] Johnson comments on the effect on the reader: 'After a half dozen writers have done this, the reader might as well leave the tale unread as far as the interest touches upon the Indian character, for an unvarying experience tells him that this convenient personage will repeat herself with monotonous accuracy. He knows what she did and how she died in other romances by other romancers, and she will do and die likewise in his (she always does die, and one feels relieved that it is so, for she is too unhealthy and too unnatural to live).'[24] The delicious alliteration and parallelism of Johnson's phrasing enact, in comic form, the exact repetition of fictional character that she finds so irritating, and they establish her weary superiority to such superficial novelistic devices. A present-day reader immersed in theories of gender as a repetitive performance might also see a deliberate invitation to read Johnson's own theatrical and highly self-conscious performances of identity as repetitions that undo by overdoing.

In the article, Johnson goes on to survey the literary productions of a number of well-known North American writers, including Helen Hunt Jackson, John Richardson, and G. Mercer Adam and Ethelwyn Wetherald, demonstrating how their fictional creations conform to type and fail of reality. Her observations range from the delightfully absurd – as when she notes the sameness of the heroines' names, which always have 'a "Winona" sound,' even if they are not actually Winona[25] – to the seriously deficient – as when she points out writers' tendency to create an animal-like character who 'grubs in the mud like a turtle, climbs trees like a raccoon, and tears and soils her gowns like a madwoman.'[26] In her brilliant and funny tour de force, Johnson reveals the errors of fact and failures of imaginative empathy of a host of acclaimed writers.

Her most scathing and politically charged criticism comes at the end of the essay. The real problem with Indian maidens in modern fiction is not simply that 'they are all fawn-eyed, unnatural, unmaidenly idiots ... merely imaginary make-shifts to help out romances that would be immeasurably improved by their absence,' but that their characters and plot function serve a particular ideological purpose: the confirmation of Native inferiority. Johnson effectively suggests such a conclusion through a number of rhetorical questions: 'And here follows the thought,' she asks near the end of her catalogue of authorial folly, 'do authors who write Indian romances love the nation they endeavour successfully or unsuccessfully to describe?'[27] She follows this question with an even more pointed linking of narrative design and colonial imperative: 'Surely the Redman has lost enough, has suffered enough without additional losses and sorrows being heaped upon him in romances.'[28] Recognizing that stories are never merely fictions but carry ideological import, Johnson saw that the stakes of textual representation were high indeed and that racialized portrayals bore a significant relationship to colonial realities. In her own writing and performance, she sought to widen the narrative possibilities available to Native women and to change the images and patterns that shaped Native/ non-Native relations in the country. Using humour and romantic stereotypes to appeal to her audience, she also challenged them with angry demands, strategic reversals, and pointed analyses, asking them to confront the realities of Native dispossession as well as their own stereotypes, assumptions, and blind spots. Her assessment of the social and political significance of representation was astute.

The wry and satirical analyses of Johnson and Duncan indicate their consciousness, as platform performer and celebrity journalist respectively, of identity as a style of address and a series of rhetorical postures to be exploited in public discourse. They were not the only women in the public eye conscious of constructing a persona from a variety of available markers of identity. As Marjory Lang has persuasively demonstrated in *Women Who Made the News* (1999), the first generation of female journalists established their careers by creating a public personality with whom their readers could identify – someone fascinating but familiar, exotic yet knowable. Hired to appeal to a female audience and to establish a new kind of 'soft' journalism with a focus on personal issues, relationships, family, and community, Lang has argued, these writers 'won their renown by creating literary personae who attracted enormous followings.'[29] Kit Coleman, for example, often teased readers about the limits to the self she allowed them to know and warned them that meeting her in the flesh, as many requested, was bound to be a disappointment; and Flora MacDonald Denison once informed a reader that her greatest interest was spiritualism, which had to be kept out of her suffrage column because it did not fit with the suffragist perspective she was paid to represent.[30] All were aware that their words communicated an alluring self as much as ideas and argument. Whether writing an anonymous society column such as that by Amaryllis in Toronto's *Saturday Night* or giving sundry advice and political exhortations to farm women, as did

Francis Marion Beynon in the Winnipeg *Grain Growers' Guide*, women writers traded on an attractive self-image.

Lang's observations about journalists' 'literary personae' apply to all the writers in this study, even those who did not write primarily for the newspaper. Aware of cultural constraints on their self-creation, all participated in shaping a persona whose words would have social power. Seeking to appeal to various cross-class constituencies – professional women in newly opened fields, women who worked mainly in the home, women whose work was unskilled, and men seeking diversion and social commentary – they filled multiple roles simultaneously. On the one hand, they represented the modern woman who was carving out new opportunities and forms of employment; on the other, they claimed affiliation with the traditional woman concerned about courtship, marriage, children, and social relations. As Machar did in her article 'The New Ideal of Womanhood,' they upheld the standard of 'separate spheres' even as they embodied the transgression of those spheres. Theirs was always a balancing act in which they established their ordinary womanhood while displaying extraordinary abilities, initiative, and ambition. Even Denison, the most self-consciously radical proponent of women's rights, who most clearly declared her desire to smash the old order, was careful to emphasize her motherhood and the maternal feminist mandate to improve the lives of other mothers and children. 'If I did not honestly believe,' she wrote, 'that woman suffrage would be a strong factor in rectifying many crimes against childhood and be instrumental in doing away with the white slave traffic, I would not work another day for it.'[31] Women who moved into conspicuously public positions were conscious of the need to establish compelling and attractive personalities that would intrigue, fascinate, and reassure a socially broad-based audience.

Even while they worked within specific strictures, however, these women found significant flexibility and variety in creating their identities. Machar's Christian commitment stands in marked contrast to Denison's exuberant heterodoxy and Coleman's lapsed-Catholic scepticism; and McClung's reassuringly homespun humour is distinct from Johnson's self-dramatizing passion, Duncan's patrician wit, and Denison's (rather humourless) crusading conviction. Perhaps more significantly, they not only differed from one another but also, as a consequence of the media in which they worked, experimented with and changed their self-presentations. Performances, public lectures on a circuit, and daily or weekly newspaper columns were, by their nature, fluid and evanescent, involving both repetition and variation: reflecting news or opinion of the day, individual texts and speeches were soon forgotten or superseded by another performance or another article. Journalists were regretfully aware that 'however good one's piece, it would be thrown out with yesterday's rubbish.'[32] While such ephemerality could be frustrating to the writer or performer seeking to establish a lasting reputation, it could also be liberating and productive, enabling her to experiment with a variety of styles, arguments, and forms of self-construction. In an interview with Isabel Ecclestone MacKay, Johnson laughed off a question about the true self behind her varied verse: '"Oh, consistency!" she shrugged her shoulders. "How can one be consistent until the world ceases to change with the changing days?"'[33] With consistency out of the question, these writers and speakers could and did try out various speaking positions, manipulating and gauging audience reaction to the particular self on display on any one occasion. For this reason, their writings are particularly worthy of attention for what they reveal about the diverse forms of self-fashioning available to women during a period of transformation and public debate.

I stress the obvious fact of their diversity and self-diversity because it strikes me that, despite the tremendous range of scholarship on this period by social historians and literary scholars (according to Karen Dubinsky in *Improper Advances* [1993], the fifty years from the 1880s to the 1920s are the most studied period in Canadian history, 'particularly among women's, labor and other social historians'),[34] there remains a tendency among feminist and post-colonial scholars of the period to condescend to their subjects – to see nineteenth-century women as simpler than we are now, as different from us mainly in their lack of awareness of important insights that we now possess, as operating under a relatively uniform set of assumptions and beliefs, handicapped by their historical limitations in a way that we have escaped. Such an attitude is subtly expressed in Rick Monture's essay on Johnson, in which he concludes that, despite the sincerity and courage of her Aboriginal advocacy, 'her writing seems to be strained at times, as if she attempted to do too much in an era when the methods and terms that exist today were unavailable to her.'[35] Veronica Strong-Boag similarly registers some disappointment in her concluding summation of McClung's politics, stressing, 'A mind formed by a Victorian belief system and a Methodist social gospel both of which emphasized the special attributes of women was limited in its freedom to develop.'[36] Surely the task of any historical scholar is not to measure a past writer by a present-day yardstick but to attempt to understand the particularities and complexities of her world view.

It is important, too, to strive against oversimplification, which is all too easy and tempting when analysing the past. Scholars of this period have tended to assume a uniformity about past peoples that would appear ludicrous if applied to our times: that all had a settled religious perspective – or none at all (or none worth bothering about); that all accepted certain nationalist or racialist tenets about the superiority of Anglo-Saxon peoples; or that notions of maleness and femaleness were much more (repressively) stable than they are at present. Such an attitude is part of the bravura assertiveness with which Valverde opens an essay on the racial politics of Canada's suffragists, proclaiming, 'Racist strategies were not confined to situations in which topics such as immigration were directly at issue. They were integral to the movement as a whole.'[37] And it leads Cheryl Krasnick Warsh, in an otherwise superb essay on attitudes to female alcoholism in nineteenth-century Canada, to generalize rather dismissively, if wittily, about the 'respectable maternal feminists who strove to sweep away vice, pauperism, disease, and alien cultures with the broom of community agitation.'[38] While it is true that historical distance enables us to recognize particular ideologies that were taken for granted during earlier periods, it can obscure the tensions, complexities, and differences of belief that also characterize these times. It is my hope that focusing on individual women's words, arguments, and self-construction will reveal how much diversity remains to be explored in the period under study.

Diversity is also, to some extent, the rationale for my selection of these writers for the study, though it does not account for the exclusion of many other fascinating figures also deserving of attention, such as Mary Ann Shadd (1823–93), the American-born black teacher and abolitionist who moved to Canada West and published a radical newspaper called the *Provincial Freeman* from 1853 to 1857, advocating full integration of blacks and whites, or E. Cora Hind (1861–1942), the renowned wheat expert and suffragist who wrote for the Manitoba *Free Press* for the first four decades of the twentieth century, astounding the world with the accuracy of her crop forecasts. I chose the writers in this study because they represent differences of opinion, style, and self-representation. No single platform or rhetorical strategy links them into a coherent group or school, though some of them knew one another or were familiar with one another's work. I was delighted to discover, while looking through the McClung scrapbooks at the

Provincial Archives of British Columbia, a 1910 clipping from the *Kingston Whig* stating that McClung was entertained at a reception of the Young Women's Christian Association by the ladies of Kingston, a group that included 'Miss Machar';[39] thus the youngest and the oldest of this group met at least once. Machar was publishing in *The Week* at the same time as Duncan and received Johnson at her summer home, Ferncliff. Coleman reviewed both Duncan and Johnson, while Denison often mentioned Coleman in her own column. The precise extent of their interaction, however, is difficult to determine. Duncan and Johnson undoubtedly knew each other, but Carole Gerson and Veronica Strong-Boag, whose work on Johnson is authoritative, hazard only cautious statements about their likely interactions. McClung and Denison were both outspoken activists for woman suffrage, but neither writer mentions the other, and McClung's biographers Mary Hallett and Marilyn Davis find no evidence of a relationship. Machar was nearly forty years older than McClung, with whom she shared a commitment to Christian activism, and aside from the one instance above, there is no evidence their paths crossed. All participated in a small, though disparate, middle-class culture of public discourse, but they disagreed about such issues as feminism, temperance, crime, and religious faith, and certainly would not all have liked or approved of one another.

I chose these six women because each is interesting and rewarding in her own right; in particular, each used language in ways at once characteristic of some segment of her society and also individually powerful and arresting. Although the extent of their formal education varied greatly, only Machar and Coleman would now be considered learned, while the others received the limited schooling commonly available to middle-class and lower-middle-class women. All, though, were avid readers with an affinity for language; all had entertained an early desire to be creative writers and published poetry or fiction as well as non-fiction prose. All made a living from writing for at least a portion of their careers, and all achieved a wide readership and significant acclaim. Their career trajectories cover the period 1875–1915 fairly neatly, and thus their work allows an exploration of distinctly different forms of self-presentation over a forty-year period.

Popularity and public visibility are key to this study, which is specifically concerned with the public personae the women developed to meet specific writing and performing occasions. Unlike literary recovery projects such as Carrie MacMillan, Lorraine McMullen, and Elizabeth Waterston's *Silenced Sextet* (1993), which considers the writing careers and literary output of six prose-fiction writers, my focus is emphatically on six public figures who accessed a wide readership. One of the particular difficulties of literary recovery work in early Canada is the difficulty of assessing influence and reception in a country flooded with cheap reprints of American and British books. Many Canadian works of imaginative literature were published in low print runs, received only brief and sketchy notices or reviews, and sank into obscurity shortly after publication. In the case of the writers in this study, there is no question of their pervasive influence. The ability to draw a crowd is amply proven in the examples of McClung and Johnson, and many contemporary voices testify to their significant national impact. In the cases of the other writers, their tenure at particular newspapers and magazines is itself an indication of popularity. Such publications existed to make money, and columnists were retained because they brought readers to the paper.

As Paul Rutherford has demonstrated, the late nineteenth-century newspaper benefited from massive increases in literacy (about 94 per cent in Ontario by 1891),[40] changes in print technology that allowed greater speed and volume of production, new forms of communications (the telegraph, for example), and an urban culture united around the consumption of leisure products, popular entertainment, and sports. These developments enabled papers to reach out to a mass audience, finding readers 'among all classes of the community.'[41] While there remained a distinction between 'quality' papers such as the Toronto *Mail and Empire* and the *Globe* and 'people's' papers, which included the Montreal *Star* and the Toronto *World*, the quest for advertising revenue led more and more news organs to attempt, through a variety of features and special-interest columns, to bridge social divisions and appeal to all. To examine the self-constructions and persuasive techniques of the figures in this study is to engage with writers whose impact and public visibility were undeniable.

In stressing the complex rhetorical choices facing women writers and public speakers seeking to establish authority and credibility, I benefit from ground-breaking scholarship on Canadian and other turn-of-the-century writing. In their book-length study of Johnson, Strong-Boag and Gerson stress the notion of identity as a performance and Johnson's careful negotiation of conventions of Indian womanhood in her on- and off-stage self-presentation. As they argue, her elaborate costume, dramatic poses, assumption of a Native name, and strategic construction of Iroquois heritage demonstrated her keen recognition that 'to an audience, the truth of an identity is created in its trappings and performances.'[42] Carol Mattingly has documented the appeal to shared values and establishment of ethos by which temperance activists in nineteenth-century America gained the trust and commitment of their audiences; in the Ontario context, Sharon Anne Cook has analysed the forms of 'self-identity, collective consciousness, and organizational strategies'[43] that WCTU organizations provided for their members. Barbara Green has convincingly examined how the militant English suffragettes turned their own suffering bodies, textualized in accounts of prison experience, police brutality, and forced feeding, into propaganda tools during the final years of the suffrage struggle. These diverse approaches share a recognition that the writer or speaker's presentation of herself was inextricable from the content of her text. Drawing loosely on Judith Butler's theory of performativity, such scholars have emphasized the performative nature of texts that present an autobiographical persona,[44] and this broad notion of performance seems a compelling way in which to approach the women in this study. Then as now, the public woman was neither entirely free nor hopelessly bound as she endeavoured, within certain discursive constraints, to create her public self.

Further benefiting from recent scholarship, I also take for granted that women of this time were neither oppressed nor revolutionary in any simple way. As Bacchi has demonstrated, the women who campaigned for suffrage and social reforms around the turn of the twentieth century often had a clear stake in the existing social order. Far from working disinterestedly for justice (though they did that too at times), they sought to shore up their own positions and to combat threats to their social privilege and sense of identity. In *Practising Femininity* (1998), Dean has argued forcefully against the 'narrative of progressive liberation'[45] that feminist scholars sometimes reproduce. Writing about Johnson, Strong-Boag and Gerson have addressed the futility of seeking a pure resistance, noting every generation's inescapable entanglement in a historical context that cannot be fully resisted or recognized.[46] I seek neither to praise nor to blame the writers in my study but rather to read them carefully and appreciatively. My goal is to understand and articulate the strategies through which they forged their public selves and to attend closely to their passionate and fascinating words. While I do feel a liking and admiration for all of them, my objective is not to defend them from charges of racism or maternalism or to hold them up as subversive models from which present-day activists can learn, but to read them as evidence of the complexity and vibrancy of writing and public performance of the age.

THE SIX WRITERS IN THIS STUDY emerged at a time when social issues were being discussed with an unprecedented urgency in Canadian society. As a young, thinly populated country with an uncertain future (debates raged in the newspapers about Canada's colonial status, economic problems, internal divisions, and the possibility of annexation by or union with the United States), Canada was, in the final decades of the nineteenth century, 'a society preoccupied with the task of nationmaking,'[47] its lawmakers and patriots attempting to forge a sense of unity, identity, and national purpose, 'a cohesive national heritage,'[48] out of a reluctant federation with a diverse, sometimes indifferent, population. Unassimilated French and Aboriginal peoples and potentially unassimilable immigrants from eastern Europe were a cause of anxiety for Anglo-Canadian commentators who believed national harmony could best emerge from racial and cultural homogeneity. Discontent over Canada's colonial submission to Britain and fears of American aggression, revived during the Civil War (1861–5), made this a period both of intense nationalism and of anxiety and speculation about the country's political and economic future. Like so many of their contemporaries, the six writers in this study frequently address questions about Canada's cultural identity and future prospects, and their visions of social betterment are also, implicitly or explicitly, calls to national transformation and renewal.

Perhaps the most worrisome social change exacerbating commentators' unease was the country's shift from a predominantly rural society to a largely urban one, and the subsequent growth of cities and concomitant urban problems. As Valverde summarizes, 'in the 1870s Canada was a very sparsely populated, barely post-colonial state where farming and staples production predominated; by the 1920s the Native populations had been firmly marginalized, the weight of the economy had shifted towards industry and finance, and urban living had become the rule rather than the exception.'[49] As Canadian industries developed and people moved to cities seeking factory work, the problems of urbanization that Canada had hitherto escaped came to the fore: slums, unsanitary conditions, homelessness, thievery, prostitution, and the spread of disease. Tramps gathered on darkened corners, grimy children darted in and out of crowds, and women painted their faces to attract customers. As in Britain and the United States, it was hard not to notice the desperation of the unemployed as well as the misery and degradation of portions of the newly emerging working class, whose grim conditions of labour, long hours, low pay, and precarious status seemed to many middle-class observers a pointed reproach. In one of her many articles on the subject, Machar lamented, 'A thousand voices unite in testifying of the pinching hunger, the desperate struggle for work, the bitter lot of uncounted multitudes, not only in London and New York but even in our own Canadian cities.'[50] Like many other commentators, she found such misery to be evidence of the injustice of the existing industrial order, asking, 'Will anyone say that this is what ought to be the outcome of eighteen centuries of Christian teaching?'[51]

For some such observers, the emergence of workers' organizations such as the Knights of Labor, considered 'Canada's most important labor organization before 1900' by Gregory Kealey and Brian Palmer,[52] was a step in the right direction. Established in Philadelphia in 1869, the organization attempted to unite all skilled and unskilled workers to oppose exploitation and inadequate pay. The Knights formed local assemblies all across Ontario in the 1870s and 1880s and reached the peak of their strength in 1885–9, when the organization oversaw numerous strikes, lockouts, and public protests. To some middle-class supporters, the Knights were a productive force resisting capitalist monopoly. For others, the prospect of a class war between workers and owners disrupted ideals of an organic society and threatened to create even more firmly entrenched social divisions. Some took up Henry George's Single Tax solution, a proposal to levy a tax on land values in order to benefit those whose labour indirectly created the increase in value. A few turned to forms of socialism or cooperative ownership. Many advocated a greater sense of personal responsibility for charitable assistance, the development of organizations to help working-class families and destitute individuals, a greater spirit of fairness and sympathy on the part of business owners, and a more thorough Christianization of society to prevent the worst abuses.

The Labour Question, as it was often referred to, remained unsolved throughout the period, and every writer considered here had something to say about it. Machar and Denison showed the deepest concern and practical consideration: they agreed in approving 'the principle of co-operation and organization among workmen as absolutely necessary to protect their rights'[53] and imagined collectivized nurseries and cooperative kitchens as aids to single mothers.[54] At the other end of the spectrum can be found the irritated condescension of Duncan, who, after reading about female workers' attempts to unionize, could not relinquish her insistence on individual enterprise: 'When a woman enters the competition of money-making she becomes, so far as that is concerned, simply the agent of her own goods, and has no right to expect to be regarded as wrapped in a sentimental halo of sex ... The only hope lies in ambition, enterprise, energy, and excellence.'[55] All six writers engaged, to some degree, with the problems and potential of the city.

Related to urbanization and industrialization, though also developing its own complex momentum, was the second major issue of the day with which these writers were concerned: the transformation in the social role of women. Many material factors influenced this change, including new forms of transportation, labour-saving technologies in the home, a decrease in average family size, and expanding social networks in the cities. There was also, as Machar had stressed, a perceptible shift in 'public sentiment'[56] about women's rights and duties and a concurrent backlash of concern and resistance on the part of conservative editors, religious leaders, and writers. Women were more mobile and less bound to the home than they had formerly been, and many sought a larger life of education, work, and influence. In an autobiographical narrative about women's entry into journalism, Duncan proclaimed the new aspirations born of 'this golden age for girls, full of new interests and new opportunities,' in which everyone 'want[s] to do something; something more difficult than embroidered sachets, and more important than hand-painted tambourines.'[57] Even the politically conservative Coleman, hesitant to support the suffrage cause in its days of controversy, advised a reader, 'I do not believe girls should remain at home waiting till husbands claim them. There is plenty of work at hand, and plenty of aims in life besides marriage, which is, of course, a good, healthy institution, but not the end of a woman's life.'[58] As low-income women swelled the ranks of factory labourers, they became a striking symbol of the modern era, while middle-class women sought educational and work opportunities in the expanding list of professions newly (and in some cases grudgingly) opening to women.

The most striking manifestation of female independence and desire for a new aim in life was the New Woman, whose rejection of conventional femininity was at times rebellious and threatening to middle-class norms: Duncan's fictional heroine Elfrida Bell, in her novel *A Daughter of To-day* (1894), flaunts her radicalism by abandoning her parents, devoting herself to her art, smoking cigarettes, and expressing scorn for the institutions of marriage and motherhood. Other New Women, such as Duncan herself, were more socially acceptable, confining their transgressions mainly to intellectual and artistic pursuits as well as a fondness for bicycles and bohemian styles of clothing. Johnson's fictional portrayals of Native women emphasized their courage and political power, while many of her journal articles stressed the necessity of physical strength and independence for young women. Her racial advocacy symbolized another facet of the modern woman's agency. Coleman, too, was interested in the modern girl, defining modern women as both much more confident than they used to be and also more humble because aware of new objects of aspiration: 'prouder because they learn more and have a more accurate understanding of the capacities of their sex' and also 'far less apt to be puffed up with satisfaction at their own little personal achievements or appearance.'[59] All of the writers in this study emphasized, from different perspectives, both the greater freedom and the greater sense of responsibility of the 'daughter of today.'

For a majority of middle-class women in Canada, the 'something' they wanted to do ran in the channel of social reform: impelled by a desire and obligation to improve their communities and benefit the weakest members, they pursued helping professions such as teaching, nursing, or social welfare; they joined organizations such as the Young Women's Christian Association (YWCA) or the WCTU; or, in the case of the women in this study, they took up their pens and raised their voices with a purpose, convinced that they had something to say worth hearing. Machar never deviated from the principle, 'Above all, Canada wants writers with noble ideals. The tendency of too many writers, now-a-days, is to lose these under the undermining influence of a debasing materialism, but, without the noblest ideals, the noblest work can never be done!'[60] Denison declared that, 'being convinced that the majority of women are anxious that every child should have a fair running chance in this world, and that their anxiety would mean something when backed up by a vote, I am going to work for this reform till we get it.'[61] The desire to reform and strengthen the nation became a major focal point of turn-of-the-century Canadian life, a rallying cry for churches, welfare organizations, and individuals, with goals ranging from practical objectives, such as ameliorative factory legislation, fairer divorce laws, and legal measures to protect girls from sexual predators, to general uplift and spiritual guidance. Coleman

sought to cheer and instruct, declaring, 'I am learning through the letters I get every day how very careful anyone who is writing for young
girls and women ought to be, and how much we all need words of
sympathy and encouragement.'[62] Johnson put it ironically in 1897 to a
reporter from the *Chicago Tribune* wanting to know her ambitions:
'Well, I am only a Mohawk with an ambition to show that even an Indian can do something in the world.'[63]

Women justified their entry into the public sphere by figuring it as
mothering writ large – a rationale often called 'maternal feminism' and
the subject of an extended debate by social historians, who have argued over its conservatism and limitations.[64] Accepting (or seeming to
accept) women's inherent capacity to nurture, protect, and care for
family, maternal feminists argued that they were well suited to public
roles that touched upon the safety of children, population health, and
morality. As Dean characterizes the debate, 'Whether this position was
a strategy adopted by canny leaders like McClung to make the revi-
sioning of women's role more acceptable to a conservative population,
or whether maternal feminism was a strongly held belief, is a matter
of contention among feminist scholars, as is the designation of such
views as feminist at all.'[65] Other scholars such as Helen Buss, reading
McClung's two autobiographies,[66] and Henderson, in her study of racial discourse at points of national tension, have argued that the maternal ideal of moral purity, self-sacrifice, and the reform of others created
a debilitating legacy for twentieth-century women. As Henderson
phrases it, the 'strategic *justification* for a demand came to replace the
demand itself, and the liberal feminist dream of broadening women's
desires and capacities was collapsed with the goal of reforming the
dangerous classes.'[67]

However one evaluates maternal feminist beliefs, the pursuit of social uplift and its organizing metaphors often had far-reaching and
radical consequences, frequently opening women's eyes to the systemic sources of the misery, filth, and vulnerability they sought to alleviate, galvanizing them to seek a greater role in creating the laws and
influencing the conditions of their society. As McClung formulated it,
'Women have played the good Samaritan for a long time, and they
have found many a one beaten and robbed on the road of life. They are
still doing it, but the conviction is growing on them that it would be
much better to go out and clean up the road!'[68] Denison explained the
thinking along explicitly maternal lines: 'In order to make homes safe,
women must not only help to make the homes but they must help to

make the laws that govern the homes. They must evolve a social soul and consider it their duty to not only protect their own children ... but to see to it that every child is protected.'[69] The demand for the vote and for higher education grew largely out of this sense of duty, or at least was articulated most persuasively in relation to it; and as women met resistance to moderate demands and recognized their relative political powerlessness, a deeper awareness of their social disabilities often complicated maternal idealism. The result was a greatly enlarged conception of what women might do to transform their societies (McClung, for example, was convinced that wars would cease when women formed governments, declaring that if there had been a woman politician in the Reichstag, she would have told the Kaiser, 'William – forget it!')[70] and a much sharper awareness of the forces ranged against them.

As will already be evident, there has been a great deal of debate over the character of the reforming zeal that gripped the country and motivated many suffrage and reforming women at this time: whether it was a progressive movement to combat injustice, as Richard Allen, Ramsay Cook, and Nancy Christie and Michael Gauvreau have suggested, or an assertion of white, middle-class power shaped by imperial politics and eugenics, as Bacchi, Valverde, and Angus McLaren have argued. Henderson, Cecily Devereux, and Daniel Coleman have recently published studies of the racial politics of the literature of this period, demonstrating how narratives of white agency, civility, self-government, and self-empowerment were entangled with the control and regulation of racial others, such that white writers' narrative self-representation was inextricable from claims of racial and moral superiority. The debate over the progressive or oppressive meanings of reform discourse does not receive sustained attention in this study. As with any widespread movement, social reform partook of the complexities and tensions of the society from which it sprang, in some ways forward-looking and hopeful; in others, conservative and fearful.

Like that society, it was informed by the shattering crisis in religious faith in the last quarter of the nineteenth century, a subject addressed by all the writers in this study. Developments in evolutionary science and in textual biblical scholarship had called into question the veracity of the Scriptures and left many churches and individual believers scrambling to justify their faith and reorient their religious practice. According to A.B. McKillop, it was a time 'when traditional Christian teleology was in the process of dissolution.'[71] In *The Regenerators: Social*

Criticism in Late Victorian English Canada (1985), Cook draws a straight line between the weakening of Christian orthodoxy and the rise of the social gospel, arguing that 'the religious crisis provoked by Darwinian science and historical criticism of the Bible led religious people to attempt to salvage Christianity by transforming it into an essentially social religion.'[72] Either convinced by attacks on traditional Christian doctrine or unable to mount a satisfying scientific or scholarly rebuttal, many religious leaders and adherents began to argue that 'the practical application of Christ's teaching was more important than theological controversy.'[73]

Given the profound social problems seething at church doorsteps and throughout Canadian cities, it was both practically expedient and morally urgent for pastors and religious people to turn away from seemingly intractable theological intricacies in order to tackle 'the social problems of the street.'[74] Whether this was an attempt, as Kealey and others have suggested, 'to make the church relevant'[75] or whether it reflected a spiritual awakening to the gospel mandate to the poor – and it was probably both – the result was a widespread conviction 'that Christianity required a passionate commitment to social involvement,'[76] with the result that Christians of all denominations – particularly Methodist and Presbyterian evangelicals but also Catholics and Anglicans – sought to apply Christian principles to contemporary social problems such as labour unrest and prostitution. In Allen's influential formulation, 'The demand "save this man, now" became "save this society, now."'[77]

All the writers in this study were influenced by the social gospel, even if, like Duncan, they resisted its rhetoric or, like Denison, they found inspiration in non-Christian spirituality. The inextricability of spiritual belief and social action, the need to take responsibility for one's society, and the possibility that individuals could profoundly change the social order for the better were bedrock beliefs for them all. Writing at the beginning of the First World War, McClung articulated three decades of social gospel thinking about how a lived Christianity could regenerate the world, and her generalized rhetoric of redemption and renewal created the kind of statement that all of the writers in this study would have embraced. Appropriating the dominant metaphor of her day, she asserted, 'Life is warfare, not one set of human beings warring upon other human beings – that is murder, no matter by what euphonious name it may be called; but war waged against ignorance, selfishness, darkness, prejudice, and cruelty, beginning always with the roots of evil which we find in our own hearts. What a glorious thing it would be if nations would organize and train for this warfare, whose end is life, and peace, and joy everlasting, as they now train and organize for the wholesale murder and burning and pillaging.'[78] Although not all these writers had such a clearly articulated sense of overarching social mission (Machar certainly did, and Denison as well), all had a vision for the country and a belief that their words could communicate that vision as well as inspire clarity and purpose. Matters of faith and its impact on conduct are fundamental to the self-presentations of Coleman, Denison, and Johnson, each of whom spoke frequently of religious, though not necessarily orthodox, convictions and inspiration. Even Duncan, who did not discuss her religious beliefs, relied on biblical language for rhetorical effect and was interested in the connection between the social gospel and the intellectual development of women. In their very different ways, each had deep convictions about women's spiritual influence in her society, and all – even the frivolous Duncan – took seriously their public positions as models and guides.

This conviction of significance undoubtedly had an impact on these writers, inspiring them to extraordinary exertion and achievement. As a number of scholars have noted, the women who established themselves in the period 1875–1915 encountered a kind of public attention and interest, and met with a degree of success, that none of their forebears could claim and that would never quite be repeated. They were conscious of themselves as pioneers, clearing a path for others to follow, and as women who were making history in their day. Once the vote had been achieved and the professions opened, at least theoretically, to women, later generations, for a variety of reasons, lacked the same motivation, momentum, and sense of purpose. In the pages that follow, I demonstrate how that sense of purpose translated into vibrant textual personae who, through stirring rhetoric and a strong connection with their audience, claimed a voice in the public sphere.

1 Agnes Maule Machar, Christian Radical

In an article for *The Week* entitled 'Voices Crying in the Wilderness' (1891), Agnes Maule Machar wrote admiringly of the impact of social reformers such as the Reverend James Huntington and General William Booth, whose words on behalf of 'suffering humanity' had recently created a 'deep impression'[1] on many Canadians. Huntington was a radical Episcopalian priest and adherent of the social gospel who had toured Ontario in 1891 to promote Henry George's Single Tax solution to social inequality, a scheme whereby a high tax on privately owned land would redistribute wealth. Booth was the founder of the Salvation Army and the author of *In Darkest England and the Way Out* (1890), an influential book about England's industrial poor that proposed a radical Christian reorganization of society to assist the destitute. According to Machar, herself an avid reader of reform literature, their 'impassioned pleas on behalf of sunken humanity'[2] were taking effect across North America, inspiring earnest citizens to confront the poverty and degradation of nineteenth-century industrial society. Reflecting on the relationships among rhetoric, conviction, and social action, Machar emphasized such men's ability to awaken audience members' 'latent aspirations for better things':

> It is an interesting illustration of the fact that despite all the pessimistic utterances, theological and otherwise, respecting the moral perversity of our race; despite the crass selfishness and stupid indifference that hang as deadweights on its moral progress; that teacher will always evoke the warmest and strongest response who rouses its latent aspirations for better things, strikes the higher chords long dormant from disuse, and, in a word, appeals to the underlying moral consciousness that antagonizes and controls the natural selfish impulses which, at first sight, seem so much the stronger.[3]

The statement aptly characterizes Machar's own writing on behalf of the poor and disadvantaged, in which, over a period of some four decades, indignant protest was leavened by Christian hope.

As the passage makes clear, Machar believed that moral appeal was most powerful when it touched the conscience and awakened a desire for right action strong enough to combat 'natural selfish impulses.' While not denying sinfulness, she did not dwell on depravity, stressing instead human beings' 'latent aspirations' for goodness and emphasizing that persuasive language could aid in transforming character and regenerating society. Such regeneration was desperately needed at a time when a 'thousand voices unite in testifying of the pinching hunger, the desperate struggle for work, the bitter lot of uncounted multitudes, not only in London and New York but even in our own Canadian cities.'[4] Adding her voice to the urgent conversation then under way about the future of the city, Machar too sought to break through 'crass selfishness and stupid indifference' in order to reach the 'underlying moral consciousness' of her readers. Although she published in English and American periodicals as well as Canadian ones, she wrote most frequently for the *Canadian Monthly and National Review* (1872–8), its successor *Rose-Belford's Canadian Monthly and National Review* (1878–82), and *The Week* (1883–96), the Canadian journals that cover the years of her greatest literary activity. Intended for an elite and predominantly male audience, they were Canada's most prestigious periodicals of literary opinion and public culture. Nancy Miller Chenier estimates that Machar published 'more than one hundred articles in less than thirty years'[5] in these venues, becoming by 1888 one of the 'best known names among Canadian literary women.'[6]

Machar wrote at a time when much seemed to be at stake for Canadian society and the Christian church during a period of rapid industrialization, social upheaval, and developments in science and historical scholarship that challenged religious certainty; as a result, her work was unashamedly didactic. In *For King and Country* (1874), an early novel about the War of 1812, she aimed both to bolster Anglo-Canadian patriotism and to convince Canadians of the possibility of continental cooperation and brotherhood (though not political union) with the United States. In 'Quebec to Ontario: A Plea for the Life of Riel, September 1885,' a poem written upon the defeat of the second Riel Rebellion in 1885, her purpose was to convince English Canada to show compassion to Louis Riel and the 'conquered race' of the Métis. Moral instruction and cross-cultural sympathy are her goals in *Marjorie's Canadian Winter*

Agnes Maule Machar.

(1892), a novel for children about the history of Quebec, in which the main characters, the American Marjorie and her Canadian cousins, listen to tales of Jesuit heroism in the New World and are encouraged to apply the situations described to their own experiences. The novel's intention was to make English-speaking readers more aware of and sympathetic to the historical accomplishments of French Canada. In *Stories of the British Empire* (1913), a collection of historical sketches intended to inspire love for Canada and imperial loyalty, she gave instructions in the preface as to how the greatest moral benefit could be derived from the book, suggesting to readers that they read just one narrative per sitting and then reflect on its lessons.

As the daughter of a Presbyterian clergyman known for his concern for the poor, Machar, born in 1837, grew up in an intellectual and socially earnest Kingston home that was often a gathering place for eminent Christian thinkers and social reformers such as George Monro Grant, principal of Queen's University and moral nationalist, and Lyman Abbott, the American proponent of the social gospel to whom Machar dedicated *Roland Graeme: Knight: A Novel of Our Time* (1892). Her sympathy for the Knights of Labor, idealistically depicted in that novel, may have been influenced by the fact that her brother John, a Kingston lawyer, was a member of the Knights. Other visitors to the manse included the British evolutionist Alfred Russel Wallace and lawyer and politician John A. Macdonald. Following in her mother's footsteps, Machar was involved from a young age in many reform and benevolent organizations, the most prominent being the Young Women's Christian Association, the National Council of Women, the Canadian Audubon Society, and the Kingston Humane Society. She also actively supported the orphans' and children's mission in India sponsored by her church, St Andrew's Presbyterian, and she was, according to Constance Backhouse, 'one of the most powerful campaigners for protective labour legislation for women in the nineteenth century.'[7] Machar's literary efforts were, from the first, equally socially conscious. Whether she was analysing a social problem, narrating a moment in Canadian history, or recounting the life story of a distinguished person, she aimed to awaken the conscience and enlarge the sympathies of readers. 'Above all,' as she argued in a short piece for *The Week* in 1894, 'Canada wants writers with *noble ideals*. The tendency of too many writers, now-a-days, is to lose these under the undermining influence of a debasing materialism, but, without the noblest ideals, the noblest work can never be done.'[8] She never married, but travelled and divided her time between Kingston and her Gananoque cottage near the Thousand Islands, devoting her long life (she lived to age ninety) to serving reform causes and writing noble literature.

Education was always of importance to Machar. She had herself received an unusually thorough training in theology and the classics at home, making use of her father's extensive library. In turn, she believed that there was no more useful work than 'molding the mind and manners of young Canada,'[9] and she frequently expressed her view that 'what is of chief importance in the education of a people is the formation of character – of a noble and harmonious national life.'[10] Expressions of such high purpose were not to everyone's taste: in her 1888 article on Machar, Ethelwyn Wetherald, a fellow poet and journalist, confessed that 'some of her poetry is produced by a collaboration of the artist and moralist within her' and that 'we are not so grateful for the moral as we are for the picture.'[11] The edge of condescension in Wetherald's comment was to grow stronger after Machar's death, when her idealism began to seem quaint and old-fashioned; the majority of contemporary reviewers, however, praised her high-mindedness, one reviewer commending 'the wonderful versatility of this gifted woman.'[12] The clarity of her faith led Machar to declare, 'We live in a world where the need of God has always been one of the most urgent needs of humanity, and the thought of God its strongest controlling power.'[13] To lead her readers to satisfy their thirst for Truth was, she believed, her greatest obligation as a writer, a duty that led her into spheres of bold inquiry and unflinching endeavour that distinguished her as a leading social thinker of her day.

IN THE LAST QUARTER of the nineteenth century, Machar was part of an international movement concerned to address, from a Christian perspective, the pressing social problems of the factory and the slum. Attempting to awaken the conscience of Canadians through the rhetoric of the social gospel, which taught that 'the service of God on earth is actually the service of man,'[14] she took up her pen to address the situation of the poor and downtrodden – the factory workers, washerwomen, abandoned children, inebriates, and disabled whose degraded lives on the edges of respectable society were too often ignored and misunderstood by a complacent middle class. Often writing under the pen name Fidelis to stress her commitment to faith, which she called 'the quality I most value, and care most to possess,'[15] Machar possessed a 'courageous and indefatiguable pen.'[16]

In an article on Machar written when she was nearly seventy years old, journalist Leman A. Guild stated, 'There is no question that attracts attention which is not interesting to her, and which she cannot discuss with ease and clearness.'[17] Indeed, she cared about all the major social and moral issues of her day, arguing passionately for temperance legislation ('The Temperance Problem') and higher education for women ('Higher Education for Women' and 'A Few Words on University Co-Education'), while also campaigning against the use of birds' feathers in ladies' hats ('Birds and Bonnets'). In addressing specifically urban problems, she supported ameliorative factory legislation, compulsory schooling for poor children, and organizations such as shelters for the homeless, adult training schools, and worker-owned shops and factories to establish loving charity and social cooperation as the basis of Canadian society. Her historical novel *For King and Country* is cited in the Ontario Department of Education's *Ontario Public School History of England and Canada* (1917), which also named her, along with the Confederation group and four other women, as the 'best known of our modern poets.'[18] According to anthologist William D. Lighthall, Machar was 'one of those who well disputes the palm for the leadership among Canadian poetesses.'[19] She was the recipient of numerous literary prizes for her reform-oriented fiction and verse, and was commended by literary critic Thomas O'Hagan in 1896 as one whose 'womanly and sympathetic mind is found in the van of every movement among Canadian women that has for its purpose a deeper and broader enlightenment based upon principles of wisdom, charity, and love.'[20] Writing out of sympathy with those who suffered and an unshakeable faith, Machar sought to make her work a form of Christian witness that would win hearts to her transformative social vision.

Ramsay Cook, whose *The Regenerators* (1985) is a major study of the social gospel movement in Canada, has argued that ultimately the attempt to bring Christian principles to bear on social problems weakened the Christian church and accelerated the secularization of Canadian society in the late nineteenth century. 'By urging Christians to emphasize social utility and to downplay or ignore doctrine, these advocates of the social gospel were in fact making the church irrelevant in a world where other institutions were better equipped to perform the socially useful roles once fulfilled by the church.'[21] Machar was part of this process, he argues, someone who believed that social reform was 'more important than the preaching of sound doctrine' and who found the essence of Christianity to be in 'its ethical teachings.'[22]

By emphasizing the social application of Christ's ministry, Cook argues, she expressed a 'Protestant liberalism'[23] that sidestepped, rather than answered, 'the intellectual problems raised by the higher criticism and the new biology.'[24] He also asserts that Machar's 'extensive reading of theological writing led her to a willing acceptance of both the higher criticism and the modernist view that there was no conflict between Christianity and modern culture.'[25]

While Cook's analysis of the social gospel movement as a whole is persuasive, his perspective on Machar is not entirely accurate. She did not 'downplay or ignore doctrine,'[26] and her linking of Christianity and social activism never subordinated faith to ethics; on the contrary, her rhetorical strategy was consistently to show their inextricability, to exhort readers to both renewed faith and a corresponding commitment to action. In the many articles she wrote on the meaning of Christianity in the modern world, she was concerned to show not only that faith was the source of moral life but also that it was the cornerstone of all effective social systems and ameliorative programs. Although Cook's assessment of Machar's life and work is a generous one – he calls her 'one of the most gifted intellectuals and social critics in late nineteenth-century Canada'[27] – his focus on her 'strong liberal tendency' leads him to overlook the fundamental importance to her thinking of the gospel of salvation. A.B. McKillop presents a different view, describing Machar as 'one of the most articulate and intelligent Canadian lay defenders of Christian orthodoxy' and one who 'never doubted the fundamental truths of her religion.'[28] But perhaps because of her refusal of contemporary doubt (doubt being more interesting to present-day scholars than faith), she receives only a few paragraphs of commentary from McKillop.

Like Cook, other modern historians and critics have assessed Machar predominantly from a secular perspective, finding much in her social ideas to praise while overlooking her faith or seeing it as an old-fashioned accompaniment to her politics. It is hard not to hear a note of condescension in Carole Gerson's usually even-handed assessment of Machar's 'pious solutions to problems of social and domestic conduct' as 'typical of the strain of Sunday-school writing which dominated so much of the women's and children's literature of her age.'[29] Likewise, in an otherwise excellent overview of Machar's religious thought that describes her as 'seeking to come to terms with new currents of thought while preserving the essentials of an inherited and much cherished world view,'[30] Ruth Compton Brouwer occasionally betrays a bias against her Christian commitment. Brouwer's central argument, that Machar's development was 'away from conventional theology on the one hand, and towards applied Christianity on the other,'[31] suggests that activism supplanted theology in her thought. But Machar was an evangelical believer for whom spiritual conversion and a personal relationship with Jesus were paramount. To say, as Brouwer does, of Machar's vision for the church that 'its mission was to apply Christianity in the world'[32] is to overlook her continuing emphasis on individual salvation. Moreover, in assessing her development towards 'applied Christianity,' Brouwer implicitly faults Machar for not progressing further in that direction. The conclusion to her article expresses this sense of limitation: 'The moderate stance [her rejection of socialism and violent revolution] was of Machar's own choosing, of course, but as a female product of her particular time and place she probably could not have sustained a more radical one.'[33] The commendable analysis ends on a note of apology for Machar's failure to achieve a social radicalism congruent with the assumptions and values of some present-day secular historians.

These scholars' reflections on Machar's faith betray their inattention to its central role in the author's vision of the future. Noting her criticism of the church, for example, Brouwer comments that 'Machar's attitude seems to have been that the church should be reformed from within, not simply jettisoned. Even to raise the latter possibility is probably to exaggerate the nature of her disaffection; for all its faults, the church represented a community of believers and she obviously found comfort and fellowship within it.'[34] Such an assessment – 'comfort and fellowship' indeed! – does not begin to account for the passion and conviction with which Machar defended the truth of Christianity and the significance of the universal church. Dianne Hallman, who also presents an admirably detailed, well-balanced, and insightful overview of Machar's historical writing, does not downplay the importance of Christian faith to Machar, but her brief and generalized references to it (she refers, for instance, to Machar's 'particular brand of historical determinism, Christian triumphalism, and Canadian nationalism') suggest that, for Hallman's purposes, it does not reward close and extended attention.[35]

In light of the secular emphasis and perspective of these studies, it is perhaps useful to reverse the accepted lines of inquiry in order to examine how and to what extent Christianity was integral to Machar's social analysis, both as a foundational principle for her arguments and as a key source of her rhetorical power. Given that quotations from or allusions to Scripture, biblical imagery and ideas, and spiritually charged language and metaphors are prominent in her writing, it seems that they were intended to have an irreplaceable role in her arguments. Moreover, that role is a flexible and multidimensional one, deserving of consideration. Christian belief was remarkably diverse in late nineteenth-century Canada, and Machar, as the daughter of a clergyman and a lay writer translating Christian debates for believers and non-believers, wrote with creative passion and authority. Having devoted much of her spiritual and intellectual energy to contemplating Scripture and doctrine, she was uniquely fitted to present Christian ideas in engaging ways. Far from expressing a straightened orthodoxy, as non-Christian writers often assume of Christian thought, Machar defended her faith creatively and boldly.

Like many other advocates of the social gospel, Machar argued that the Christian church had been for too long complacent about social injustice. The 'human side of the Christian religion' had been ignored, she contended in 'Voices Crying in the Wilderness,' with the result that the church had opened itself to the charge of having forgotten Christ's commandment to 'love thy neighbour as thyself.'[36] Horrified by General Booth's analysis of England's impoverished millions, she regarded the spectacle of urban pain as a direct challenge to the church requiring immediate action: 'Could it have been so had the Christian church been faithful to her divine charter? Is it not time that easy-going, self-indulgent Christians should be confronted with the question, in tones as stern as those of an Amos or an Isaiah: *What are you going to do about it?*'[37] The church, Machar believed, must be involved in the problems of the world. But, as her reference to its 'divine charter' made clear – and as suggested by her figuring of Christians' interrogators as Old Testament prophets – Machar's calling of the church to social commitment did not mean a turning away from God's word; social action was nothing less than a passionate living of Christ's commandments, not a secular application of the most attractive ones. The church must engage with the world but must not become 'like the world' in serving the rich or advancing the causes of social elites. It must turn back to its core doctrine, the 'great principle of brotherhood.'[38]

Machar wanted to demonstrate the relevance of Christianity to the problems of urban life, as Cook contends of proponents of the social gospel, but more importantly, she also wanted to live Christianity, and encourage others to live it, as a daily practice of God's love as expressed through the atoning death of Jesus Christ. For her, the social and the spiritual could not be separated, and engagement with social problems was an urgent spiritual necessity both for the victims of urban poverty and for middle-class reformers, two groups equally endangered, though in different ways, by the combined squalor and opulence of an inequitable social system. Speaking of the attitude of wealthy Christians, she lamented the 'assumption that the employing class have a prescriptive right to live in spacious, and generally luxurious houses, to "wear purple and fine linen" and to "live sumptuously every day"'[39] while the poor must struggle to live. The reference to fine clothing and sumptuous living is an allusion to Luke 16:19, which tells of a rich man who, because of his indifference to a beggar at his gate, suffers eternal separation from God after death. His pleasure in sumptuous living and fine linen has hardened his heart, and Machar suggests that the comfortable middle class of her day faced the same peril. Social action was for Machar a matter of salvation, representing not only a duty to God but a necessary spiritual discipline. Part of her rhetorical and political effectiveness involved erasing the distinction between the social and the spiritual so that, far from de-emphasizing theology, she evoked and interpreted Scripture with the twofold purpose of spiritual chastening and call to social action.

Political economy, then, was not merely a pressing social issue for Machar but also a pressing Christian issue because the foundational principles – if not all the economic details – of a just economic order were to be discovered in Scripture. The Bible taught 'that great principle of brotherhood which, faithfully carried out, would regenerate society.'[40] Her use of the word 'regenerate' communicated her belief not only that society would be improved by implementing principles of cooperation and justice, but also that it would be brought to God, renewed and filled by the Holy Spirit in preparation for the Saviour's return. The title of 'Voices Crying in the Wilderness' clearly indicates this scriptural and eschatological focus: the voice crying in the wilderness is, in John 3:17, the voice of John the Baptist calling people to 'prepare the way of the Lord.' That first preparation had involved repentance and the opening of hearts to the message of Jesus; now, Christian workers would advance the Kingdom of God on earth in preparation for His Second Coming. To engage in social reform work, then, was both to fulfil the divine law of charity and to carry on the work of world evangelism, bringing into being the earthly kingdom of the Lord.

To demonstrate her overarching concern with divine justice, Machar repeatedly buttressed references to economic questions with expressions of faith. Speaking of the Single Tax, the social panacea much debated by reformers and economists of every political shading and promoted in Henry George's best-selling *Progress and Poverty* (1879), Machar comments, 'If it be, as its enthusiastic advocates declare, founded on eternal justice, in other words, if it be of God, it must go on, as other reforms have done, and cannot be brought to nought.'[41] The allusion is to Acts 5:38–9, where a wise Pharisee warns his fellow Jews not to harm the apostles teaching in the name of Jesus. He tells them that 'if this counsel or this work be of men, it will come to nought; / But if it be of God, ye cannot overthrow it.' For Machar, God was present in human affairs, working through the thoughts and proposals of reformers: social commitment, therefore, should not take the place of prayer and scriptural study, but must accompany these essential practices. This aspect of her thought and writing, far from being a quaint element of her personal theology, is a key to her power as a writer and thinker. In her commitment to stressing both the human side of Christianity and also the Christian side of social action, Machar distinguished herself as a Christian radical in command of a rhetorical power few of her contemporaries could match. She went much further than many other reformers in expressing support for workers' organizations, trade unions, and, where necessary, disruptive job action. And she went further than most Christian reformers in invoking God as the source of truth in social and industrial matters, encouraging her readers to find inspiration not in social theories merely but in the Holy Spirit working through the words of men.

MACHAR'S ARTICLES ON SOCIAL ISSUES were designed to 'apply' Christianity in word and deed. In 'Unhealthy Conditions of Women's Work in Factories' (1896), she summarized the findings of the Royal Commission on the Relations of Labour and Capital, published in 1889, and expressed her shock at the many abuses – the harsh discipline, unsafe equipment, poor ventilation, inhumanly long hours – in 'a so-called Christian society' and 'among our free-born Canadian people.'[42] The royal commission was an inquiry, established by the aging prime minister John A. Macdonald, into all aspects of labour in Ontario, Quebec, New Brunswick, and Nova Scotia. According to Susan Trofimenkoff, nearly 1,800 people testified before the commission on subjects ranging 'from factory laws to wages, from apprenticeships to rents, from arbitration to immigration, and from convict labour to strikes.'[43] Of these, 102 were women, many of them employed by textile mills, shoe factories, and match factories for long hours (nine hours per day in Ontario, ten in Quebec, eleven in the Maritimes) and low wages. Largely unskilled, they were paid substantially less than male workers, with punitive deductions for fines, work slowdowns, and temporary closures. They frequently had extra time added to the workday without increased pay. For Machar, the royal commission report was a revelation of appalling abuse; the young women's rights, health, and moral well-being had been sacrificed on the altar of industrial prosperity. She even used the metaphor of pagan sacrifice to emphasize the horror of the report's findings, comparing the girls to the human sacrifices offered to the mythological Cretan Minotaur. However, 'The exactions of the Pagan Minotaur,' she declared, '... were moderate compared with those of so-called Christian society,'[44] which was consuming the lives of thousands of girls and women in Canadian factories and mills. Stressing Canada's youth and Christian origins in the opening paragraph, Machar sought to establish the shared values and national mythology, especially the appeal to Canadian justice and egalitarianism, that underpinned her analysis.

Throughout the essay, Machar presented material and humanitarian concerns alongside spiritual ones in order to confirm their fundamental interconnection. The abuse of female workers mattered on personal, social, and spiritual grounds. In terms of 'ordinary humanity,'[45] the overwork and poor pay were the cause of considerable suffering, wretchedness, and justifiable resentment. The practice of fining workers for trivial infractions was particularly pernicious, and Machar provided a number of vivid examples of managerial pettiness and injustice. On larger social grounds, too, the exploitation of girls and women led to 'imprudent premature marriages' and thus, in her view, to 'the abject poverty which perpetuates itself and other evils to succeeding generations.'[46] One girl's distress and desire for escape from unpleasant work could become an ongoing generational cycle of impoverishment, as personal suffering led to family and community dysfunction. But the most significant harm was spiritual, involving the moral danger to which innocent girls were exposed. Long hours and fatiguing work led the girls to seek 'exciting amusement' as an escape. Machar was circumspect about the danger and its results, saying only that the craving for stimulation 'often takes forms fraught with great danger to their best interests, and has led many an unfortunate into the paths of despair,'[47] but she was explicit in defining moral harm as a surpassing danger for which both workers and their society would suffer deeply.

This unspeakable harm was almost certainly sexual immorality caused by late nights, alcohol, and dissipation. Immorality was one of the preoccupations of Victorian urban reformers generally and an abiding focus of the authors of the royal commission report, who, according to Trofimenkoff, assumed 'that immoral behaviour was a necessary consequence of the mingling of the sexes in the factories.'[48] As Valverde has also shown, it was not unusual for reformers to fret over the temptations facing young working women in the city, and it might seem here that Machar is at her most conventional in worrying that the dehumanizing effect of factory work led girls to sexual sin. Indeed, for her, spiritual corruption, which had eternal consequences, would always be a graver concern than earthly suffering, no matter how heartbreaking. But Machar's concern with sin and punishment did not linger, in conventional Victorian fashion, on the spectacle of feminine sexual degradation; instead, it moved to the question of moral responsibility for such sin. Referring to the Last Judgment, she stated, 'When all evil is judged aright, on which will fall the severest condemnation of eternal justice – on these victims of a heartless industrial system, or on the society that apathetically tolerates conditions which naturally lead to such results?'[49] The burden of sin, she concluded, rested most heavily upon those who might have changed a system that encouraged it. Few reformers would have gone so far as Machar to claim that social justice was not all that was at stake in arguments over working hours and wages: that individual standing with God might ultimately depend on one's commitment to the factory operative, that one might be held to account for the corruption of an innocent under such circumstances. Whether or not she was actually suggesting that whole classes of people could face judgment for their failure to change the social order, Machar certainly meant to clarify her conviction that social action was an essential component of faith in Jesus, the 'works' to enliven and embody a passionate 'faith.'

She ended the essay by stressing the parallels and intersections among her various justifications for protective labour legislation. The grounds of humanity, economic efficiency, and patriotism were all linked, for the moral and economic prosperity of the nation rested largely on the physical vigour and moral health of its working class, who made up the bulk of the population. Therefore, even if a reader was not moved by Machar's account of the physical and moral suffering of working girls – and not touched by her reference to God's judgment – he or she might be moved by considerations of community prosperity and national productivity. But Machar could not end with an appeal to economic self-interest. Her final sentence stressed the Christian motive once more, emphasizing how it encompassed and superseded all other considerations. Quoting Frederick Robertson, a mid-century Anglican theologian admired for his inspiring sermons at Trinity Chapel, Brighton, she closed by stressing that 'the kingdom of Christ can never be established ... until we have done all that in us lies, not only to preach and teach the truth, but to take away the hindrances in the way of truth.'[50] Christians were called to labour for their fellows' salvation, and if demoralization and bodily degradation were barriers to conversion, as they undoubtedly were, it was a Christian duty to attempt to remove them.

Machar's insistence that Christian and social commitment were inseparable is also demonstrated in 'Our Lady of the Slums' (1891), her tribute to the Salvation Army, an evangelical organization active in Britain and North America that provided both practical succour and enthusiastic gospel ministry to the poor. Founded in 1856 by dissident Methodist minister William Booth, the Army dispensed with church hierarchy and liturgy, holding informal street meetings that involved song, Bible preaching, and testimony; it also fed the hungry and tended the sick. Machar commended the Army as one of the organizations that most fully practised Christian principles. Taking the gospel message into the darkest corners of the urban underworld, it gave 'the most striking expression of Christian love and service for the perishing, of the spirit of the Good Shepherd who goes after that which is lost until he finds it.'[51] Jesus calls himself the Good Shepherd who lays down his life for the sheep in John 10:11, but here Machar refers most closely to the parable he tells in the Gospel of Luke to justify his ministry to sinners. Scorned by the scribes and Pharisees for spending time with disreputable people, Jesus asks, 'What man of you, having an hundred sheep, if he lose one of them, doth not leave the ninety and nine in the wilderness, and go after that which is lost, until he find it? / And when he hath found it, he layeth it on his shoulders rejoicing' (Luke 15: 4–5).

To be a follower of Christ, Machar stressed, was to risk comfort and safety for the lost, and the Salvation Army was an arresting modern example of such self-sacrificing love. And yet social action could never become an end in itself apart from the work of salvation. The Army was succeeding in its work with the poor where many had previously failed, not because its sociology was better, but because its evangelizing soldiers worked with love 'to surround and soften their hard lots, and too often, also, hard hearts.'[52] Only such a double process of softening could achieve the miraculous transformation of slum dwellers that the Army was effecting, and only Christ could soften the sin-hardened heart.

While Machar's focus in the essay included the material good the Army achieved, her greatest rhetorical energy was devoted to its work of salvation. Her special sympathy for the Army's women workers led her to a series of passages in which she characterized the future of the activist church in feminine terms, evoking the Madonna of her title as the spirit motivating the Army's women:

> As we think of the multitudes of devoted women who leave comfortable homes, and in some cases West End drawing rooms, to live amid the wretchedness they seek to relieve, whether they wear the garb of a sisterhood or the familiar Salvation Army bonnet, it seems as if it were scarcely a metaphor to personify the tender compassionate spirit which inspires this multitude of ministering angels under the suggestive name of 'Our Lady of the Slums,' walking, living, amid the foulest surroundings with unsullied raiment kept pure amid the evil by the invincible panoply of faith and love.[53]

The convoluted phrasing here, which perhaps suggests self-consciousness about the Roman Catholic figure, pictures these women workers as embodying the deepest Christian love, types of the Madonna herself in their self-sacrificing faithfulness. A spiritual gift that could maintain such purity amidst such corruption seemed nothing less than a special anointing from the Mother of God. That Machar was led to such an effusive trope reveals her passionate admiration for the work of women in the Army and other evangelical organizations and her desire to acknowledge their particular sanctification.

At the end of the essay, Machar went further to characterize the church as a whole using the same metaphor. She began by noting that for too many years, the Christian church had 'passed by on the other side' of the miserable and destitute, like the wealthy priests in the story of the Good Samaritan. Next, she emphasized the maternal metaphor, stressing that the church of old had been like a cold stepmother, willing to receive a properly penitent prodigal son yet unable to embrace her role as the selfless nurturer of the unrepentant and the erring. Finally a change was coming, and some Christians were adopting a new model of divine motherhood: 'But she is beginning to see the spirit of the true mother in "Our Lady of the Slums," who goes forth to seek for the wandering prodigal in the lanes and by-ways; to throw round him the pleading arms of persevering unquenchable love; to melt his heart with the tender compassion of her gentle voice and love-lighted eyes; to dare scorn and suffering in the painful search, and, if need will, to follow her divine Lord in laying down her life for the lost sheep.'[54] In Machar's conception, commitment to the victims of the new industrial order would lead to revival within the church as well as a transformation of social relations. She was certainly not alone in stressing that service to God meant service to humanity, but she is notable for insisting emphatically on the evangelical and eschatological implications of community service and on its necessary grounding in the 'persevering unquenchable love' of the Holy Spirit. Moreover, Machar's recourse to the figure of the Madonna in the essay enabled her to highlight both a feminine dimension of Christian ministry and a Christian foundation for the maternal metaphors so prevalent in feminist discourse of this period. As I have already suggested, Machar's strength was not in formulating a new kind of language to address social problems or in devising an original approach to the questions of the day, but rather in her ability to clarify the simultaneity of the spiritual and practical dimensions of complex social problems. Addressing a diverse audience, she used every writing occasion as an opportunity to teach believers their social obligation and to teach non-believers the scriptural underpinnings of social service.

THE TEXT TO WHICH secular interpreters of Machar turn most frequently for evidence of her lack of interest in Christian doctrine and her preference for 'applied Christianity' is her 'Creeds and Confessions' (1876), a long, learned essay published in the *Canadian Monthly and National Review*. Machar's focus in the essay is on the many unfortunate schisms in the church that have resulted from human attempts at constructing theological systems to explain God. Because God's truth would always be, to some extent, beyond human grasp, Machar argued, the effort to order, delimit, and codify all the details of the Christian faith could only end in distortion and division among Christians. However, far from suggesting that believers should turn away from doctrinal questions to focus on the practical problems of the age, she stressed the importance of a renewed understanding of Christian essentials and a return to the Bible as guards against confusion and doubt.

In 'Creeds and Confessions,' Machar praised the apostle Paul for refusing to 'sound the mysteries of God's Providence, past and present,' and declared that 'nothing in all the teaching of the "chiefest Apostle" is so remarkable as the mutual toleration he commands in regard to minor differences of opinion concerning days, meats, and even the more important question of circumcision, which at that early period threatened to divide the Christian Church.'[55] A brief history of the divisiveness and bloodshed caused by traditions of belief illustrated how 'the cold corpse of dogma'[56] inevitably quashed charity and truth. Such schism was, she believed, a sin for which the churches must take responsibility in their 'demand for uniformity of assent to non-essential and debatable propositions.'[57] Rejecting dogma as presumptive, totalitarian, and dishonest, Machar asserted the primacy of the individual conscience and the inevitability of differences of opinion. 'Just as no object in nature is perhaps seen exactly alike by any two individuals, so truth, however absolute and unchangeable in itself, may, and perhaps *must*, appear somewhat different to each receiving mind.'[58] For Machar, human uniqueness mandated liberty of interpretation for the conscientious believer.

Yet despite the radicalism of such a demand for liberty, Machar was in no sense rejecting Christian doctrine or, as Brouwer phrases it, moving 'away from conventional theology.'[59] On the contrary, the essay reveals the extensive theological training that Machar had received under her father's guidance and her zealous defence of the 'sound doctrine' Cook erroneously sees her as abandoning. Although she comments approvingly that Paul and the other apostles cared less about 'doctrinal orthodoxy' than about 'visit[ing] the fatherless and the widows in their affliction and [keeping] oneself unspotted from the world,' a biblical allusion to James 1:27, she also insisted that a pure heart and selfless human love could only flow 'from love to God.'[60] Rejecting the 'letter that killeth,' Machar would never have advocated an 'ethics' without 'the spirit that giveth life.'[61] Her quarrel was precisely with 'the determined adherence to unscriptural tests of Church adherence' and insistence upon 'absolute uniformity of opinion with regard to some complicated system of human theology.'[62] The key words in this statement are 'unscriptural' and 'human.' Rather than downplaying doctrine, Machar wrote to rescue doctrinal truth as found in the Bible from erring human systems and non-scriptural ideas. Her call, then, was to return to Scripture, not to abandon it.

Modelling her own practice after that of Paul, Machar emphasized that the 'Word of God' was 'the only authoritative source of Christian truth';[63] as a divinely inspired document, the Bible was the Christian's ultimate moral authority. Far from placing her faith in the ability of human beings to forge practical applications and ethical principles from Scripture, Machar was wary of 'the inherent limitations of the human mind' and 'the further limitations caused by the constant tendency to moral evil or sin, which we believe clings to the best and purest Christians while still "in the flesh."'[64] She advocated renewed attention to Scripture and extreme caution regarding 'human definitions and dogmas,'[65] insisting that 'the Divine revelation given to man contains all that it is necessary ... to know'[66] and encouraging all believers not to rely on denominational creeds but to 'search the Scriptures diligently.'[67] So certain was Machar of the inerrancy of Scripture and the fallibility of human systems that she wrote of her longing for a purer reading experience, an approach to the Bible unencumbered by human traditions of interpretation: 'Who has not wished sometimes that he could read the Scriptures for the first time, free from all traditional bias?'[68] This dream of a pure and direct experience of the Word – an almost mystical oneness with the mind of God – strongly militates against any understanding of Machar as a social activist uninterested in scriptural issues or happy to reject the divine authority of the Bible.

Throughout the essay, Machar's love for the Bible and her horror of sectarian debates combine with her commitment to the gospel to create a compelling defence of each individual's freedom and obligation, following Luther, to 'endeavour to enter into God's thoughts in his own Word.'[69] Her very citation of Luther should give pause to those who would insist on her liberalism. Her commitment to seek personally the mind of God inspired some of her best writing. In the essay's concluding paragraph, she used parallel structure, scriptural allusion, and unifying metaphors introduced earlier in the essay to convey an urgent and prophetic message about the ultimate revelation of Truth:

> And in proportion as each division of the Church remembers that at present it only possesses a broken ray of the perfect Light, seen through the glass that distorts even while it reveals, will it prepare the way for the dawn of the light which shall combine all the rays into the whiteness of Divine purity; and divisions shall be no more, for all shall see face to face.

In proportion as each division keeps in view the fact that it has not the perfect statue of Truth, but only a fragment awaiting its place in the complete figure, shall it tend towards the perfection of the now broken statue, and the time when, crowned at last with its Divine Head, it shall shine forth in a perfect and now inconceivable beauty.[70]

Here, once again, Machar expressed her belief that human systems were inevitably flawed and partial and that all formulations of doctrine must be undertaken in a spirit of humility. Yet she did not waver in her conviction of the perfect Truth recorded in Scripture, a Truth that would ultimately be revealed on the Last Day. Her yearning for the time of Revelation, with its 'perfect and now inconceivable beauty,' reveals an intense spiritual focus. It is correct to call Machar a 'theological liberal' only so long as we bear in mind that the designation refers to her insistence on individual freedom to accept or reject denominational creeds and formulations; it did not mean, as for others then and now, resistance to the divine authority of Scripture or denial of the divinity of Christ. For Machar, all understanding began with 'the great facts of Christ's life, death, and resurrection.'[71]

In *Roland Graeme, Knight* (1892), Machar's most complete fictional articulation of her social gospel beliefs, labour unrest and spiritual doubt are two interconnected problems whose solution the novel proposes. The main character, Roland, wants to play some part in the social betterment of his fellow men: he works to improve factory conditions and agitates for ameliorative legislation through his newspaper, *The Brotherhood*, and has joined the Knights of Labor. Some years earlier, he lost his faith after a disillusioning experience at college and a devastating confrontation with the 'rigid, scholastic, one-sided theology' of his church,[72] which he had formerly planned to enter. In explaining Roland's troubles when he began to read theology, Machar highlights her objection to rigid dogma: 'He found there [in his father's old textbooks] not only statements that seemed to conflict with the teachings of science, but also declarations concerning the deepest mysteries of Divine purpose, against which his heart and his sense of justice alike rose in passionate revolt, and which he could never have dreamed it possible to conjure out of the love-lighted pages of his New Testament.'[73] Although she does not specify what these statements were, Machar may have been referring to ideas about the damnation of infants who died before being baptized and of heathens who have never heard the Christian gospel, unscriptural aspects of doctrine that many nineteenth-century Christians found horrifying. In the novel, further doubts follow the initial shattering until 'a "horror of great darkness" seemed to have swallowed up the very foundations of Roland's faith.'[74]

While he maintains his Christian activism, he does so as an unbeliever until, near the novel's conclusion, he has a faith-restoring conversation with a friend and clergyman, Reverend Alden, who shares his interests in social reform and is sceptical of elaborate theological systems. For Alden, difficulties such as scriptural obscurity and elaborate creeds are met and overcome by his recognition of divine love in Christ's death on the Cross. As Alden tells Roland, 'The central doctrine of Christianity is far greater than any human theory, or all of them together; – one proof to me that it never was of human origin!'[75] Much in Scripture, especially all the details of God's plan for salvation, is beyond human understanding, and to attempt a comprehensive theory is to 'attempt to force into a rigid mould of human formulae, mysteries which, because they belong to the workings of infinite Wisdom and Love, are quite beyond the compass of human thought.'[76] While we cannot comprehend God's plan, we can know His righteousness and mercy, and without that knowledge, all endeavour for human improvement will fall short of achievement.

At the end of the novel, Roland is planning to begin a cooperative factory, as well as to work for various legislative reforms through his writing, but he stresses in the novel's final scene that real happiness can only come about through 'the growth of the *brother-love!* And that must come from the Source of Love.'[77] The gathering strength of Roland's social convictions is finally rightly grounded in his renewed faith. Critics have been disappointed in the ending, finding Machar's 'remedies for industrial strife ... vague and optimistic'[78] and regretfully noting her 'acceptance of the class basis of her society.'[79] For Machar, however, social brotherhood did not mean socialism, and she necessarily saw transformation of the heart as at least as important as structural and legislative change. In this narrative, she was challenging both Marxist revolutionary conceptions and the comfortable maxims of laissez-faire traditionalists from a position significantly to the left of the political centre and also firmly *at* the centre of orthodox faith.

ONE OF THE MOST STRIKING FEATURES of Machar's work is the boldness with which she entered public debate with the leading intellectuals of her day. Perhaps her pseudonym had opened a space for self-assertion

without scruple, though it is unclear how long 'Fidelis' preserved anonymity; writing in 1888, Wetherald commented that her identity had
been known 'for many years,' despite her strong 'distaste for everything approaching publicity.'[80] Certainly, Machar's fearlessness in
debate suggests how intellectual acumen and righteousness could together obviate a gendered timidity in essays that enact the triumph of
faith over modesty.

In undertaking to defend the role of Christianity in modern life,
Machar wrote a series of essays on morality, science, and faith in which
she demonstrated her wide general knowledge and revealed herself a
critic for whom purity of intention, concern for accuracy, and peda-
gogical purpose governed method. In the latter half of the 1870s until it
ceased publication in 1882, the *Canadian Monthly* showcased an extended debate between theists and sceptics about the implications of
Darwinian science, the continuing relevance and truth claims of Christianity, and the philosophical foundations of morality. The major representative of Darwinian-influenced scepticism was William Dawson
LeSueur, an Ottawa civil servant, philosopher, historian, and social
critic who came to be known as the 'Sage of Ottawa'[81] for his wide
learning and commitment to intellectual inquiry; according to his biographer Clifford Holland, he was 'the pre-eminent Canadian Victorian
intellectual' who 'did much to mould public opinion in Canada and
even beyond its borders.'[82] Machar took on the task of debating with
this enthusiastic supporter of the theory of evolution and avowed critic
of religious orthodoxy. Throughout the series, she showed herself scru-
pulously fair yet determined to make her case, both generous and uncompromising. She sought every opportunity to find common ground
with her adversary, to commend that which she found true in her
opponent's discussion, and to concede areas of ambiguity and uncertainty. At the same time, though, she could, when necessary, chastise
him vigorously, exclaiming over instances of wilful blindness, conceptual sloppiness, or moral error. Ultimately, LeSueur would admit that of
the three writers who had attempted to answer his arguments, her reply
was 'the most detailed, and, so far, the most satisfactory.'[83]

An issue that occupied pages of the *Canadian Monthly* concerned
prayer, specifically whether Christian claims about God's answering
of prayer could be made to correspond with the facts of science. For
LeSueur, the orthodox Christian position was entirely unbelievable,
and Machar wrote a series of essays, including 'Prayer for Daily Bread'
(1875) and 'The Divine Law of Prayer' (1876), to defend faith in the

miraculous. Her genius for clear definitions, precise distinction, and close analysis serve her well in these carefully argued responses. In 'The Divine Law of Prayer,' she worked to show how LeSueur's rational positivism, which presumed greater sophistication in thought and scientific understanding than Christianity, was in fact crude in its beliefs about prayer, inadequate in its conception of the Almighty, and, perhaps most tellingly, mistaken in its grasp of scientific principles. LeSueur's central contention was that prayer could not alter the unalterable laws of nature. But such a conception of nature, Machar was at pains to demonstrate, was in fact a rather discredited and debatable one. Nature was no longer conceived to be fixed and static but rather was recognized as a dynamic exchange of forces and fields of energy. Such new understanding – and the awareness of how much was still unknown – actually made it easier to conceive of God's power acting through nature from moment to moment. Given that the laws of electricity, for example, were previously unimaginable and considering how many other such laws remained to be discovered, it became increasingly tenable that the Divine Spirit, all powerful and all knowing, should manifest His will in accordance with these complex laws in a process both dynamic and ordered. New scientific understanding actually 'makes it more instead of less easy to conceive of the physical efficacy of prayer,'[84] Machar explained.

Moreover, Christians did not see prayer, as LeSueur implied they did, as directly affecting physical events 'as if it were a kind of natural agency which had only to be put in motion to produce a uniform result.'[85] The Christian understanding was much subtler and more nuanced than LeSueur acknowledged. It was the God of the universe who granted prayer, not the prayer that changed the universe, and then only when the petition was in accordance with God's cosmic and omnipotent will. Moreover, LeSueur falsely separated God from His universe, whereas an appropriate conception of the Divine Spirit, one that took into account divine 'foreknowledge and foreordination,' enabled some apprehension of how 'an all-wise Ruler of the universe could adapt His moral to His physical government.'[86] Machar was delighted to discover that LeSueur conceded the impact of prayer in the spiritual realm, and she went on to show, citing contemporary scientists, that the distinction between the physical and the spiritual was in the process of being broken down; to concede effects on the spirit was in essence to accept physical change.

Dealing point by point with LeSueur's objections, Machar not only uncovered the failures of coherence or full understanding in his argument but also undertook to demonstrate how the Christian answer could supply the deficiencies of his positivism. She argued carefully throughout about the many different ways that prayer might be answered and about the complex relationship between human effort and prayerful petition. Most importantly, perhaps, she addressed the crucial difference between probability and provability, showing how argumentative claims and procedures shifted according to this difference. Her object, she clarified triumphantly, 'was not to *prove* the physical efficacy of prayer, inasmuch as from the nature of the case either proof or disproof is impossible ... But where the disproof is limited solely to considerations of improbability, we do not need, in reply, to go farther than to show the inadequacy of such objections to disturb our well-grounded faith.'[87] Relentlessly pursuing LeSueur's misconceptions and illogicalities in order to shore up her case, Machar conducted a calm and sometimes audacious rebuttal of his position.

As in the above example, in which she responded at some length to LeSueur's quoting of her own words out of context in order to clarify that she had never claimed to 'prove' the results of prayer, Machar was often alacritous in pointing out where she had been misrepresented, where objections had already been met in a previous article, or where the criticism of an opponent was based on misunderstanding. Moreover, she was not afraid on occasion to imply that her opponent was disingenuous, prone to oversimplification, or ill-informed; on one occasion, blunt contradiction expressed her sense of his ignorance. She quoted his contemptuous words in order to contradict them flatly, offering the authority of her position in a community of believers as irrefutable proof of superior knowledge: 'Mr. LeSueur "cannot think that any human being, in uttering sincerely and fervently the words, 'Thy will be done,' can ever have felt that they implied petition." It remains true, however, that many sincere and fervent Christian petitioners in all ages *have* felt this to be a real petition.'[88]

At another point in the article, she observed quite sharply that a certain objection of LeSueur's 'merely repeats, in different words, a misrepresentation of our position, the inaccuracy of which has been pointed out by the present writer in a previous article.'[89] She was annoyed when he cited a Christian as disbelieving in prayer as petition 'on the foundation of a few words *said about him*, which, however, were never meant to assert' LeSueur's construction of them;[90] where the faith of fellow Christians was concerned, Machar could be fiercely protective. She also vigorously rebuked her opponent when he failed to fulfil her standards of argumentative conduct, finding one of his objections to be of the sort 'which was not to have been expected from an able and thoughtful pleader for truth.'[91] And her final direct address, more in sorrow than in anger, impugned his motives and moral conception in spreading doubt about prayer: 'While, therefore, there is much in the latter part of Mr. LeSueur's article that we can sympathize with, we cannot but regret that the writer of it should "spend his strength for naught," in trying to accomplish that which is impossible and which, if it were possible, would be hurtful, not beneficial.'[92]

Logical rebuttal and appeals to scientific authority were not Machar's only resources. In defending faith against unbelief, she sought to engage her reader on the emotional and spiritual as well as the intellectual level, believing as she did that only through the spirit could the heart 'reach out into the darkness and touch the Divine, as it never can do through the mere intellect and reason.'[93] In one instance, a carefully phrased analogy was immediately followed by a passionate claim of personal conviction intended to strike the heart of her reader and to awaken a different order of discernment:

> That much debasing superstition has been engrafted upon the intuition of prayer, is no more an argument against its intrinsic truth, than the superstitions of Polytheism are an argument against Theism, or than the Mohammedan vision of a sensual Paradise is a proof that immortality is a delusion. No! we believe that the divinely implanted and ineradicable instinct of prayer is no delusion, but is our Divine guide to the unseen and uncomprehended love which lies around and about us; just as the instinct that draws the child to its mother's breast is its guide to the uncomprehended mother-love, which is the necessary and blessed provision for its opening years.[94]

In cases such as this, it is clear that Machar was not only refuting LeSueur but also attempting to win him, and other sceptical readers, to a saving faith. To that end, she sought to persuade readers to suspend doubt and to seek through prayer the infilling of the Holy Spirit, confident that conviction would not be denied to anyone who sought it. Speaking of the unmistakable blessing afforded those who pray, Machar added, 'Here, we apprehend, is the true prayer test, and we would earnestly recommend every sceptic to try it for himself.'[95] Frequent references to God's abundant mercy leavened her closely reasoned rejoinders as she assured readers that 'no humble, praying Christian will ever be left to wander in darkness'[96] and declared her conviction that even when a prayer might seem to be unanswered and even when all material hope was gone, Christians could rest assured of 'the loving care that guides the sufferer through that parting pang of agony into the nobler life beyond.'[97] While these emotional appeals were of little logical value to her argument, they demonstrated Machar's deep conviction about how much was at stake in the debate.

Concerned less to win the argument per se than to win readers away from doubt and despair, Machar created in all of her writing a powerful ethical appeal based on her earnestness and concern. Admitting the barriers to persuasion in a sceptical age, she articulated the sense of Christian obligation that motivated her work. While she accepted that there was 'little hope of convincing by argument' those who regarded intellectual difficulties as 'insuperable barriers to belief,' she expressed not embattled frustration but heartfelt regret at 'their bearing the burden of life without availing themselves of this unspeakable privilege [of faith].'[98] Her strongly stated conviction that the real issue under discussion could never be satisfactorily resolved in the pages of the *Canadian Monthly* gave evidence of her integrity: 'It is not by argument or discussion that any truth can become the possession of the soul; and all that we would desire would be that they should fairly test the matter in their own experience, a test which would be of infinitely more value than many "doubtful disputations."'[99] In advising her reader *not* to trust in words and debate, she confirmed unimpeachable motives. Moreover, she frequently stressed her desire to avoid presumption so as not to attempt to explain *how* or *why* God manifested His purpose in the way that He did (or did not), thus revealing the tender and confiding faith that her argument was designed to defend. Added to all of these features of her discussion, her tendency to paraphrase Scripture in the course of the argument so that biblical phrasing mingled with her own, as when she referred to a God perfectly able 'to care for the fall of a sparrow and answer the prayer of a trusting child,'[100] lent to her discourse a potent moral authority.

Such creation of authority at the levels of logic, ethos, and emotion is evident also in 'The Source of Moral Life' (1880), an essay Machar contributed to an ongoing conversation in the same journal about the relation between social morality and Christian belief. Once again, Machar

rebutted LeSueur's central propositions, picking through his arguments to uncover their misapplications. She deftly overturned many of
his assertions, targeting especially those that he proposed to be self-
evident. Quoting, for example, his assertion that 'no system of religion,
past or present, can claim to have invented [morality], or to be alone
capable of maintaining it in vigour,'[101] Machar forcefully concurred,
dismissing the charge as unfounded and supplying a neat analogy to
reveal LeSueur's illogic: 'But no one on either side of the present discussion would assert that either religion, or any system of religion, "invented morality." To do so would be to honour neither religion nor
morality, and would be as rational as to speak of sanitary systems as
inventing the laws of health. Christ Himself made no such claim, when
He appealed to the Jews to judge Him by His words and works.'[102] To
the charge that Christianity's focus on life after death made this life 'a
thing of little value,' not treated with 'due seriousness,' she responded
by pointing out that 'nothing could make this life of such momentous
seriousness as the consciousness that its issues reach out into a vista
of infinity.'[103]

Analytical precision and adroitness were never, however, deployed
merely in the cause of besting her opponent or having the last word:
throughout the essay, Machar sought to lead her readers, through
logical reversals and compelling rearticulations, into new avenues of
thought, away from a worldly wisdom incapable of discovering truth
and towards a spiritual apprehension of divine mystery. In the following example, she transformed what might seem a weakness of her position – the unreasonableness of the Christian account – into evidence of
its truth: 'We do not need to be told that [Christianity's] central doctrine
is distasteful to the pride of natural reason – conclusive evidence that
natural reason never could have originated it.'[104] Moreover, Machar
was obviously emboldened and invigorated by the opportunity to clear
up misconceptions that could stand in the way of faith, delighting in the
clarity and confidence of her own theological position. For example, she
rebuked her opponent for his weakly conceived articulation of Christ's
sacrifice and chastised him for implying Christian foolishness to believe
it. 'In the paper entitled "The Future of Morality,"' she noted, 'we have a
curiously crude and incorrect statement of what Christians understand
by this great central belief [of the doctrine of the Cross]. Can the writer
really believe that the doctrine, as *he* states it, is that which drew forth
the adoring love of such intellects and hearts as those of Paul and
Augustine, and Luther and Chalmers?'[105] Triumphant in claiming a

vibrant intellectual tradition, Machar clarified the Christian position to enlighten readers (and perhaps to prove membership in the august company she had cited): 'Christians are asked to believe – not that they are held guiltless because "an innocent person" has died for their offences – but that "God was in Christ reconciling the world to Himself" – that Divine Love itself descended into the conditions of sinful humanity, and submitted itself to the penalty of sin, that it might raise humanity, through the love and trust which we call Faith, to receive forgiveness and help, and the renewed communion with God, which must be the true source of moral life.'[106] Christians did not celebrate Christ's death but His resurrection, she reminded readers, which made possible reconciliation with God, triumph over sin, and the earthly comfort and guidance of the Holy Spirit. Left to his own faulty reason, man would eventually choose wrongly.

To lead her readers away from reliance on 'natural reason,' Machar pinpointed her opponent's crucial neglect of the spiritual element in mankind. Here, once again, she sought to touch the emotions of her readers, tracing that wellspring of loss, fear, and longing that was, for her, the irrefutable sign of a spiritual reality. In passages that give evidence of the many emotionally stirring sermons to which Machar had listened all her life, measured analysis is replaced by impassioned refutation. In the following statement, for example, the very long conditional structure, with its agonized string of descriptions and analogies defining existence without God, crescendoes to a fervent declaration of God's presence:

> Were man, indeed, the mere transitory product of blind material forces, owing no allegiance and feeling no aspirations beyond these, with nothing either to draw him upward or to draw him downward from the inevitable progress of his being through the action of his 'environment,' like a mollusc on the sea-shore, with no perception of spiritual beauty or of spiritual need, – no sense of warfare between that which his higher nature admires and that which his lower nature is impelled to do; then, indeed, his so-called 'morality' might develop as instinctively as his senses or his passions, and religion, and indeed anything worth calling virtue, would be alike superfluous and inconceivable. If, in short, we lived in a world of the secular moralist's creation, his theory would be unexceptionable. *But we do not!*[107]

Rhetorical questions and pitying exclamations give evidence of unshakeable conviction and sympathy for the lost, as when Machar asks,

'Is then the deepest consciousness of humanity "nothing?" Or is it a delusion that has forced from the noblest hearts the cry, "My soul thirsteth for God, for the living God?" No! the delusion lies with those who, apparently for the sake of a favourite theory, throw away their noblest birthright.'[108] Compassion marked her admission, while rebuking her opponents for an error devastating to their peace and welfare, that 'when we are told that to lose Christ, and life, and immortality is to lose nothing material from our moral life, we can scarcely find words of reproach for those who so cheat themselves with "vacant chaff well meant for grain."'[109] Machar closed the essay on a rousing note designed to comfort the beleaguered faithful and inspire the doubting, a message affirming ecstatic certainty in an uncertain age: 'Infidelity, in all its guises, may for a time vaunt its destructive triumphs in the borrowed language of the heavenly kingdom. But the Church of Christ knows her leader will not fail ... The Star of Bethlehem still lights earnest seekers to the spiritual king, and its light shall not wane till the whole sky is radiant with that fuller glory which many think is already dawning.'[110] To be such an 'earnest seeker' encouraging others along the way and looking for the 'fuller glory' was Machar's purpose in everything she wrote. The paradoxical combination in her essays of urgency and serenity came from her righteous desire to combat injustice coupled with her faith that, whether she succeeded or not, divine justice and truth would ultimately prevail.

In 1924, a few years before Machar's death at age ninety, F.L. MacCallum sounded the note of affectionate condescension that would characterize modernist attitudes to so many Victorian writers: visiting the elderly author at her home, MacCallum felt 'ushered into the 1860's'[111] as he met the 'tiny, old lady,' who seemed worlds away from the 'hilarious squad of very modern young things'[112] he had seen enjoying themselves outside her house. At the end of the interview, the 'derisive bray' of a 'passing runabout'[113] seemed to signal a modernity that could no longer appreciate moral earnestness. Yet only a few decades earlier, Machar had been at the centre of Canadian cultural life, claiming a powerful position as an advocate of social and spiritual regeneration. In the *Literary History of Canada* (1965), Roy Daniells was more admiring than MacCallum in summing up her legendary status, claiming, 'Her tenacity of purpose, her consistency of aim, her articulateness, and her ability to fuse religious, patriotic, and cultural interests give her all the force of a legend.'[114] Remarkable for the fearlessness and effectiveness with which she entered Canadian public debate, Machar did not hesitate to pronounce upon a range of subjects, from the theological to the industrial, that many other women avoided. Her identity as a Christian radical, I argue, was a particularly important feature of her rhetorical self-positioning, enabling her to claim and exercise a degree of authority that might otherwise have eluded her. Drawing inventively on Scripture to discuss social issues while deploying a range of rhetorical strategies to mark her earnestness and faith, Machar found a way to exercise her intellectual acumen and learning while impressing her opponents as a gentlewoman of humility and integrity.

2 The Uses of Wit: Sara Jeannette Duncan's Self-Fashioning

'Dear Garth Grafton,' wrote a reader of Sara Jeannette Duncan's 1886 column in the Toronto *Globe*, 'I take much pleasure and profit reading the themes that are discussed in the columns of "Woman's World." But I think sometimes you are rather severe on some of the characters which are introduced.'[1] Such was a typical response to the sharp-tongued persona Duncan created in her newspaper columns of the mid-1880s. Although sometimes finding her 'rather severe,' readers seemed to enjoy being teased, corrected, and edified by the ebullient Garth, who never hesitated to point out flabby logic or chide them for infelicities of grammar and expression. They in turn appealed to her with an affectionate combination of deference and raillery. Duncan was a popular columnist, credited by journalist Hector Charlesworth with single-handedly creating the 'fame' of the *Globe*'s women's department,[2] and the paucity of critical attention directed to her newspaper work is a baffling oversight given its charm and iconoclasm.[3] Witty, complex, and carefully structured, peppered with literary references and wordplay, Duncan's columns of social observation and argument were a flexible, dynamic medium for the young writer in which she experimented with parody, invective, and comic scenes to skewer social pieties and proffer unorthodox opinions. In doing so, she proved the newspaper an effective platform from which a young woman could construct an alluring public identity.

Duncan is now known, if at all, for her Jamesian novels of social manners and national types, which she wrote after she married Everard Cotes, a civil servant in colonial India, and moved to Calcutta in 1890. There she established a moderately successful reputation for novels that presented North Americans in Europe or examined Anglo-Indian society, focusing on cultural misunderstanding and the difficulty of putting ideals into practice. She also contributed articles to the *Indian Daily News*, which her husband edited. Serious novels such as *A Daughter of To-day* (1894) and *Set in Authority* (1906) remain fascinating portraits of their time and place. But before her twenty-fifth birthday, she was developing through journalism the subtle distinctions, ironic double-voicing, and polished social comedy that later became hallmarks of her fiction. Born Sara Janet in 1861 in Brantford, Canada West, a go-ahead manufacturing town that she could not wait to escape – the entire province of Ontario she scorned at the ripe age of twenty-four as 'one great camp of the Philistines'[4] – she seems always to have looked upon the convictions and enthusiasms of her fellows with an ironical eye; and from an early age, she knew that she wanted to write and to reinvent herself. After training to be a teacher and realizing that the work was uncongenial, she was fortunate to launch her literary career at a time when Canadian newspapers, keen to attract female readers in order to secure advertising revenue, were just beginning to bring women on staff.[5]

Duncan began with determination, covering the New Orleans Cotton Centennial early in 1885 and then contributing to the *Globe* over the summer, and finally making her name when she was hired in the fall as literary editor of the *Washington Post*, where she continued until June of the following year. On the basis of her U.S. credentials, she was able to secure full-time employment at two major Canadian papers, the *Globe* (1886–7), where she wrote as Garth Grafton, and then the Montreal *Star* (1887–8). While she was working at the *Post*, she also became a regular contributor to the most prestigious Canadian weekly of the period, Goldwin Smith's *The Week* (1886–8), to which she submitted many of her *Washington Post* articles. Although she was very young and relatively inexperienced, Duncan established a name for herself quickly, becoming the first Canadian woman to declare in print her support for woman suffrage[6] and serving as parliamentary correspondent during her tenure with the *Star*. Unlike most other female journalists of the 1880s, she was not limited to writing about recipes, housekeeping tips, and social etiquette. Although she wrote her share of fashion news, she more often covered diverse and controversial subjects, attending women's conventions, visiting institutes for the destitute, interviewing professional women, reviewing serious literature, and reflecting on social problems. Through her interviews, book reviews, sketches, travel articles, and tirades, in prose notable for its buoyant self-confidence and wit, Duncan made herself the bright and insouciant public voice of the New Woman in Canada.

Sara Jeannette Duncan.

IN 1890 THE JOURNALIST-EDITOR E.E. Sheppard commented in *Saturday Night* on the public fascination with the new breed of female journalist, who made herself and her adventures the subject of her journalism. 'Trifles such as would hardly be read if written by a man,' observed Sheppard, 'become thrilling or picturesque as an episode in the life of a woman.'[7] He was referring to the much-publicized world tour of Duncan and fellow journalist Lily Lewis,[8] which provided the subject for the most popular book Duncan ever published, *A Social Departure: How Orthodocia and I Went round the World by Ourselves* (1890). According to Marjory Lang in her study of early Canadian journalism, 'the newspaper of [the late nineteenth century] both catered to and stimulated popular curiosity about the unconventional woman.'[9] The feminine persona of female journalists was a source of fascination to readers of the 1880s to the extent that women writers became 'part of the news-making formula'[10] and keenly scrutinized public commodities.

Duncan herself thought her era was a 'golden age for girls, full of new interests and new opportunities.'[11] Part of her own success was surely the unconventionality that she flaunted. Writing her 'Woman's World' column, where one might expect a fairly predictable canvassing of domestic instruction and fashion news, Duncan could do nothing in the ordinary way, even when she did stoop to such commonplace material as housecleaning or fashion tips. Once, conveying instructions on how to kill cockroaches, she described with mock solemnity the efficacy of cucumbers, whose peel was both attractive and deadly to the 'horny black pests.'[12] As often happened, Duncan's language took on a biblical and bombastic inflection when she wrote of matters slightly ridiculous: 'More fatal than the unripe apple to the small boy is the cucumber unto the cockroach,' she explained sententiously. 'He simply partakes once, turns his face to the wall in vain repentance, crosses his legs, and dies.'[13] Whether or not anyone could take such a recommendation seriously, it made for amusing copy.

On another occasion she took pleasure in responding to an anxious reader who asked for 'a recipe for freckles on the face.'[14] Duncan's pretended misunderstanding – did the writer want to cook the said freckles, and in what manner? – indicated both her amusement at the poor word choice and her elaborate indifference to the conventions of feminine beauty. Her mocking answer combined the overly formal with the colloquial commonplace. 'If it were pickles now,' she replied, 'but freckles, and on the face, too – I don't believe I've got anything reliable. But it becomes clear to my kindred consciousness that your desire is rather unto the banishment of your present supply than to the "putting down" of indefinite quarts for next winter's use, my subscribing sister. Well, I've heard that vinegar is good – or is it lemon and the whites of two eggs? – but they come on worse the next day ... I'm afraid I can't give you a sure cure for freckles on my own responsibility, but I can tell you how many I've got – exactly twenty-three, if that will be any comfort to you.'[15] The implication of the playful rejoinder seems clear: modern women had more important things to worry about than freckles. On other occasions she was even more pointed in teasing her readers, telling one correspondent who asked for directions on the use of sulphur and molasses for clearing a 'muddled complexion'[16] that her question was simply beyond reason: 'My Dear Girl – I think you will find this department at all times and under all circumstances willing to answer any reasonable question that the curiosity of man can suggest or the ingenuity of woman devise, but I leave it to the general public if that's a reasonable question!'[17]

As these examples suggest, one of Duncan's favourite strategies of self-fashioning as a journalist was to set off her own wit, irreverence, and linguistic verve against another's naive conformity, intellectual dullness, or boorish self-satisfaction, confident that her witty tirades and expressions of irritated superiority were stylish and amusing enough to satisfy readers. Even when she made a mistake in the column – as she did once in referring to the death of old-fashioned heroines such as Florence Nightingale, who turned out to be still alive – she turned it into an occasion for cheeky self-assertion: 'Florence Nightingale is not dead,' she wrote a few days later in mock abasement after receiving a flood of corrections. 'Would it be sacrilegious at this juncture and under these unhappy circumstances to wish that she were? It would, but she is not.'[18] On other occasions she vented high-spirited spleen on examples of smug pomposity, as when she took aim at the tendency among married men to use their wives as examples in discussing women's proper roles and duties:

It is the unanswerable argument with which he confronts all questions relating to femininity. He would have all womankind cut upon the pattern he has honoured with his selection. He rises – this married fiend! – smirks, and we know that the wife is coming – there is no dodging her – 'I have a wife,' and she does this or that, or abstains from doing this or that, yet I find her a perfectly satisfactory spouse, *ergo* the sex can do no better than comport itself accordingly. I have never been able to fathom this confiding person's desire to unburden himself to the public concerning the state of his domestic relations. I think, however, that when he stands up there in his deacon's tail coat, or his broadcloth cut-away, with a comfortable sense of good things within, and says he has a wife, he feels snugly conscious of having done well by society in general, and womankind in particular, by committing matrimony, and wants the respect deserved for the exercise of such an expensive proprietary right, and one would fancy from the invariable applause that greets him from his fellow Benedicts, that he usually gets it.[19]

The zest with which Duncan enumerated such irritating foibles illustrates her fondness for exercising her verbal facility at another's expense. A favourite tactic was to seize upon a conventional opinion or banal remark found in another newspaper (she read voraciously) or to respond at length to a remark overheard in the cafeteria or on the street.

Duncan's tendency to play off the statements of others is perhaps most complexly revealed in her interviews, of which she conducted a significant number for the pages of 'Woman's World.' In an era when female journalists were themselves news, female journalists in interview with other professional or publicly active women were particularly noteworthy. Duncan's interviews provide examples of the kind of woman-to-woman encounters that sparked widespread interest among newspaper readers in the mid-1880s. As a newly emerging journalistic genre, the interviews reveal not only Duncan's own, often ambivalent, attitudes to unconventional women in her society but also something of the manifold public assumptions and expectations that shaped women's choices and self-constructions in Victorian Canada.

An interview, for Duncan, was never just a conversation: despite its claim to spontaneity and informal exchange, it was a fairly elaborate performance, with elements of ritual and improvisational bravura. Her columns were always, as I suggest, about self-display, and in interviews that element was heightened through a carefully staged encounter with another whose words she guided, framed, and played against. Though friendly interest was often a part of the tone Duncan created in these dialogues, darker notes of condescension and aggression were also sounded. It may have been that, as a woman in conscious revolt against the domestic realm of conventional femininity, she was profoundly engaged by – but also ambivalent about – other women who were likewise forging identities that distinguished them from their more conventional peers.

One category of such women included those Christian activists whose causes – temperance, homes for fallen women, institutes for working girls, havens for the aged or for orphans – were attempts to ameliorate the evils of contemporary urban life, to better the lives of other women, and to spread the good news of salvation among the vulnerable and the erring. For these women Duncan, in line with the society around her, seems to have felt a mixture of admiration and gentle contempt. Their Christian fervour was both unsettling and compelling; although Duncan was a nominal Christian, a Presbyterian who knew her Bible and attended church, she avoided serious discussion of faith and often used Scripture for comic purposes. She once wrote in annoyance about temperance women who opened meetings by proclaiming, with tears in their eyes, that theirs was 'a good work and ordered of the Lord'[20] – presumably irritated by the presumption and emotionalism of such rhetoric. But she also found herself strangely drawn to a rhetorically unpolished young Salvation Army woman preaching in Toronto's Queen's Park, her face 'pale with excitement, her ugly poke bonnet pushed back, her hands moving in untrained, ungraceful gestures as she battled with an imaginary spiritual foe to the welfare of mankind.'[21] The girl was surrounded by men, Duncan noted, 'some of them of the variety of mankind from whom might be expected the most flagrant disrespect.' But there was no disrespect. The woman had, Duncan declared, 'this one infallible source of power over her wayside congregation; she believes implicitly what she is telling it.'[22] Despite being struck by this girl's sincerity and courage, Duncan in general seems to have believed religious faith a private issue not to be discussed or demonstrated.

In the first interview under consideration, a mixture of gentle mockery and hesitant admiration betrays Duncan's ambivalence in interviewing an organizer in a local chapter of the Woman's Christian Temperance Union (WCTU), the foremost reform organization in Ontario, dedicated, as Sharon Anne Cook has shown, not only to prohibition but also to sexual purity and the abolition of vice, crime, and cruelty to women and children. Duncan's interview subject was a gentle lady so retiring that she did not wish to have her name or personal details published in the paper; she was addressed throughout the column as Mrs Y. For a professional writer such as Duncan, such extreme modesty could only have seemed quaint. Duncan appeared to like Mrs Y, telling readers that though her mood had been dark on the day of the interview as a result of a dreary fall of rain, it brightened through contact with the benevolent lady. 'People who lend their lives to doing good, I find, usually manage to wrap themselves in a very delightful atmosphere,' she comments.[23] The remark is ambiguously approving, for 'doing good' was, for the intellectual and ironical Duncan, always somewhat of a doubtful accomplishment. And in her report of the interview, Duncan could not help but have a little fun at the expense of Mrs Y's cheerful earnestness and humourless sincerity. Discussing the overall increase in WCTU membership, Mrs Y explained the languishing of individual chapters and the sudden expansion of others using the metaphor of a tree: 'As a tree grows, you know, its imperfect fruit falls, and the sickly twigs dry up and drop, yet that doesn't interfere with the tree's vitality. We ought to be very well content with forty-six new shoots this year.'[24] In Duncan's response, we catch her amused reaction to the rather clichéd and pious metaphor: '"Yes," I said, "it is pretty rapid progress for vegetation of any sort."'[25] There is no indication that Mrs Y smiled her discernment at Duncan's wit.

And in the discussion that follows, one notes the satirical edge to Duncan's questions and responses, her seemingly irresistible urge to highlight Mrs Y's innocent hopefulness with her own slightly world-weary irreverence. Responding to Mrs Y's statement that some of the most important work being carried on by the WCTU was in the hands of the youngest members, Duncan initiated the following exchange, in which her own ebullient overstatement and mock-serious inquiry are contrasted with Mrs Y's literal-minded conventionality:

'I am glad to hear that that besatirized, belectured young person, the Modern Girl, has done something at last which may be approved of in the newspapers,' I rejoined. 'Please tell me about it that I may print it in *The Globe*, to the dismay of her enemies, and the everlasting confusion of face of those who perennially rebuke her.'

'Well, Miss Scott, of Ottawa, took the chair, and filled it with both grace and dignity. Miss Scott is naturally of a very quiet, shy, retiring disposition, but that evening she took courage, and really distinguished herself by her good management.'

'Now this, Mrs. Y., would be a good opportunity to settle public opinion in the Province of Ontario as to the proper form in addressing a lady in the chair. Did you call Miss Scott "Miss Chairwoman," "Miss Chairman," or what?'

'It is a vexed question, isn't it? I don't think she was addressed in her capacity as the chair, so nobody called her anything.'

'If we could only have settled, it,' I sighed, 'one half the horror of pre-
siding over a public meeting would, I am convinced, have been done
away with! But go on.'[26]

And so on. Duncan must have taken pleasure in writing up the interview to display the markedly distinct sensibilities – the one high-
spirited, arch, and worldly; the other sincere, earnest, and devout – of
interviewer and interviewee. In the end, however, she summed up
Mrs Y's significance by pointing to the development of a new spirit of
active citizenship among 'club' women across the country: 'The work
of the WCTU shows to Prohibitionist and anti-Prohibitionist alike
many things, apart from its mission and its motive, which the most forward caviller could find inspired by nothing but good. It shows a
growing ability in women to organize, and sustain, and control. It
shows a lively awakening to their individual responsibility, not only as
women but as subjects and citizens. It shows a deepening sense of the
importance of opinion and an increased desire to grapple with wrong –
the wrong that affects other people. These are not little things.'[27]
Whether or not Duncan believed as fervently as Mrs Y in the benevolent reform principles of the WCTU – and she was certainly no
supporter of prohibition – she approved, as did most readers of the
high-minded *Globe*, the seriousness and social commitment of the
women involved.

It was a different Duncan – sober, awed, even reverent – who interviewed Mother Anselme of the Notre Dame des Anges, a superior who
operated a convent and single women's boarding house.[28] For most
late nineteenth-century Protestants in Ontario, the Roman Catholic
convent was a place of secrecy and superstition, and Duncan from the
first emphasized the enchanting strangeness of her encounter with the
mother superior. Usually alert and ironically observant, she found herself so stricken with awe by the robed sister before her that 'the information she imparted during the first five minutes of her conversation
will never be given to the world through the columns of the Globe and
the agency of me, for ... I heard none of it; so absorbed was I in listen-
ing to the quiet, musical voice, in watching the gentle, reposeful deportment, and in speculating upon the strange withdrawal of all pain
and care from the placid face of my informant.'[29] The interview became an occasion not for jaunty banter but for extended reflection on
mystery; frequently, Duncan acknowledged her inability to comprehend the inner life of the woman before her and her sense in the

woman and her sisters of access to a source of power and peace beyond her own understanding. 'What years of fast and penance and
sore chastening of the spirit has it required to efface every footprint of
life and love and vanity from these pale faces, and to invest these quiet
personalities with so great a degree of spiritual force that they seem
even in moving and talking to exhale a perceptible odor of sanctity!'[30]
Perhaps there is an implied criticism here of the effacement of 'life and
love' in the pursuit of 'sanctity,' but if so, it is a hesitant one. In the final
exchange recorded, as the mother superior shows Duncan the room in
which the nuns do their work, any trace of irony or insouciance has
been extinguished from the chastened Duncan:

> Then we went down into the nuns' quarters, or what my guide called the
> 'community room,' where she and her seven subordinates meet for work,
> occasionally prayer, and recreation. The 'community room' is very plain
> and bare, but for a few prints of the saints. The walls are lined with
> presses for the nuns' work. The Superioress showed me a brown piece of
> cloth upon which she had been embroidering in white silk I.H.S. and the
> emblems of the cross, crown, and anchor.
>
> 'This,' she said, 'is a scapular worn by the members of the Order of
> St. Carmel when they are laid out in death. The entire robe is of this
> brown cloth, and the scapular is laid on the breast. They are constantly or-
> dered, so they are made, blessed, and put away in readiness.'
>
> I shivered involuntarily. 'It doesn't seem to be very pleasant work or a
> very pleasant room,' I said.
>
> 'But in time we become accustomed to it and would not have it other-
> wise,' she responded gravely. 'We would not enjoy the luxuries of the
> world, for we could not feel that they were consistent with our vocation.'[31]

Duncan ends the interview without further comment. For the Protestant Duncan, the nuns' life apart from men and in dedication to God
gave them a remote and disquieting fascination that commanded her
respect and rapt attention. While she could not help being amused by
the staidly earnest Mrs Y, she recognized in Mother Anselme an inaccessible dignity and power.

An entirely different attitude and self-presentation are evident in
what is one of Duncan's most intriguing interviews: that with the
part-Mohawk poet E. Pauline Johnson, an emerging celebrity from
Duncan's home town of Brantford. The interview in the Globe[32] was

published the day after Johnson's poem '"Brant," A Memorial Ode' (1886) was read out at the unveiling in Brantford of a statue to Joseph Brant, Mohawk Loyalist. As Duncan described it, Johnson's poem had received 'a storm of applause,'[33] and Duncan took the occasion to introduce her, somewhat proprietarily, to the public: 'I have had the pleasure of her acquaintance for some time, and while it is a privilege that cannot, unfortunately, be extended to the general public, it seems to me that all *Canadiennes* deserve at least to enjoy it by proxy.'[34] There is something fulsome in this beginning, a note of insincerity and over-formality in Duncan's professed regret that all her readers cannot be 'privileged' by acquaintance with Johnson. For a writer sceptical of the mere cult of personality, and especially for one who bristled at all forms of cant and empty rhetoric, this was a rather hollow tribute; one wonders if its strained formality was a deliberate snub resulting from professional rivalry or whether, annoyed by what seemed undeserved recognition for a mediocre talent, Duncan simply could not praise Johnson sincerely. She described Johnson's physical appearance in more detail than she normally gave to interview subjects, and again one detects some artificiality – perhaps condescension – in Duncan's stereotypically flattering word portrait: 'You want to know what she is like first, of course. Well, she is tall and slender and dark, with grey eyes, beautifully clean cut features, black hair, a very sweet smile, and a clear, musical, pleasant voice. I have always thought her beautiful and many agree with me. She has certainly that highest attribute of beauty, the rare, fine gift of expression. She is charmingly bright in conversation and has a vivacity of tone and gesture that is almost French.'[35] Duncan's exclusive focus on Johnson's physical beauty and her use of formulaic romantic language (she refers later to Johnson's 'dusky locks')[36] have the effect of turning her interview subject into an exotic stereotype.

The false note struck at the outset continues for the rest of the interview, during which Duncan approaches Johnson not in the manner of a friendly acquaintance and still less as a fellow writer with her name to win and an interest in literary matters, but rather as an Anglo-Canadian gentlewoman self-consciously confronting a specimen of Canada's past. As Johnson shows Duncan various relics of her Native heritage, Duncan foregrounds her own horrified fascination. Confronted with a tomahawk and a scalping knife belonging to Johnson's father, she gasps out her confused interest: '"But don't they – didn't he – I mean, isn't it usual for people who indulge in that kind of amusement to do it with their tomahawks?" I inquired rather delicately, for I wasn't at all sure that their fair descendant would relish this allusion to the peculiarities of her warrior ancestors.[37] Duncan's so-genteel discomfort with the 'amusements' of Native life seems calculated to reflect the strangeness of Johnson's mixed heritage, which has made her an elegant poetess whose 'warrior ancestors' only recently renounced barbarism. Perhaps the effect was intended to be humorous; perhaps it was even stage-managed by Johnson as a personal marketing strategy – a few years later, after all, she would don a buckskin tunic with bear-claw necklace and attach a scalp to her waistband. Whatever the reason, the interview seems to demonstrate Duncan's discomfort with female literary competitors and her tendency to position herself in an adversarial relationship with other young women writers.

The sting of condescension apparent in the interview with Johnson is entirely missing from a conversation Duncan recorded with an old school friend who was working as one of Toronto's first female medical doctors in a general practice. Eschewing any attempt at reportorial objectivity, Duncan from the outset of the piece is warm and personal, even nostalgically sentimental. She reflects upon a time in the past – even dating it to 1880, when she would have been eighteen years old – when three friends picnicked together in the park, indulging in dreams of future glory. They were 'three very earnest and enthusiastic young persons indeed,' spending the afternoon in avid conversation on all subjects imaginable, but especially 'the Future and the Sex,' pronouncing both 'with capital letters.'[38] It soon becomes clear that Duncan is one of these three confident and ambitious young women, anticipating future achievement of the sort only youth, with 'a wildly exhilarated opinion of itself,' can hold.[39] One of her most undisguisedly autobiographical reflections, the passage gives an implicit accounting of the personal dreams and promising social climate that had brought her and other aspiring girls to their present state. As Duncan makes clear, although the girls could not predict the future, their youthful determination and eagerness were not without foundation:

I said three girls, but one had committed the indiscretion of matrimony the year before. Her fate, of course, was settled in the pessimistic opinion of the other two. The second had just received High School honours and had college ambitions; the third, who hated such things, looked affectionately upon a large and ambitious daub in oils that was secured in the fork of a sapling near by, as in some way typical of a dazzling future career in art. Today the married girl occupies with credit a professor's chair in the Kingston Women's Medical College. She occupies another chair in different quarters with equal credit, I believe – a rocking-chair. There is one baby in Canada that will receive scientific attention from its earliest youth. The second girl is now a practicing physician in the city of Toronto with excellent prospects. The third – well, it doesn't matter about her.[40]

It would take a dull reader indeed not to recognize that Duncan is the third girl in the story, one whose artistic ambitions have been succeeded by a rather more prosaic career in journalism. Her ease with and admiration for her two successful friends is also evident; here is the type of woman she likes and understands: worldly, capable, bent on success – propelled not by a spirit of religious fervour, renunciation, or reforming benevolence but by a desire to exercise her talents and to carve a place for herself in the public sphere. Such ambition need not overshadow domestic concerns, as is indicated by Duncan's playful and somewhat laboured reference to the other 'chair' occupied by her friend 'with equal credit.' What is remarkable about these women is not their difference from other women, although they are different, or their conscious attitude towards their femininity, but their sublime indifference to the question of difference and their sense of entitlement to both the domestic and the professional realms. As Duncan describes her interview subject, the practising physician, she stresses the almost unconscious ease with which she has taken on the mantle of medical authority. She is a female doctor for whom womanhood and professional identity exist in harmony:

I went to see number two yesterday in her professional capacity. No, you shan't be told her name, at least in this column, but a very little enquiry will convince you that she is no hypothetical M.D. She came in with an aspect of professional seriousness which she dropped, however, upon recognizing me, and at my special request, did not assume again while I stayed. As she led the way into her cosy little office I carefully observed her for evidence of that loss of womanly attributes which is so necessary a result of a medical course, but I was disappointed. She didn't stride, she wasn't a guy, she didn't use slang, her manners weren't aggressive. *Tout au contraire.* She walked well, she was dressed with taste, she talked excellently, and her manners were admirable. Most astonishing of all, when a small boy came in with a fishhook driven as far into his middle finger as the self-destructive instinct of that queer little animal can drive it, she didn't go about it in any cold-blooded or brutal manner whatever, but extracted it just as deftly and tenderly as if she had been the little fiend's mother, plus firmness and knowledge and minus hysterics.[41]

It is rare to encounter Duncan in interview so entirely without guile or ironic interrogation, so completely in accord with her subject, who seems as close as possible to an embodied feminine ideal as Duncan could find. The rest of the interview focuses on the prejudice faced by women doctors, a subject discussed without surprise or rancour. 'It is the effect of time,' her interviewee tells her, 'and time only can efface it.'[42] Her confidence, humanity, and reasonableness are emphasized throughout. As Duncan leaves, with a laugh at the idea that medical training might in any way be inimical to femininity, one senses that the golden glow of the opening sketch casts its mellow light over this portrait of female achievement.

Duncan's account of the idyll on the summer afternoon expresses as clearly as anything she wrote her sense of the almost limitless possibilities available to women in her day. Frustrated as she might have been by setbacks to women's progress, she did not doubt that her generation was uniquely privileged and that most barriers to women's free self-development would soon fall. She might not have understood or respected all the forms that women's public identifications took, and there were elements of condescension and competition in her exchanges with them, but she believed in their right to self-determination, just as she was obviously excited to be young, smart, and in charge of her own personal and intellectual destiny.

A NUMBER OF SCHOLARS have remarked on 'the charm of [Duncan's] prose style,'[43] Thomas Tausky noting how many of her rhetorical techniques serve 'to draw attention to the clever, lively, imaginative and unconventional character of the writer.'[44] Rae Goodwin has analysed her creation of a 'fresh, clever, and cultivated' persona[45] and 'manner of gay feminine imperiousness,'[46] and Marian Fowler comments on her 'distinctive voice'[47] and 'decisive, opinionated' persona.[48] Misao Dean has written extensively on the importance of irony in the prose fiction.[49] Style was important to Duncan, who prided herself on the acuity and intellectual sparkle of her prose as evidence of equivalent qualities of mind. She did not want it said, as she had remarked of an American journalist, that her prose was merely 'amiably discursive' or 'vapidly just.'[50] An omnivorous reader and judicious reviewer, she frequently commented on the strengths and weaknesses of other journalists, critics, creative writers, and orators. These comments not only provide a fascinating glimpse into Duncan's rhetorical preferences and objectives but also demonstrate her awareness of how language reflected and shaped social identity.

For Duncan, wit was the route to power. That she admired ironic intelligence above all is evident from her reaction in *The Week*[51] to a review by Julian Hawthorne, son of the famous American novelist. The review, an indictment of Adam Badeau's exposé of *Aristocracy in England*, condemns Badeau's writing and observations with a pen dipped in vinegar, and Duncan quotes some particularly piquant extracts to illustrate how good a damning review can be. She was particularly impressed by the review's biting irony and uncompromising intelligence, an intelligence that did not seem to care whether its ironies were accessible or not. In fact, Hawthorne's review was so ingenious that it was likely to be misconstrued by an undiscerning reader: 'It is difficult by extracts to give any idea of the veiled irony of the whole, the finished art which has doubtless ere this conveyed to Mr. Badeau and half of the *World*'s readers the impression of Mr. Hawthorne's genial admiration, and to the other half the impression of his supreme contempt.'[52] 'Veiled irony' was, in Duncan's assessment, the supreme device for testing an audience's intellectual penetration, leaving dull readers in the dark.

Her approval of such difficulty is evident in her assessment of the review's effect: 'It is almost dishonest, so double is its suggestiveness, and yet we cannot withhold our approbation, so fitting is the treatment to its subject.'[53] Good critical writing was not necessarily clear or accessible: it was double, suggestive, elusive ('almost dishonest'), and 'fitted to its subject,' a 'finished art'[54] of conscious difficulty. Duncan's own subtle and challenging ironies give evidence of how seriously she valued this conception of the writer's craft. When she wrote for *The Week* of the average reader's boorish taste in literature that he 'is particular about the ending, and it not infrequently determines the whole merit of the book for him,'[55] she might well have been illustrating Hawthorne's 'veiled irony.' Only a bright reader would take her point. On another occasion she ironically mitigated a criticism of a book of political economy with a devastating dismissal. Commenting on the author's strenuous objection to regulation of the free market, she noted, 'We cannot agree with the author in the length to which he carries this principle, but its occasional absurdity is so manifest as to be comparatively harmless.'[56] Duncan used every writing occasion to exercise her ironic wit.

Writing that relied on formulas and clichés to produce a sentimental effect was, of course, to be avoided. On this score, Duncan singled out for particular disapprobation certain female journalists, especially the society columnists whose style, she felt, was gaudy and undisciplined. Speaking of the 'lady correspondent' who wrote of social life in Washington, Duncan observed disparagingly, 'With an occasional notable exception, this is usually a person of boundless adjective eloquence, a fulsome ability to flatter, a gossipy instinct, and no discrimination whatever.'[57] Her linking of triviality, insincerity, and lack of discrimination with the overuse of adjectives illustrates Duncan's assumptions about the relationship between style and gender. Adjective use indicated to her a flowery insubstantiality associated with feminine discourse and habits of thought. On another occasion in the *Globe*, she parodied the style of writing typical of the lady correspondent in the press gallery:

> With the best will in the world, a lady correspondent in the gallery takes up her position directly opposite a favourite Senator who is rising to make an important speech. With true feminine eye for detail, she notes admiringly his silvery hair, his classical forehead gleaming like polished ivory, his steel-blue eyes snapping sarcasm at his opponent, his drooping moustache that seems to quiver with the eloquence proceeding from immediately behind it, his cheek ruddy with the hue of hale old age, his graceful gesticulations – everything about him, in fact, but his speech. This doesn't usually get down, but that, of course, is an insignificant omission, compared with the graphic value of what is recorded.[58]

In Duncan's estimation, the typical 'lady correspondent' used an insipid language drawn from the clichés of sentimental romance. Her own preference for subtlety, irony, and complexity, then, were at least in part a strategy to avoid the straitjacket of feminine style.

In her own work Duncan usually cast herself as the anti-society columnist, the inventor of unflattering portraits and cynical aphorisms, as when she observed of American society, 'Democratic usage and tradition not permitting rank by heredity, the democrats hasten to create it by notoriety.'[59] The verbal concision, structural elegance, and syntactical complexity – as well as the sardonic assessment of American republicanism – are characteristic. Rather than gush predictably about prominent people and their doings, she preferred to be the social analyst who stands at an ironic distance from received opinion. Speaking of 'Society at the American Capital,' she noted approvingly that the diverse regional types gathered in Washington presented 'an *embarras de richesse* for the sociologist.'[60] As a satirical observer of the age, her voice was arch, knowing, bright, and often mocking; she made it her business to find occasion for insight and provocation in every subject she tackled. Only such a sharp-witted chronicler could write, as Duncan did in an article about the Canadian government's dealings with Native peoples, 'We are all lineal descendants of the person who stood upon the street corner and thanked the Lord that he was not as other men.'[61] On another occasion she formulated a clever maxim to illustrate the inevitable failure of dress reform schemes: 'The evil-disposed go to reformatories and the criminals to prisons,' she wrote, affecting an emphatic cadence and biblical mock-echo, 'but the vulgar we have ever with us, and vulgarity is a law unto itself.'[62]

Duncan's conviction that the journalistic persona should be keen, clever, and dispassionately analytical is evident in 'A Study in Monochrome,' a report of her visit, while she was living in Washington, to a black Baptist church, where, she tells us, 'I watched "the old year out and the new year in" on the 31st of December in the voluble society of nine hundred negroes.'[63] As the only white person in attendance at the service, she would have been keenly aware of the opportunity to report on an experience with which few of her white readers would be familiar, yet her report is less a story of human interest than it is an example of her own clinical amusement and descriptive flair. The reference to the 'volubility' of the gathering forms a keynote of the piece, in which Duncan emphasizes the peculiar accents, startling volume, and discordant harmonies of the preacher and his large, excitable congregation. Interested to note the entrance of Frederick Douglass and certain that no one else in the room recognized the venerated abolitionist writer,[64] she is the silent and superior watcher of an exotic scene in which church members work themselves into a frenzy of religious adoration while she records it all.

Throughout the article, Duncan is observant and detached. In her own words, 'I watched the people attentively and was amply repaid'[65] – repaid not because she has participated in a community event, even less because she has enjoyed herself or learned something (certainly not from the sermon, which she mocks), but because she has gathered material for a story of the 'Negro' element in the American capital. The fact that she is attending a religious service at which church members praise God and testify to changed lives underlines the rigid separation drawn between the dispassionate Duncan and the impassioned body of believers, whose swaying, chanting, writhing, and singing are presented in vivid contrast to the reporter. The rather malicious care with which she transcribes dialect and records the volume of words demonstrates her appreciation of the service as a supreme journalistic opportunity, as in the following description of the preacher's words:

> 'Is you red-a-a-ay, brethren!' he shouted, with an awful dying inflection. Then an inimitable Negro touch. 'Suppose the Lawd was to git offen His throne dis bery night, brethren, an' put on His warm clo's, an' come straight down heah to-night, is you red-a-a-ay, brethren!' The chorus that answered was beyond all description. Ancient crones arose and danced up and down. One man and two women writhed upon the floor in an agony of hysteria; they howled and shouted and screamed with laughter, and the preacher sat down and fanned himself.[66]

Duncan's repeated assertions of her own incapacity to record the sound and tumult of the service seem rather to confirm her enjoyment in the attempt, the enjoyment of the social critic who has found a subject worthy of her descriptive efforts. The note of spent triumph – and the punctuating exclamation mark – in the concluding sentence of the article suggests an artistic consummation almost equivalent to, though of a different order from, the emotional and spiritual one she has witnessed: 'But how,' she concludes, 'shall I convey an idea of the eager black faces, the swaying to and fro, the abandon, the unutterable tumult, and the absolute and reigning sense of enjoyment that pervaded the whole body!'[67] Whether Duncan truly believed (or recognized) that there was anything in the scene that she had not been able to convey, she took pleasure in the exercise of her descriptive powers to master the scene.

One of the strengths any columnist must possess is the ability to write well about ordinary experiences, and Duncan possessed this ability to a significant degree. She could find something of interest to say about nearly anything, and she often found matter for clever and penetrating reflection or whimsy in the minutiae of the everyday. One detects a delighted consciousness of ability in such pieces, as when, in 'W.D. Howells at Washington,' she expatiates playfully on the experience of encountering the soiled boots of W.D. Howells, the acclaimed American novelist, sitting out on the landing of the fashionable Washington boarding house where Duncan herself was living while she worked for the *Post*. One recognizes the note of happy confidence, the consciousness of imaginative resource, from the opening paragraph as Duncan, climbing the stairs to her room late one night, spies the boots sitting before a previously unoccupied suite:

> Whereupon I fell to thinking. It had been for some time currently reported in the gossip of mine inn that our next distinguished guest was to be the Master of American Realism. The air was athrob with it, the landlady radiated it, we all expected it. There was nothing especially realistic about these boots; they were buttoned boots, dusty and undistinctive. But it flashed upon me that these were the apartments newly garnished and set aside for the occupancy of the notable person aforesaid. These, then, were the boots of the Modern Novelist. In all human probability the Modern Novelist was within. I hereby confess that I deliberately listened that I might report the snoring of the Modern Novelist. But the beating of my own heart was the only sound I heard.[68]

Like so much in Duncan, the passage is neither entirely serious nor entirely mocking; her playfulness sets off an underlying engagement. The comic drama of the passage – created through the archaic language, rhetorical parallelism, suspenseful narrative pacing, portentous declaratives, and comic juxtapositions of banal detail with hushed reverence – allows Duncan both to comment ironically upon and to endorse the myth of the Great Writer. When she tells us, following this paragraph, that 'the boots, however, afforded ample scope for speculation,'[69] we are under no apprehension about her speculative ability. No one else, surely, could have riffed with more beguiling assurance on so trivial a subject, including a fanciful paragraph detailing 'how vastly humanity was indebted to their [the boots'] pilgrimages' through lands now preserved in literature for all to enjoy.[70] As Duncan was well aware, Howells had travelled through parts of Canada on his honeymoon, and he made a honeymoon tour to Quebec City the occasion for his first novel, *Their Wedding Journey* (1871). 'Our own Quebec,' she reflects appreciatively, 'how well her quaint old thoroughfares must know their pedestrian pressure.'[71] And so on. By the time she was able to provide a physical description of Howells over breakfast the next morning, Duncan had amply proved her ability to rival the realist novelist in finding the materials for art in everyday realities.

Despite the keen time pressures under which she worked and the necessity to produce copy on demand, Duncan took pride in the complexity and stylistic polish of her prose, which was characterized by vivid detail, memorable phrasing, and striking metaphors. In an article published in *The Week* on 25 March 1886, entitled 'Woman Suffragists in Council,' she turned to metaphor to define the significance of a suffrage gathering in Washington, where she had 'heard no new thing'[72] but was impressed anew by the earnestness and commitment of the activists and the logic of their cause. Until woman suffrage became a reality, she concluded, there was no 'new thing' to be said on the subject: 'Till then, these gatherings are simply tentative fingers on the public pulse – pebbles, perhaps, thrown into the stream of popular opinion, to mark the growing influence of the subject as the circles widen yearly, where once a laugh and a ripple marked the plunge.'[73] Her reference to 'fingers on the public pulse' is so conventional an expression as to barely rank as metaphor, and pebbles in the 'stream of popular opinion' is little fresher. But the comment is saved by that final clause – 'where once a laugh and a ripple marked the plunge' – which makes us aware of Duncan the artist: vivid, exact, and sensitive to nuance and rhythm. She liked the phrase so much that she carried the idea into the next paragraph, amplifying it with metonymy to indicate how the 'ripples' of the suffrage movement were beginning to touch lives previously impervious to it: 'Slowly but steadily these circles broaden and deepen. Odd, fantastic objects are gradually being drawn within their influence – French slippers, smelling-bottles, and things – and eddy about not without a certain illustrative value.'[74] Notable here is the way that a fairly commonplace metaphor is particularized by Duncan: in her decision to identify the 'fantastic objects' that 'eddy about' in the widening circles of suffrage opinion, in the combined humour and seriousness that enable her to dub them 'not without a certain illustrative value,' and in the restrained superciliousness of the double negative marking her recognition that the recent interest of society women in suffrage is both slightly absurd and telling. Such rhetorical touches indicate the care with which she crafted her prose, as well as the lofty cleverness with which she treated the social issues of the day.

For Duncan, ironic cleverness was a way of being liberated without being doctrinaire, of caring about issues without succumbing to the dull earnestness or hysteria of the reforming woman. Wit was thus a shelter from anger and bitterness as much as their tool. But there was one subject on which her ironic detachment often deserted her. When she wrote of reforming Canadian society, her concern was not moral degeneration, religious disarray, or social injustice to women. Rather, it was the nation's failure to produce a vibrant national culture. 'We are still an eminently unliterary people,' Duncan announced soberly in her 'Saunterings' column of *The Week*.[75] Six months later she again addressed Canada's need for a cultural 'renaissance,' and although there is more than a touch of comic irreverence in her cheeky opening salvo, which begins, 'What we need in Canada more than the readjustment of the tariff or the total extinction of the Catholic population,' her conclusion is sincere: 'We may be said to be suffering for a renaissance.'[76] Likewise, her comic description of the Canadian reaction to home-grown cultural productions is meant to produce a laugh of recognition, but it is the prelude to an impassioned exploration of the crippling effects of cultural colonialism:

> The publication of a Canadian work of poetry or fiction, or any of the lighter arts of literature, by a Canadian firm, among Canadians, is apt to be received with peculiar demonstrations. Their facial form is that of an elongation of the countenance, a pursing of the lips, a lifting of the eyebrows. This is usually accompanied by the little significant movement of the shoulders which we have borrowed from our French-Canadian relations-in-law expressly for use in this regard. We pick up the unfortunate volume from the bookseller's counter to which its too trustful author has confided it, and we turn its leaves in a manner we reserve for Canadian publications – a manner that expresses curiosity rather than a desire to know, and yet one that is somehow indicative of a foregone conclusion.[77]

It may be that Duncan's reference to the 'too trustful author' of a Canadian novel suggests her own thoughts in the direction of fiction writing. She was perhaps the first Canadian to so wittily formulate the dilemma of the writer in a colonial culture: the difficulty of creating art in a culture that did not believe in itself, in a climate of such 'enforced political humility' that 'We are ignored, and we ignore ourselves.'[78] Consequently, one senses that Duncan's privileging of obscurity, complexity, criticism, and provocation was more than personal preference; it functioned also as a form of cultural commitment on her part – a commitment to educating Canadian readers towards sophistication and away from philistinism. Part of this commitment involved waging a rhetorical guerilla war, in which the young journalist fashioned herself as a word soldier sniping at insincerity, foolishness, and cant.

A SIGNAL MOMENT OCCURS in a report Duncan wrote of the annual meeting of the Women's Mission Society of the Elm-street Methodist Church.[79] Duncan was at the meeting incognito, the 'good ladies of the Methodist denomination' having resolved to meet without reporters present. 'And here in neither more nor less than a reportorial capacity was I, all in my "tailor-made" disguise,' Duncan explained triumphantly, calling herself 'a traitor in the camp!'[80] She could not avoid an 'unbecoming chuckle' as she took out her lead pencil. Trying to look like the sort of woman who cared enough about mission work to attend an evening meeting, Duncan found it 'good fun to sit there unsuspectedly,' training her journalist's eye on the variety of feminine types in attendance.

Directly in front of her sat one who seemed a 'typical woman mission advocate': plain and repressed, with 'a long face, a sharp chin, an expression of extreme saint-ship, a black straw bonnet, and a Paisley shawl.' Unable to hear the speaker, Duncan was scribbling this rather unsympathetic verbal portrait of the woman when suddenly her subject 'turned around and observed' her.[81] Expecting a reproof, perhaps an accusation, Duncan instead received her gentle encouragement. '"That's right, my dear," the woman nodded in benevolent misunderstanding, "We're always glad to see people in'rested in the work an' takin' notes. She's a beautiful speaker, ain't she?"' At such unmerited kindliness, Duncan claimed to feel deep 'remorse' – 'I wanted to get down in utter abasement and stay under a hassock for the remainder of the service' – but her shame did not prevent her from recording the woman's infelicities of speech as well as the 'amusing' rhetorical habits of the evening's presenters, who exhibited, she noted with interest, 'a tendency to imitate the mannerisms of the minister they have "sat under."'[82]

The moment in which Duncan finds the woman's gaze upon her dramatizes the self-conscious ambivalence in her self-positioning as a woman journalist. Pencil in hand, a woman reporter 'disguised' as a mere woman, she represents her note-taking presence at the meeting as a kind of betrayal in which she, despite a pang of guilt, takes evident pleasure. Although the well-intentioned Methodist lady did not discover her deception (at least not until the publication of the column), Duncan stands self-condemned by her own unflattering self-portrait, which emphasizes her ungenerous scrutiny and cool detachment. One might read the scene as enacting one of many moments in which Duncan chooses to identify against her sex.

She did not always, of course, use her pen against women – quite the contrary – but her (half-proud, half-abashed) determined non-alignment was a key part of her self-conception. Attending the woman suffrage convention in Washington, Duncan wrote a sympathetic but gently satirical account of the meeting, noting the enforced conformity and scripted assent such gatherings seemed inevitably to produce: 'From its genuflecting beginning to its undulating close, one was conscious of being confronted with a stern interrogation point, before which several pompadoured heretics felt constrained to announce fervent admiration for a cause which, up to that inquisitorial hour, they had amused themselves and their masculine attachments by prettily reviling.'[83] Mocking the occasional fakery of the movement's public aspect, Duncan's elaborately religious language demonstrates her own preference for the role of heretic over that of genuflecting adherent. And she enjoyed her ironic detachment in declaring, on the occasion of having attended too many meetings derailed by self-indulgent sentimentality, that she 'should like to go to a temperance meeting without running the risk of being called a "dear sister."'[84]

Ironic doubleness and witty non-alignment are central to a piece of satire written for *The Week*, entitled 'Extracts from the "Woman's Journal," May 2, 2001.' It purports to be a newspaper report from a future in which women are the dominant sex, having gained the vote and transformed the social order to their advantage. The once-tyrant man has been disenfranchised and fully domesticated, and women engage in parliamentary debate over dress reform, the extirpation of the Masonic Order, and the admission of men to the professions. As virtuoso comedy that is also biting social analysis, the piece shows Duncan, as always, sceptical of the orthodoxies on both sides of the Woman Question.

The report is divided into a number of sections: 'Ottawa Correspondence,' a report of parliamentary debates; 'News Notes,' a survey of political scandals and social issues – in this instance the recent admittance of men to Vassar College and its implications for other universities; and 'Pour les Hommes' and 'Fathers' Department,' two personal-interest columns for men, with advice on fashion and housecleaning. As the latter titles indicate, much of the humour and irony of the piece rests on its coy gender reversals, which are played for laughs and satirical suggestiveness. In the last, most lighthearted of these sections, Duncan parodies the rhetoric of domestic instruction and its condescending treatment of household work. Her parodic portrait of a 'much-tried husband crying in a corner of the coal shed'[85] highlights, through its mock-epic language, how newspapers trivialized even while they mandated domestic labour and also peddled the associated consumer products:

> The house-cleaning season, with all its attendant miseries, is upon us. The air is thick with carpet dust, the whitewasher's harvest is at hand, the silver teaspoon, missing since January, has turned up in the debris of the back yard. The weary wife returns from her labours at the office or the counter to find her evening meal promiscuously laid out on the top of an empty barrel, her much-tried husband crying in a corner of the coal shed, his highly-wrought nervous organisation having given way before the fiendish conduct of the paper-hangers in reversing the order of the patterns on the drawingroom wall. It is a pessimistic season, but it will not last always. The attention of husbands and fathers is requested to our advertisement of the new Patent Muscle-Saving Fluting Iron, in another column.[86]

The demands of household work in the 1880s were considerable, as Duncan well knew, and she detested male journalists' tendency to speak of domesticity with contempt even as they held women to ever-higher standards of housecleaning and decorative achievement. She had once professed her mock gratitude for the 'magnanimous desire for the elevation of the sex that possesses that man who, sitting down, doth mourn over the imperfections of the average housekeeper,'[87] and she took every opportunity to suggest areas of possible male improvement.

Such areas are precisely her subject in the 'Pour les Hommes' section, which parodies the moralizing tone of fashion news. Men are exhorted to remove their hats at the theatre or be forced to do so by an act of Parliament: 'Either the young gentleman of the period should withstand the wiles of his milliner more successfully, or he should be compelled – barbarous as it may seem – to remove his headgear altogether upon taking his seat and hold it in his lap while the performance is going on.'[88] The joke reflected a real debate taking place in the pages of Duncan's *Globe* column about the ethics of hat-wearing by ladies at the theatre, demonstrating her ability to turn a genuine (though tongue-in-cheek) discussion of fashion etiquette into a parody of patriarchal directives. The censoriousness that so often accompanied advice on dress and deportment is emphasized in a passage chastising men for imitating the clothing of the more powerful sex: 'Owing to the foolish tendency on the part of young men to imitate feminine fashions, it has become almost impossible to distinguish from the rear a youth of the day from his escort. Draw the line at hoop-skirts, gallant gentlemen!'[89] One can guess that Duncan chose the hoop skirt as a particularly ludicrous example: no sane Victorian gentleman would wear this symbol of ornamental femininity; yet under a different gender arrangement, she suggests, the status of the hoop skirt might be rather like the tall top hat. A reader could enjoy the titillating image of a cross-dressing male and, without thinking much about it, be alerted to the way that dress and the enforcement of dress codes reveal social power. Moreover, the coy reference to the view from (and presumably of) 'the rear' suggests Duncan's clever challenge to the fashion adviser's male gaze and her humorous, slightly risqué, textual revenge.

The more ambiguous satire in the piece comes in 'Ottawa Correspondence.' This section, in which men petition women legislators for the ballot, is a journalistic version of the Mock Parliament skits that were to become a crucial prop of feminist activism during the suffrage campaigns of the later nineteenth and early twentieth centuries. As later feminists would do, Duncan parodies the condescending language and irrational fear-mongering of the anti-suffrage forces. The report describes the women interrupted while discussing a 'Bill for the Extirpation of the Masonic Body' by 'the familiar whiskered face of the Male Re-enfranchisement Measure.'[90] The men are greeted with undisguised indifference (a 'cavernous' yawn, the distribution of caramels, and sleepy inattention) and predictable opposition:

> In a stirring speech, the leader of the Radical wing of the Dress Reform Party compared the length of time disenfranchisement has been visited upon men with the period during which women were deprived of the glorious privilege of the ballot, according to which, she said, justice, working with compound interest, should withhold its voices from the subject sex for eons yet to come. Looking at it from the standpoint of mere expediency, their probation, she said, was comparatively short, and it was extremely improbable that its lessons could as yet have been thoroughly learned. The political depravity of man was not a thing to be eradicated in a century or two. Re-enfranchisement might mean, even in this advanced and enlightened age, a return to the intolerable tyranny of the days of that arch-fiend, Sir John Macdonald, who had once, as everybody knew, gratuitously insulted the whole sex by offering it the voting privilege in return for a kiss! With a few general observations on the mischief the male vote would probably effect in the progress of certain highly-desirable domestic reforms then being dealt with by the Provincial Legislatures, and a ·

feeling reference to the discord that would undoubtedly ensue from it about the sacred fireside, which caused pocket-handkerchiefs to be sought for in every hand-bag in the room, the speaker assumed her *fauteuil*, having augmented the defeat of the measure at the previous session by seven votes.[91]

Here Duncan parodies what were already standard elements of the anti-suffrage arsenal, particularly its strategies of delay and the appeal to sentiment. Recent debates in the House of Commons about extending the franchise[92] had furnished her with ample matter for ridicule. She had obviously been following the debates and had written bitterly, as early as 1885, about the defeat of an enfranchisement bill put forward by the government of John A. Macdonald, noting, 'But again, the qualified widows and spinsters of the fair Dominion have been requested to devote their restless energies to the achievement of marvels in crazy patchwork, to confine their over-reaching aspirations within strict housekeeping limits.'[93] References to the inevitable 'discord' that would disturb 'the sacred fireside' if women had the vote had been part of the House debates, and Duncan was never less than savage about such male worries.

But a careful reading of her male suffrage bill scenario suggests that it does not confine its satire to parodic reversal alone; its very elaborateness – the detail about the various bills the women discuss and the particular objections they make to male suffrage – shows Duncan taking a few satirical swipes at the women's movement itself, particularly its tendency to retaliatory fervour and what would now be called 'reverse sexism.' It is surely no accident that the speaker who defeats the bills is 'the leader of the Radical wing of the Dress Reform Party,'[94] dress reform being a cause for which Duncan, who prided herself on dressing attractively, had limited sympathy (she once quoted a lady of her acquaintance that heaven would be 'a place where there are no dress reformers').[95] The insistence on injury and the feminist focus on male sexual depravity were elements of the women's rights platform that, in Duncan's opinion, bordered on the irrational and the vengeful. While male political rhetoric was often hollow, bombastic, and self-serving, women's rhetoric – if it hardened into uncritical orthodoxy or dogmatism – was vulnerable to the same errors.

I have argued elsewhere that Duncan's journalism offers a fascinating window onto the complexity and ambivalence of her feminist self-positioning, which was always a mixture of conviction and strategic display, and the above examples demonstrate once again her preference for double-edged satire and ironic detachment. Duncan did not want to be pigeonholed as a feminist with an axe to grind, aiming instead to occupy the wide field of the social critic, humorist, and cultural arbiter, one whose light touch enabled laughing rejoinders as well as vituperative denunciations. On one occasion she responded to advice by a French journalist that women should 'veil their learning' with a string of outraged rhetorical questions that demonstrate intense irritation with conventions of feminine modesty: 'Are we to veil our indiscretion in venturing beyond the covers of the cookery book for fear of beguiling some unwary sister from her rightful contemplation of pickles and preserves, who might otherwise have developed into a housewife extraordinary! Or is it that some of us, having come short of the absolute stupidity required for perfect patient womanhood are to propitiate fate by trying to look as stupid as possible in deprecation of intelligence that is our misfortune and not our fault!'[96] Even without the exclamation marks, Duncan's indignation is obvious. But she was also capable of shrugging off insult and condescension; responding to *The Week*'s editorial disapproval of a new fashion in gaudy hairpins, she suggested pointedly, 'If we can't select our representatives, you must at least give us choice in hairpins.'[97] She always liked to flaunt her femininity, as when, in the same column in which she stated her support for woman suffrage as a sign of civic responsibility and intelligence, she also exhibited girlish frivolity, confessing herself 'not as much interested in it [voting] as the importance of the subject deserves' and objecting 'to being supposed an elderly female with spectacles and side curls and an aversion to bangs.'[98] And she chose withering irony when commenting on a report in the *Globe* entitled 'Row in the Indiana Senate' about a physical brawl among the legislators: 'Clearly we must add to the present legislative incapacities of woman her muscular unfitness for the task.'[99] Writing as a woman (her pseudonym, Garth Grafton, was never a real disguise) about one of the great social questions of her day, Duncan was by turns angry and dispassionate, provocative and conciliatory, and often amused, flippant, or coy: a flirt with a formidable intellect and a horror of predictability.

She could be bitterly angry in her denunciations of male condescension and brutality, as when she attacked an item in the *Dublin Free Press* critical of a woman's right to sue for divorce on what the editor considered the rather too lax grounds of drunkenness, desertion, and violence.[100] Duncan launched a stinging assault on the suggestion in the editor's discussion that 'a black eye in the family circle'[101] was a triviality. At other times, she was equally angry with feminist critics, as when she levelled a withering blast at one who celebrated the dying out of female emotional 'slavery' to husband and family; Duncan declared in response that womanly self-sacrifice for family 'never will die out, for its roots are beyond the envious digging of any spinster social reformer whatever.'[102] That the feminist writer might have been responding to attitudes like those of the editor at the *Dublin Free Press* would certainly have occurred to Duncan, who would probably have retorted that misogynistic dismissal of women's real injuries in one quarter did not excuse feminist misrepresentation of them in another. But one also wonders whether Duncan's fervent celebration of so-called slavery, in which she declares the 'unemancipated' woman 'the happiest being I know,'[103] might not have invited a satirical assault by Duncan herself on a different day.

Changing her line of attack as the situation invited or her mood dictated, Duncan embodied the multiplicity of the modern woman, a being who, in her opinion, would sacrifice none of her charm, gentleness, and essential femininity with her assumption of responsibility, independence, and intellectual development: 'If with the helpless dependence of our grandmothers must go the graceful little characteristics that have come to be regarded as exclusively feminine,' she conceded, 'nobody would preserve them by sacrificing the present self-helpful, progressive position of the sex. But is it a question of choice?'[104] Duncan claimed – perhaps rather disingenuously – that there was no such question, and her own column, in which she vowed to 'wear not one glove-button or yard of embroidery the less,'[105] even while claiming women's new opportunities, was, in its rhetorical variousness and experimental boldness, a demonstration of her freedom. Criticizing feminists who asked for political rights based on women's traditional virtues and presumed moral superiority, Duncan again suggested that the modern woman must and could have it all: 'In the political field as everywhere, women will need all their moral superiority; but to ardour they must add acumen, and to sincerity sagacity, and to disgust with the present conditions the ability to improve them.'[106] Her teasing manner with intellectual topics and refusal to adopt a singular identity were her way of claiming, rhetorically, her feminine sensibility, her masculine responsibility, and above all her witty individuality.

Answering a reader who asked about the 'emoluments' and 'difficulties' of journalism, Duncan ironically enumerated the joys of mediocre pay, criticism from the public, and poor working conditions, adding ruefully that there were also 'invitations to the festive affairs of public charities, and free tickets to church socials, to say nothing of the muscular development attendant upon climbing Grub-street stairs.'[107] Journalism was hard work, and Duncan seems to have wearied of it quickly. In 1888 she left home for her world tour with Lily Lewis, during which she met her future husband in India and set in motion the events that would take her away from Canada permanently. She probably felt relief about leaving a homeland 'where literary sensations are about as infrequent as earthquakes'[108] and about leaving a job that was frenetic and ephemeral. But Sara Jeannette Duncan's irreverent and witty work also testifies to the sense of possibility and excitement that journalism once held for her and other women at a time when barriers to their advancement were falling and they were defining new forms of usefulness and self-expression. To have been 'news' as well as 'newsmaker' must have been a heady experience, and the tremendous energy, curiosity, and high spirits it inspired still rise off the crumbling, 120-year-old pages of Duncan's articles.

3 'This graceful olive branch of the Iroquois': Pauline Johnson's Rhetoric of Reconciliation

When Sara Jeannette Duncan interviewed Pauline Johnson for the *Globe*'s 'Woman's World' column on 14 October 1886, she called her a 'graceful olive branch of the Iroquois.'[1] Although she did not elaborate on the comment, Duncan appeared to suggest that the poet embodied, both in her mixed-race parentage and in her promotion of Indian dignity within a framework of Canadian nationalism, a process of peacemaking between the First Peoples of Canada and the Anglo-Canadian majority. That Johnson also saw herself in that way is evident not only in her dedication of *Canadian Born* (1903), her second volume of poetry, to both her 'paleface compatriot' and her 'dear Red brother'[2] but also in the body of work on Native themes that she produced over the course of her successful career as a writer and performer. Daughter of a British-born Quaker mother and a Mohawk father and privileged by birth, beauty, and opportunity, Johnson relished her role as an ambassador for the Iroquois, enthusiastically assuming an identity as a fierce defender of Native interests to English Canada's white population. She wrote to her friend Archibald Kains that her objective was to 'upset the Indian Extermination and Non-education Theory' and generally 'to stand by my blood and my race.'[3]

Some of the problems Johnson faced in this endeavour are hinted at in the *Globe* interview, which focuses largely on her Native heritage with almost no reference to her opinions, literary aspirations, or published work. The interview was published the day after a poem of Johnson's was read out in the town of Brantford, Ontario, at the unveiling of a statue of Joseph Brant, acclaimed Mohawk ally of the British during the American Revolutionary War. As Duncan well knew, the unveiling and its related fanfare signified a tension at the heart of the

Anglo-Canadian view of Native peoples, who in the late nineteenth century were at once honoured heroes from the past and a problem in the present, a people whose diminished stature both legitimated and shamed those who claimed a benevolent conquest. While a few commentators, including author and anthologist W.D. Lighthall and poet Charles Mair,[4] celebrated the noble deeds and future potential of Canada's Aboriginal peoples, many Anglo-Canadians looked forward with relief to their eventual disappearance.

Despite the politically charged occasion and Johnson's literary triumph, Duncan does not, in the interview, question Johnson about the poem, her writing life, or her assessment of Brant's historical significance. Instead, the subject of their conversation is Indian exotica. Johnson displays to Duncan various ancestral relics, including ceremonial cuffs embroidered with wampum beads, deer-bone rattles made to adorn dance moccasins, a Cayuga tomahawk given to her father, and a scalping knife he made himself. She also tells a gothic story of murder and revenge associated with a rusty knife dug up on the grounds of Chiefswood, her family home on the Six Nations Reserve. Throughout the encounter, Duncan plays up her role as the fascinated and slightly horrified white observer, pointedly confusing the tomahawk and scalping knife in an awkward, titillated question about their respective uses and confessing to readers her uncertainty about whether her interview subject 'would relish this allusion to the peculiarities of her warrior ancestors.'[5]

Duncan's assumption that Johnson will be embarrassed by elements of her ancestry makes clear her consciousness of the gulf separating these two acquaintances. When Johnson tells Duncan that her last name was given to her great-grandfather when he was baptized and that the Johnson family's 'real name' is Te-ka-hoon-wa-ke, Duncan's somewhat malicious response is a pointed 'aren't you glad he was baptized?'[6] Although it seems that Johnson participated enthusiastically in – or perhaps even directed – the exchange between them, at times laughing and encouraging Duncan's genteel awkwardness, the interview confines her within a narrative of Indian origins seen as piquant yet also potentially degrading. When Johnson demonstrates why a tomahawk would not be useful for scalping, Duncan describes with relish how she 'raised one of her own dusky locks and made a mimic circle around it.' The word 'dusky,' as the literary Duncan was perfectly aware, signalled the tired representational stereotype she would normally have scorned. Both young women were published authors

E. Pauline Johnson.

enjoying their first glow of public recognition, but they do not meet as fellow writers in this interview preoccupied with relics of war and tales of Indian superstition.

At the close of the article, Duncan does mention Johnson's relationship, on her mother's side, to W.D. Howells, a novelist Duncan greatly admired. Yet a reference that might have opened discussion of the literary side of Johnson's heritage seems mainly to reinforce her exotic status and to remind readers of Duncan's own acquaintance with the acclaimed American author. Noting that Howells was a 'second cousin of Miss Johnson's,' Duncan reflects that he 'spoke in terms of the liveliest interest of his "Indian cousins" when I met him last winter in Washington.'[7] In other words, Johnson is a curiosity to Howells, and Duncan is his literary compatriot. She concludes her account of the interview with muted praise for Johnson's style, in which she notes 'a dreamy quality that is very charming,' and with the comment that she 'writes best of her own people, whom she dearly loves.'[8] Given that Duncan understood her own subject to be the whole field of human endeavour, it is significant that she believed Johnson's poetic range to be limited to tales of the Indian past.

It may have been that jealousy or professional rivalry created the edge of condescension in Duncan's piece; perhaps she had been irritated by the 'storm of applause'[9] that, she reported, had greeted Johnson's poem when it was read out at the Brant celebration, or perhaps she simply did not regard Johnson as a talented poet. Whatever the explanation, her rhetorical framing of Johnson highlights the assumptions and reactions Johnson would typically encounter in her role as Mohawk ambassador and Canada's most famous poet-performer. Celebrity status meant, as Lorraine York has demonstrated, both possibility and limitation for the poet-performer.[10] Often greeted with titillated curiosity as much as respectful interest, she negotiated a variety of conflicting expectations as she attempted to satisfy both popular tastes and her personal artistic standards. Her livelihood depended on her ability to soothe and stimulate the audience she also sought to instruct and to guide, and her subject – relations between Euro-Canadians and the people who had lived on the land for centuries – was arguably the most charged and overdetermined issue of late nineteenth-century Canada. Moreover, she began to write at a time when the banning of the potlatch and the institutionalization of residential schools signalled Anglo-Canadian society's most forceful attempt to assimilate and pacify its Aboriginal population. Belonging to a mixed-race family with close ties to Indian Affairs officials as well as the Anglican church, Johnson's own Aboriginality was not without strain, and it appears that she never performed on the Six Nations Reserve, where she grew up.[11] Yet despite the challenges she faced, she was successful in creating a body of work whose appeal to popular tastes softened but did not obliterate its serious intent to unite Red and White in 'one common Brotherhood.'[12]

After nearly a century of academic neglect, the poet who in 1889 was called by Theodore Watts-Dunton in the *Athanaeum* 'the most interesting English poetess now living'[13] has quite recently regained the prominent position she once occupied in Canadian culture and letters. Charlotte Gray's *Flint and Feather: The Life and Times of E. Pauline Johnson* (2002), Carole Gerson and Veronica Strong-Boag's *Paddling Her Own Canoe: The Times and Texts of E. Pauline Johnson, Tekahionwake* (2000) and their edited *E. Pauline Johnson, Tekahionwake: Collected Poems and Selected Prose* (2002), and a cluster of articles and book chapters in recent years have confirmed a range of approaches to her work and life. As in the case of any significant and complex historical figure, interesting disagreements are to be found in the scholarship, with all commentators noting degrees of tension and contradiction, what George Lyon calls 'semiotic confusion,'[14] in Johnson's self-positioning as writer, stage personality, and political advocate.

Yet while biographers Betty Keller and Charlotte Gray have been content to see Johnson as a complex personality, 'aggressive, manipulative, talented, and utterly charming,'[15] who both exploited her Mohawk ancestry as 'an asset to her career'[16] and defended Native peoples with a message few whites wanted to hear,[17] academics have been more polarized. Daniel Francis, author of *The Imaginary Indian* (1993), writes rather scornfully of her fake Indian outfit and sees her as someone who 'had to make compromises with the expectations of her White public' and therefore as a 'White Man's Indian'[18] who 'demanded little from her White audience beyond sentimental regret.'[19] While more sympathetic to Johnson than Francis, Rick Monture also faults her for avoiding 'overt political statements' and for reinforcing 'a subordinate relationship to the Crown'[20] for Mohawk people. In contrast, Strong-Boag and Gerson paint a much more positive picture of Johnson as a bold advocate who 'spoke back' to the dominant culture in a spirit of resistance that is 'sometimes blunt, sometimes ironical, and sometimes so subtle as to be barely perceptible, but rarely entirely absent.'[21] Sabine Milz, extending their argument, suggests that Johnson's performances not only challenged stereotypes of First Nations people but also unsettled the Euro-Canadian privileging of the published text over the oral performance.[22] In his tribute to Johnson, her stage partner Walter McRaye asked, 'What need is there to prove whether the source of her inspiration was in her white or red blood?'[23] For present-day scholars, however, Johnson's racial allegiance remains very much a live issue.

Despite such extensive discussions of her public identity, there has been relatively little sustained attention to individual texts, especially to the rhetorical strategies she deployed in her role as an 'olive branch' seeking to strengthen the alliance between Aboriginal and non-Aboriginal peoples in Canada. Readings of select poetry, prose fiction, and essays enable consideration of how Johnson both accommodated and challenged her audiences, crafting a deceptively simple, but also compelling and at times unsettling, appeal to their sympathies, sense of justice, and deeply held beliefs. I argue that she was neither subversive, in its contemporary post-colonial meaning, nor complicit with non-Native expectations, but instead an effective rhetorician capable of inspiring assent not only on the basis of easy emotionalism, as Francis would have it, but also through logic and ethos. Though her words did not always find a full hearing, they spoke powerfully in the patriotic and idealistic language of her day.

NEWSPAPER ACCOUNTS of Johnson's performances, from her debut in 1892, at age thirty, until she retired in 1908, suggest that her staging of her double identity always involved negotiation with audience assumptions, expectations, and desires. Even as she aimed to revise stereotypes and stimulate respect for indigenous peoples, she also relied upon the voyeuristic thrill evoked by her romantic costume, a buckskin outfit purchased through the Hudson's Bay Company and embellished with a fur pelt on one sleeve, a bear-claw necklace, and a Sioux scalp. She was careful to stress her Mohawk ancestry, playing up associations of imperial loyalty and military prowess (as well as cultural superiority to other indigenous groups), and she failed to correct many reviewers' and interviewers' assumption that the costume was authentically Mohawk, a regal outfit befitting the daughter of a chief. Furthermore, a poem such as 'Ojistoh' (1895), one of her most popular performance pieces, presents Native life before colonial contact as a drama of violent splendour, probably confirming audience fantasies about the Aboriginal past and about Johnson's identity as a storybook Indian come to life. Another frequent recital piece was 'As Red Men

Die' (1890), a poem about a Mohawk warrior bravely enduring torture; as Lyon argues, it 'undoubtedly confirmed many readers' [and listeners'] suppositions about the bloodthirstiness of native people.'[24] A reviewer in an undated article from the *Sun* expressed relief that her performance 'was "only in the play," and that there was no immediate danger of a too free use of the scalping knife and tomahawk.'[25]

Johnson's emphasis on the Aboriginal past, on the Iroquois brave who 'bends to death – but never to disgrace,'[26] surely confirmed stereotypes about Natives as a vanishing race. As Francis has argued, it was easier for some portion of her audience to accept her championing of a people seen to be a remnant of the dying: as early as 1886, a poem by an admirer in the *Globe* paid tribute to her as a 'sweet prototype of a passing race':[27] and an undated *Saturday Night* article is representative of many reviews in noting that 'the race that has gone speaks with touching pathos through Miss Johnson.'[28] Writing for the *Literary History of Canada* many decades after her death, Roy Daniells speculated that much of her popularity was based on 'the continuing secret desire of all Canadians to reach back into an innocent and heroic world of wild woods and waters before the white man came and the guilt of conquests ... was incurred.'[29] Recently, Mary Elizabeth Leighton has suggested that the periodical press's romantic identification of Johnson with a past at once foundational to Canada and fading into legend 'successfully undermined the validity and specificity of Johnson's position as a Native woman in the present.'[30]

Yet Johnson's range was greater and audience response more complicated than these comments suggest. Some of her most popular performance pieces were angry denunciations of present injustice, such as 'A Cry from an Indian Wife' (1885), about the Northwest Rebellion, and 'The Cattle Thief' (1894), about starvation and land loss on the prairies; such poems, targeting the 'greed of white men's hands'[31] and exhorting whites to 'Give back our land and our country'[32] were often singled out by reviewers as moving and eye-opening experiences. Passionate anger was to some extent, it seems, tolerated and even expected from a Native advocate such as Johnson, who was part of a small but significant tradition of elite First Nations spokespeople,[33] and reactions of empathy, regret, concern, and affiliation were not uncommon among her audience. One commentator emphasized the 'shrinkage of the conscience' that came upon him when Johnson 'stood before the audience and said "the land is ours."'[34] Another asserted that 'when the anger of an Indian maiden, feeling from experience the suffering of her race, is depicted in every line, dull indeed is the man that cannot be aroused by Miss Johnson's recitations.'[35] Although such responses might not go as far as present-day activists would wish, they were far removed from the complacency and self-congratulation that often characterized mainstream perceptions of the Native situation in Canada.

If Johnson's anger often commanded respect and empathy, however, it was also linked in the public mind with nature and artlessness. One reviewer, after commending 'The Cattle Thief' as 'probably the best number of the evening,' went on to note approvingly, 'It was read with the intensity which is not a product of art but of nature.'[36] He may well have been referring to her lack of formal training in elocution, but the notion that she was a child of nature was a popular perception. Charles Mair similarly claimed of her Indian poems, in a tribute to Johnson upon her death, that 'they flow from her very veins.'[37] Audiences and reviewers were often ready to forgive passionate outbursts as well as moments of petulance – such as her irritated response in 1897 to an American interviewer for the *Chicago Tribune* to whom, when he did not seem appropriately interested in her Native heritage, she exclaimed, 'If you don't want to hear about the history of my people, what did you come to see me for?'[38] – so long as Johnson made them part of a mercurial display of emotional intensity that also included romantic idealism, unbridled ardour, and rollicking good humour.

To that end, she became skilled at balancing angry demands for justice with lighter material, often contrasting her emphasis on 'might's injustice'[39] with lilting nature pieces about the Canadian landscape, dreamy moods, and the romance of the canoe. Marcus Van Steen has emphasized Johnson's remarkable ability to shift registers: 'In delivering her Indian ballads, she was all savage, her deep rich voice harsh with blood-lust, her eyes flashing fire, her whole personality suffused with pleasure in her ability to make people's spines tingle with delicious excitement. Then she would change completely for a quiet lyric of the delights of nature, her voice liltingly musical, caressingly smooth, her dark eyes becoming as deep and mysterious as one of her beloved river pools.'[40] Denunciations of injustice were also softened by comic monologues and teasing exchanges with audience members. One review of a New Westminster, British Columbia, performance reveals the crucial role of humour in establishing an unthreatening relationship with listeners. Celebrating as 'splendid' 'one or two monologues in which she whimsically describes some experiences in different parts of the world as an entertainer,' the reviewer asserted that 'it was evident that this part of the program was the most appreciated.'[41] Johnson was not averse to joking about her 'own' people too, telling audiences on one occasion that 'Indians are, above all, a nation of boasters.'[42] The fact that the same people who delighted in her performances also enjoyed Walter McRaye's recitations of the French-Canadian patois of William Henry Drummond's poetry may indicate that for many, her performance art was as close to vaudeville as it was to serious recitation.

Many reviews emphasize Johnson's ability to move quickly from pathos and anger to light satire and humour: an unidentified review, dated 11 May 1892[43] described how 'her hearers weep with her and laugh with her as she wills,' suggesting that audiences enjoyed an emotional release during the performance. Her costume change – almost always from Native to European-style dress – also defused the anger of early poems. As Monture has argued, 'For her contemporary audience, it would have been easier to ignore her politically charged messages as long as her transformation – from the Mohawk Tekahion-wake to the Victorian Pauline – was enacted in the second half of her readings, somehow negating the reality of Native oppression and subjugation, as if all was forgotten and forgiven.'[44] Furthermore, if audience attention seemed to flag or reaction to cool, Johnson knew how to evoke patriotic fervour with poems celebrating the Mounted Police, Canadian national pride, and Iroquois loyalty to the Crown.[45] As Gray notes ironically, she knew well that 'crowds love uplifting patriotism and a great outfit.'[46]

Given these incoherencies in Johnson's self-presentation and in audience expectations, it is not surprising that responses to her serious side were mixed. Many commentators were so preoccupied with the beauty of her person and allure of her heritage as to be seemingly oblivious to the content of her poems. A commentator for the *Spectator* in 1892 heard exactly what he wanted, commenting blandly that 'the subjects were just what one would expect to hear from a poet of Indian origin – stories in graceful, rhythmic narrative of fertile grassy plains, of rushing rapids, of smoothly flowing rivers, of forests, or of Indian life and character.'[47] Another, in an unidentified review dated 18 November 1896, was mesmerized by her exoticism: 'Slender and graceful as a mountain gazelle, with her long, black glossy hair hanging down her back and her buckskin dress covered with the mystic, symbolic jewels of the Mohawk tribe, she presented a picture seldom seen outside the imagination.'[48] A majority of the reviews, as Strong-Boag and Gerson note, 'demonstrate greater comfort in praising her stage skills than in acknowledging her challenge to European hegemony.'[49]

In a few cases, the responses of reviewers seem even to have been precisely the opposite to what Johnson must have intended, as when one writer summed her up as 'a living example of what environment will do for a person,'[50] making her not a spokesperson for her race but an example of the triumph of the civilizing mission. Others simply rejected her representation as overstated, exaggerated. One reviewer dismissed 'The Corn Husker' (1896), which includes a portrait of a people 'banished from their lands,' as 'an excess of poetic licence, not a statement of fact.'[51] Another mocked her for romanticizing Native peoples, commenting that 'though we like to hear of the Indians' virtues, and fully believe at least in their wrongs, the fiery strains of "Tekahion-wake" leave us unmoved' because overstated.[52]

Despite such misunderstandings and refusals, Johnson's message came through clearly for a significant portion of her audience. One reviewer was impressed by 'her love for her native land and people, and scorn for those who would take her parentage from her.'[53] A review entitled 'Canada's Favourite Poetess' strongly commended the poet's ability to 'make ... one realize the other side of the question, the "Red Man's" side.'[54] An undated review from the Michigan *News-Reporter* stated, 'Her work thrilled the audience and held them spellbound, for beneath the surface there was the deep undercurrent of feeling that cried out in strong protest against the wrongs of her race.'[55] Mair commended Johnson as one 'who spoke out loud and bold ... and sang of [her race's] glories and its wrongs in strains of poetic fire.'[56] If her works and presentation strategies sometimes spoke at cross-purposes, many who heard her were moved to reflection, empathy, and awakened conscience. Strong-Boag and Gerson have commented of the performances that through them she reached a much larger audience than would have read her poetry on the page. It is possible, too, that her performances caused many to read or reread her poetry with a heightened attention to questions of race, sympathy, and national justice.

EXPLICITLY NATIVE CONTENT was never the major part of Johnson's verse or prose fiction, but it was nearly always the work that her audiences found most remarkable, and it is therefore appropriate to examine this material as a distinct subgrouping in her oeuvre. Strong-Boag and Gerson have argued that Johnson's Native identity came to the fore in 1892 after she began to appear on stage and to identify herself through her Native costume, but commentators at least as early as 1886, when she was publishing poems in newspapers and magazines, identified her as an 'Indian maid' and assessed her message as a challenge to white ignorance.[57] In these Native-content texts, certain techniques of address and persuasion occur frequently enough to be identified as key rhetorical patterns. Especially in early poems such as 'The Re-interment of Red Jacket' (1884), 'A Cry from an Indian Wife' (1885), and '"Brant," a Memorial Ode' (1886), Johnson worked to rearticulate the Anglo-Canadian myth of identity, seizing on the ideals, promises, and self-images that English Canada used to define itself and applying them to the contemporary situation of Native people. In expressing those ideals in poetry designed for dramatic performance, she sought to reinvigorate Canadians' deeply held convictions about their society by embodying their cherished myths of equity, justice, and compassion. In essence, she challenged the nation to live up to its own imagined identity.

In later prose pieces such as 'My Mother' (1909), 'Catharine of the "Crow's Nest"' (1910), 'A Red Girl's Reasoning' (1893), 'As It Was in the Beginning' (1899), 'A Pagan in St. Paul's Cathedral' (1906), and 'We-hro's Sacrifice' (1907), that challenge is made even more forcefully through Johnson's evocation of familial analogies to stress the potential, and fragility, of a close national and cultural partnership between Anglo-Canadian and Native peoples. Throughout these texts, she carefully balances between enthusiastic affirmation of Canadian ideals and forceful examination of inequitable practices. While she was not afraid to name injustice where she saw it, she did so predominantly to invoke and affirm Canadian national values, rather than to undermine them fatally. She sought to inspire and enact a radical empathy that simultaneously reassured audiences about their ideals and guided them to changed perceptions. Although her poems' and stories' 'disruptive potential ... was often lost on her contemporaries,'[58] they nevertheless spoke deeply to some portion of her listeners and remain a provocative legacy to twenty-first-century readers.

An early piece demonstrates the skill with which Johnson often links her themes of reconciliation and challenge. 'The Re-interment of Red Jacket' is her first extant poem to address the meaning of the

North American Native past and its continuing relevance in the present and future. It was written for the Buffalo Historical Society's 1884
commemoration of Red Jacket, an acclaimed Iroquois orator, and was
published in the *Transactions of the Buffalo Historical Society* shortly
after the ceremony for his reinterment, to which Pauline and her
sister Evelyn were invited. In the poem, Johnson 'boasted of her Indian lineage and expressed sympathy with her Indian forbears.'[59]
She also, as Strong-Boag and Gerson observe, 'attempted to knit a
new nationalist narrative'[60] and experimented with a message combining Native pride, elegy, and exhortation. The couplet near the
conclusion in which the speaker asks white North Americans to
'Forgive the wrongs my children did to you, / And we, the red skins,
will forgive you too' is frequently quoted as an example of the
caution and conciliatory tone of Johnson's message, but these lines
cannot be understood apart from the rest of the poem, which insists
upon the high standard of fairness and truth set by Red Jacket
for those who come after. Commemorating the great Seneca leader's
wisdom, commitment to peace, and generous heart, Johnson praises
her white audience ('O, rising nation of the West') for carrying
out the reinterment while also challenging them to emulate Red
Jacket's nobility.

As in a number of the poems in which she laments the 'waning' of
Indian power, Johnson begins the poem by stressing the still hush of
the landscape ('So still the tranquil air') and allegorizing in a single individual's death the decay of his nation ('But deeper quiet wraps the
dusky Chief / Whose ashes slumber there'). As she reflects on Red
Jacket's life, she also grounds hope for the future on his legacy, and
thus although the poem might be seen to betray the cause of Native-
white coexistence in overemphasizing the inevitability and finality of
Native cultural 'decay,' it also insists on the multiple connections
between past and present as well as on the vital need both to honour
ancestors and to base future national conduct on the ground (here
made literal as burial space) of a heroic inheritance. The 'honoured
place' that Johnson celebrates for Red Jacket is both physical and cultural. With this motive in mind, we can recognize that the encomiums
she lavishes on Red Jacket are all coded references to present-day
white obligations. As 'stubborn hearts' were stirred by Red Jacket's
eloquence in the past, so whites owe a respectful hearing to the
eloquent voices (such as Johnson herself) of Red Jacket's heirs in the

present. Just as 'Factious schemes succumbed whene'er he spoke,' so white conquerors are obligated to pursue peace in the present. And remembering both Red Jacket's political might and his tenderness for the weak, whites are exhorted to emulate the 'mental sight' and liberality of a compassionate ruler:

> Early he learned to speak,
> With thought so vast, and liberal, and strong,
> He blessed the little good and passed the wrong
> Embodied in the weak.

Johnson's puzzling insistence on the absolute extinction of Native power (puzzling given her own statements to the contrary elsewhere, that is) may be explained as a strategy not merely to appease white anxieties – and thus perhaps to encourage a conqueror's benevolence – but also to emphasize the fragility of political power: in a few short years, the poem stresses, Red Jacket's 'superhuman might' has been utterly reduced. Readers are surely meant to recognize the potential personal application of Johnson's reflections on earthly power, an application heightened by her generalizing rhetoric:

> The world has often seen
> A master mind pulse with the waning day
> That sends his waning nation to decay
> Where none can intervene.

Noble action is the only enduring earthly legacy, she suggests, and therefore whites too can learn from the moral example of Red Jacket in order to claim a lasting good:

> And so ere Indian Summer sweetly sleeps,
> She beckons me where old Niagara leaps;
> Superbly she extends her greeting hand,
> And smiling speaks to her adopted land;
>
> Saying, 'O, rising nation of the West,
> That occupies my land, so richly blest;
> O, free, unfettered people that have come
> To make America your rightful home,

Forgive the wrongs my children did to you,
And we, the red skins, will forgive you too;
To-day has seen your noblest action done,
The honoured re-entombment of my son.'

Although this is certainly one of the most conciliatory poems Johnson ever wrote, it is not without serious moral challenges to its white audience. The speaker's stress on her own proud heritage from Red Jacket – declaring her 'copper-tinted face' to be her 'proudest claim' – and the symbolic suggestiveness of the poem's repeated references to 'Indian Summer,' the resurgence of warm weather after summer seems to be over, form an understated elegiac counter-text suggesting the continuity and potential renewal of Native cultural strength.

'A Cry from an Indian Wife,' first published in *The Week* in 1885 and then revised for inclusion in *The White Wampum* (1895), her first published volume, is one of Johnson's well-known performance pieces that also attempts to balance reconciliation and challenge, presenting a complex articulation of the burden of history and of cross-cultural understanding. This poem has often been commented upon, with Francis targeting its vagueness as evidence of Johnson's soft-pedalling and Strong-Boag and Gerson commending the poem for 'demand[ing] recognition for the silenced figures of colonial history.'[61] It is generally taken to be a poem in which the speaker articulates her divided loyalties as, simultaneously, the wife of a Plains Indian rebel and a British subject loyal to the Union Jack, alternating 'between advocating the cause of the dispossessed natives and expressing sympathy with the Euro-Canadian perspective.'[62] Strong-Boag and Gerson find particularly dramatic the manner in which the poem 'oscillates across an unresolvable either/or, White/Native dichotomy.'[63] Others have simply seen it as confused. The poem may be, though, much clearer in its allegiances than is generally assumed. Johnson deploys the figure of the 'Indian wife' to underscore the intellectual and emotional effort required for an appropriate empathy, but she does so not so much to dramatize national conflict as to chart the way towards a re-envisioning of national history. In keeping with her effort to enlighten rather than dismay her audience, her point throughout the poem seems to be that the oppositions at the poem's heart – between white and Native, patriot and rebel, coward and brave – are *not* irresolvable and that divided sympathies must accompany, but cannot replace, the enactment of justice.

In introducing a speaker bidding farewell to her warrior husband, Johnson carefully establishes the obvious and undeniable causes of the rebellion: the 'bare' plains from which the bison have disappeared and the dispossession of the now 'fallen' warriors who once occupied it un-challenged. Thus, well before the speaker pursues her agitated reflec-tions on the war's multiple victims, she links the horror of war to the material effects of colonial injustice:

> Curse to the war that drinks their harmless blood.
> Curse to the fate that brought them from the East
> To be our chiefs – to make our nation least
> That breathes the air of this vast continent.

Johnson's reference to 'fate,' found frequently in her poems about colo-nial domination, allows her to detour around matters of intent and cul-pability but does not soften her stress on the unjust and unnecessary diminishment of once mighty peoples. The pathos and courage of white sacrifice are appropriately recognized ('They all are young and beautiful and good,' the speaker says of the Anglo-Canadian soldiers marching to crush the rebellion), but Johnson makes it clear that these young men have been marshalled to a war that is fundamentally unnecessary, given the 'vast continent' that the Indians ask to share. Expressions of sympa-thy for 'this stripling pack / Of white-faced warriors' and for 'the pale-faced maiden on her knees' do not offset the powerful irony that accom-panies the Indian wife's recounting of the Anglo-Canadian perspective. If that perspective is not entirely dismissed, it is heavily qualified by the ironies, omissions, and contradictions pointed up by its context:

> Still their new rule and council is well meant.
> They but forget we Indians owned the land
> From ocean unto ocean; that they stand
> Upon a soil that centuries agone
> Was our sole kingdom and our right alone.
> They never think how they would feel to-day,
> If some great nation came from far away,
> Wrestling their country from their hapless braves,
> Giving what they gave us – but wars and graves.

There are no divided allegiances here. In this section of the poem, Johnson implicitly calls her white audience to the same kind of radical empathy being demonstrated by her speaker, who insists on the enemy's innocent forgetting. In order to claim such innocence, white readers must now remember and understand. Just as the speaker imagines the grief of white mothers and wives, white listeners must imaginatively enter Native suffering and oppression. The extreme asymmetry of these acts of imaginative exchange is subtly recognized in the poem through Johnson's reference to the abundant prayers for Canadian soldiers and the military inequities that pit 'a thousand rifle balls' against a single 'tomahawk.' Yet if she recognized that whites owed Native nations more than they were likely to give – a belief expressed in the anger of the poem's concluding lines – her main concern in the poem was to provide a model of empathy and recognition that some listeners might embrace. The speaker's contradictions and hesitations are not only laudable oscillations of feeling but also a rhetorical demonstration of the difficult but necessary work of cross-cultural understanding. Such understanding involved not an 'unresolvable either/or,' as Strong-Boag and Gerson suggest, but a thoroughgoing 'both/and' that recognizes the suffering of the 'enemy' and chooses historical clarity and the cause of truth.

Not nearly so well known but also significant in its work of reconciliation is '"Brant," A Memorial Ode.' This is the poem that was read to thunderous applause at the unveiling of the Brant statue in 1886 and was followed by the interview with Sara Jeannette Duncan. It too has been read as overly conciliatory. Gray stresses its failure 'to challenge the status quo of race relations,' concluding that 'either she didn't see the need to rock the political boat or she was more concerned to establish herself as a literary figure.'[64] But like so many of the poems in which Johnson attempts to teach an Anglo-Canadian audience about Canadian history, the poem balances between celebrating and complicating the founding myth of British justice. It applauds Britannia for offering protection to her Indian subjects but also places emphasis on their unmerited suffering. It praises Young Canada's growing might while making clear that the nation owes its very existence to its Native allies during the American Revolutionary War. In moving adroitly between a number of seemingly contradictory positions, the poem asks its readers to recognize the complex historical debts that Canadian patriots owe their Loyalist Indian forebears. It *is* conciliatory, but it is also unsettling.

It is perhaps worth pausing here to note the impact the poem seems to have had on Duncan, despite the flippancy with which she conducted her interview afterwards. When she wrote about the Brant celebration for *The Week*, she was led to reflect with uncharacteristic compassion on the cruel contrast between Native peoples' historical might and their present diminished status. 'One felt in a vaguely sentimental way,' she reflected as she watched Mohawk dancers honouring Brant, 'the pang of the usurper at the sight of these early Indian freeholders of the soil, joining to honour him who had given allegiance to a power that robbed them of their right of tenantry and all their wild ancestral life; and one thought instinctively of the time which cannot be many centuries away, when these people shall have vanished as a dark, impotently-forbidding shadow from this continent, and the bronze incarnation of their being will be all that the sun and wind will find of the tribes they knew before they knew us.'[65] Both Duncan's 'pang' at the dispossession of Native peoples and her confidence in their historical passing, common motifs of the Vanishing Race discourse, find their source in Johnson's poem, which laments the fading of the race and stresses British obligation to Native courage. While the certainty that Native races were doomed to die out was a commonplace of this period, Duncan's consciousness of herself as a 'usurper' was not, and must be credited to Johnson's effective presentation. 'Brant' pays tribute to the Six Nations' valour, loyalty, and extraordinary self-sacrifice. Drawing on the Loyalist ideals at the heart of the English-Canadian – especially Upper Canadian – founding myth, Johnson emphasizes how the Iroquois left a beloved homeland at Brant's behest to honour an allegiance. Without Iroquois sacrifices, Canada might not have attained her nationhood; the country's present peace and independence rest on 'allegiance from thy Indian son.'

In *The Imaginary Indian*, Francis's main criticism of Johnson is that she challenged her white audiences to little more than an easy regret, asking them to experience a pleasurable sadness in contemplating the inevitable extinction of Native power. Although he does not mention 'Brant,' the poem would seem, particularly in light of Duncan's response, to support his reading. Yet while Francis makes a crucial argument overall about Euro-Canadian understandings of the Indian at this time period, he oversimplifies Johnson's texts and intentions, for despite its elegiac qualities, 'Brant' contests the Indian extinction theory and works insistently to circumvent a response of complacency. Duncan, after all, expresses *guilt* rather than sweet sadness, and I believe that the poem calls its readers to changed attitudes as a result of an awakened historical consciousness. Although it does begin with sorrowful reflection on loss, it moves quickly to affirm the Native role in the building of Canada, not only in the past but also in the present.

Indian power is fading, Johnson affirms, as the sun fades at twilight:

> For as the carmine in the twilight skies
> Will fade as night comes on, so fades the race
> That unto Might and therefore Right gives place.

One notes the irony of 'Might and therefore Right,' an assertion designed to unsettle audience complacency and to reverberate ironically with the ideals of justice and allegiance that are the poem's keynotes. Johnson reflects that a time is coming 'when the sun / Shall rise again, but only shine upon / Her Indian graves, and Indian memories.' These reflections are elegiac indeed, but read in the context of the whole poem, they do not necessarily signal Native extinction. At the time of the poem's publication, the power of Native nations was without doubt on the wane, a fact that did not mean that as individuals and coherent cultural groups, they would not become vigorous participants in the new nation. When Johnson pictures the sun of a new age dawning on 'Indian graves, and Indian memories,' the ambiguity of 'Indian memories' (memories of Indians? or Indians' memories of former might and power?) enables us to read these passages retrospectively as a comment not on the extinction of a race but on the passing of Native independence – distressing, certainly, but not the end of all hope (suns, as the poem makes clear, do rise again). This reading is supported by Johnson's claim, a few lines later, of 'one common Brotherhood' between white and Native, who meet 'In peace and love, with purpose understood.' The specific purpose is the honouring of Brant, but a more general purpose can be reasonably deduced: that of building together a mighty Canada whose citizens are 'guard[ed] from all fear of wrong.' Furthermore, this reading is supported, not undermined, by the metaphor of sunset, which seems at first such an unfortunate confirmation of popular prejudice. Johnson elaborates the metaphor of sunset to emphasize the debt of gratitude owed to Brant and his followers:

> And as white clouds float hurriedly and high
> Across the crimson of a sunset sky,
> Although their depths are foamy as the snow,

Their beauty lies in their vermillion glow,
So Canada, thy plumes were hardly won
Without allegiance from thy Indian son,
Thy glories, like the cloud enhance their charm
With red reflections from the Mohawk's arm.

Just as the white clouds gain their beauty from the vermilion of the set-ting sun, so Canada's majority white population gains its proud na-tional identity from the red race whose power is now on the wane. Out of the elegiac metaphor, Johnson builds a powerful image of mutual interdependence designed to link patriotism ineluctably to respect and protection for Native peoples.

These three poems are characteristic of Johnson's most challenging early poetry. Memorializing historical persons and events, they enabled her to address the place of Native peoples – both their heroism and their suffering – in Canada's past and to articulate why Anglo-Canadians owed them respect and sympathy in the present. The poems are re-markable for their careful insistence that true patriotic commitment to British ideals and Canadian nationality requires an active recognition of Native peoples' contributions and needs; even more remarkable, perhaps, is the manner in which Johnson launches a thoroughgoing challenge to Anglo-Canadian complacency precisely by appealing to foundational beliefs about British justice and equity. Far from attacking or directly criticizing the stories by which Anglo-Canadians affirmed their self-identity, she reassured readers that Native peoples could also appreciate (and participate in) such national narratives; justice could be accomplished, she suggested, not through divisive confrontation but through a cooperative, full implementation of Anglo-Canadian princi-ples. The poems, then, do not resist and subvert so much as radically embrace and extend dominant narratives of Anglo-Canadian national-ism, a technique responsible for their enduring and unsettling power.

TOWARDS THE END OF HER LIFE, Johnson turned increasingly to the writ-ing of fiction to supplement her income. Stories for the American *Mother's Magazine* were more remunerative than poetry and gave her a widely circulated narrative forum for her ongoing conversation with her readers. Many of the stories address the question of how relations between Aboriginal and non-Aboriginal peoples should be understood in the past, present, and future. In keeping with the domestic focus of much magazine fiction, Johnson employed stories of family life – parent-child relations, adoption, courtship, and marriage – in order to articulate the intimate and complicated dynamics of national belonging and reconciliation. The note of patriotic fervour and idealism struck in her poetry is often present, but increasingly there is a darker suggestion of the peril and loss to be faced in the future if Anglo-Canadians abuse the pride, goodwill, and right to dignity of Native peoples.

An autobiographical narrative published near the end of her career demonstrates clearly the allegorical dimensions of Johnson's family stories. In 'My Mother,' a fictionalized biography of her parents' courtship originally published in *Mother's Magazine* in 1909, Johnson presents a carefully structured, highly romanticized account of her pedigree, emphasizing the moral rectitude, dignity, and tender sympathy that characterized her parents' partnership. By repeatedly linking the figures of her mother and father with English Canada and the Six Nations respectively, she emphasizes how individual lives could provide the literal and symbolic pattern for national harmony. Her parents' happy marriage is both an idealized image of the nation's origins and a blueprint for its future.

The story is prefaced by a statement by Johnson about the absolute accuracy of the contents, a claim immediately undercut by her use of fictional names and some obvious reshaping of plot for symmetry and emotional intensity. The romantic passion that suffuses the family narrative makes it an ideal vehicle for Johnson to justify her own claim to be a mediator between Iroquois and English-Canadian cultures. Her mother is characterized as a dignified gentlewoman of true heart and settled purpose, capable of great courage and committed to honour; her father is a strikingly handsome, well-spoken and talented Native leader with polished manners and deeply instilled courtesy, respect, and compassion. Throughout their married life, the couple are united by their love for Canada as a nation and especially for the Iroquois people of the Six Nations Reserve. Pauline's mother becomes, in essence, a mother to all the Six Nations: 'Her marriage had made her an Indian by the laws which govern Canada, as well as by the sympathies and yearnings and affections of her own heart.'[66] The couple in turn instill in their children the best qualities of both cultures, teaching them 'the legends, the traditions, the culture and the etiquette of both races'[67] and an equal commitment to them. In describing her parents' profound domestic happiness, Johnson emphasizes the ability of deep love to harmonize seemingly incompatible allegiances:

Their loves were identical. They loved nature – the trees, best of all, and the river, and the birds. They loved the Anglican Church, they loved the British flag, they loved Queen Victoria, they loved beautiful, dead Elizabeth Evans [her sister], they loved strange, reticent Mr. Evans. They loved music, pictures and dainty china, with which George Mansion filled his beautiful home. They loved books and animals, but, most of all, these two loved the Indian people, loved their legends, their habits, their customs – loved the people themselves. Small wonder, then, that their children should be born with pride of race and heritage, and should face the world with that peculiar, unconquerable courage that only a fighting ancestry can give.[68]

Through this lavish endorsement of her upbringing, Johnson was able to outline how all Canadian children might gain a rewarding bicultural heritage, and she evoked a vision of thoroughgoing reconciliation between Canada's diverse peoples.

Johnson's narrative is not only a loving tribute to her parents but also a detailed allegory of the nation's origins and potential. 'English Canada' is symbolized through her mother, who, in addition to her principles and loving heart, is desperate for rescue from the rigid authoritarianism of her background. Her father has admirable principles but is personally cold, an unloving, neglectful, and physically volatile parent. Though 'made for love,' his daughter has never had an opportunity to realize her potential; her marriage to George Johnson (Chief Mansion, in the story) allows her to escape a stifling past, a 'checkered and neglected life,'[69] and to enter into a vibrant and fulfilled present. The allegorical implications of this aspect of the story are quite clear: Native culture has much to offer English-Canadian peoples, who are too often stifled by a rigid parent. Pauline's father, representing the Native rescuer, is both passionate and canny: his aristocratic lineage and heroic history as a valued British ally mean that, while undoubtedly Lydia's equal, his qualities perfectly complement hers. He is her protector and rescuer, an honourable and loving man capable of adapting to English culture while continuing to uphold his family traditions. In describing the love between her parents, Johnson was not only establishing her romantic origins and legitimating mixed-blood families – much debated in turn-of-the-century Canada – but also retelling a myth of national origins with which she and many of her readers would have had some familiarity, that of the allegorical marriage between Old and New World figures.

As scholars such as Anne McClintock in *Imperial Leather* (1995) have demonstrated, this common imperial motif often represents New World nation-building as a union between a New World female (untutored nature, beautiful and awaiting development) and an imperial male conqueror, who asserts his rights through both superiority and force. In her reversal of this gendered pairing, Johnson emphasizes the partnership between the New World and Britannia as an honourable choice, rather than an act of imperial conquest. Equal partnership could not be claimed by conquered victims, and therefore in her narrative the two individuals fall in love at almost the same moment of mutual need and awareness. That Johnson was fully aware of the allegorical implications and emotional resonance of the familial narrative is made clear in the frequent use to which she put it in her political poetry. In 'Brant,' for example, she describes the situation of the present-day descendants of the Mohawk leader in the following terms:

> Encircling us an arm both true and brave
> Extends from far across the great Salt wave,
> Though but a woman's hand 'tis firm and strong
> Enough to guard us from all fear of wrong,
> A hand on which all British subjects lean –
> The loving hand of England's Noble Queen.

In this representation, the Mohawks have sacrificed their homeland and right of dominion out of loyalty to the British crown, and they are recompensed (a recompense that by no means cancels the debt they are owed) by the 'loving hand' of their British queen. Similarly, in 'My Mother' Pauline's father sacrifices his right, as a hereditary chief, to pass the title to his children, therefore partially renouncing his racial privileges out of love and loyalty to his white bride. He is rewarded by the 'arm both true and brave' of Pauline's mother, her unswerving gratitude, loyalty, and devotion. The two of them live in perfect amity, and on those unusual occasions when even a minor discord threatens, they turn to admire the trees Pauline's father has cultivated around his mansion, and 'these groups of trees bridged the fleeting difference of opinion or any slight antagonism of will and purpose.'[70] The allegorical implication seems to be that joyful appreciation of a shared land can buttress and maintain a loving alliance; regardless of who built what, Aboriginal and English Canadians can find common ground in love of place and mutual respect. Johnson was, of course, fully aware that British gratitude to Iroquois allies had faded in recent decades with the diminishment of the American threat and the expansion of settlement, and that the recompense of just protection was more often seen in the breach than in the observance; her familial allegory was not a description of reality but a vivid demonstration of what relations of honour might look like, an uncompromising reminder of historical debts, and an assertion of faith that reparation for Mohawk sacrifices might still be made.

Such familial allegories, especially those focusing on mixed-race marriages, adoptions, and alliances, appear in many of the stories that Johnson published in *Mother's Magazine* in the final years of her career; clearly, she found the pairing of a domestic focus with a political message congenial to her purposes. The form enabled her to imagine how reconciliation and mutual recognition might take place. In 'Catharine of the "Crow's Nest"' (1910), the newly settled territory of western Canada offers possibilities for new kinds of alliance. In the story, Wingate, a railway camp leader in the Rocky Mountains, discovers that his child, believed drowned with her mother before he came to the camp some months or years earlier, is being raised by Catharine, the Native woman who cooks for the men in his camp. Familial connection is both restored and extended through the agency of Catharine, the inscrutable and compassionate grandmother figure, whose 'mournful eyes'[71] and keen intuition recognize Wingate's sorrowful paternity by tracing his features in the child she is raising. Sensing his pain, she grieves for him as if he were her own son; she longs to restore his daughter and yet dreads the loss of the little girl she has been raising. Even before she is revealed to be his daughter's saviour, Wingate, too, is drawn to the woman, captivated by her 'strength of character'[72] and concerned for her well-being; something about her sorrowing, sympathetic gaze reminds him of his own mother's love. Johnson prepares the way for the restoration of family ties by emphasizing both characters' intuitive recognition of the other's loneliness and tender heart.

Significantly, Wingate lost his wife and child when he forfeited his role as husband and protector to search for gold in the Klondike: 'For three weeks the fascination of searching for the golden pay-streak had held him in the mountains.'[73] He was so bedazzled by desire for wealth that his wife and daughter were missing for many days before he could even be informed (and, as we learn later in the story, Kootenay Natives had to bury his wife's body and rescue his half-dead child). The implication seems to be that in the booming West, whites need the example

of Aboriginal loyalty to kin and to the earth as a counter to their materialism and enterprise. Ever since learning of the death of his family,
Wingate has been working feverishly to distract himself from pain and
to keep his emotions dead. Yet when he believes Catharine to be lost in
a snowstorm, love awakes in him again, and his 'old grief was knock-
ing at his heart once more.'[74] The melodramatic scene in which he re-
gains his daughter and acts on his love for the old woman by claiming
her as part of the family is infused with Johnson's idealistic formula for
reconstituting relationship in the 'contact zone' of colonial encounter.
Rather than taking his daughter from Catharine, Wingate requests that
she continue to care for his child and declares himself the old woman's
adopted son, her 'white boy.'[75] His white daughter will grow up with a
bicultural heritage, owing her life and the restoration of her father to
her adopted Native (grand)mother. Here again, bonds of gratitude,
self-sacrifice, and shared love unite white and red into one family.

There is perhaps some irony in the fact that this story, with its solitary and self-sacrificing Native woman character, displays some of the
very features Johnson had criticized quite a few years earlier in 'A
Strong Race Opinion: On the Indian Girl in Modern Fiction.' Published
in the Toronto *Globe* in 1892, the essay reveals the wit and freshness of
insight characteristic of Duncan's literary analyses in the previous
decade, offering an astute critique of the assumptions, misunderstandings, and white fantasy that underpin the Euro-Canadian myth of Indian womanhood; Johnson's central point was that the 'Indian maiden'
of modern fiction exists merely to confirm the cultural superiority of her
white readership – a pathetic, fawning, and suicidal maiden 'never dignified by being permitted to own a surname' and possessing an 'unhappy, self-sacrificing life.'[76]

Although Johnson departs from the standard narrative in making
Catharine a dignified elderly woman who is not in love with Wingate
and not inclined to suicide, her character is a solitary creature inexpli-
cably cut off from her people and from any family ties; it is her very
aloneness that makes possible her role in the regeneration of Wingate,
and the narrative emphasizes her 'Indianness' in somewhat stereotypical terms through broken speech, impassive countenance, and stubborn
determination. Most tellingly, her personal sacrifices for Wingate and
his daughter seem unmotivated and excessive. Romantic as the vision
of equal partnership between Native and non-Native might be, it seems
Johnson could not ignore the tremendous losses Native peoples had already suffered, and she recognized that the costs of accommodation

and reconciliation in the future would almost inevitably be borne more heavily by the Indian nations than by white Canadians. Despite this concession, however, she repeatedly emphasized, as in this story, that Native people were much more than expendable accessories in the drama of white lives; on the contrary, Native presence – especially Native female presence – was essential to the literal and emotional survival of non-Native families.

In other stories depicting mixed-race family relations, Johnson makes this same point about white need even more forcefully. An earlier story, 'A Red Girl's Reasoning' (1893), can be understood not only as a narrative about the pride of a mixed-race heroine who will not be reconciled with her husband after he insults her parents but also as a warning to Anglo-Canadian society about the devastating consequences of neglecting their Native partners. Whites must take care not to irreparably damage Native trust and loyalty for fear the union will be severed past repair. The words of Christie's father to his new son-in-law point to the inflexible reciprocity in Native responses to white actions. 'It is kindness for kindness, bullet for bullet, blood for blood,' he cautions the young man. 'Remember, what you are, she will be.'[77] Outlining how Charlie McDonald loses his wife's love, the story allegorizes both the promise and the peril of Native-white relations. At first Charlie is proud of his mixed-blood wife and eager to have his friends admire her; beautiful and intelligent, she is for a time '"all the rage" that winter at the provincial capital'[78] and sincerely in love with her husband. But when she reveals that her parents were married according to Indian law rather than Christian rites, he is appalled. They quarrel, and when Charlie suggests that he might not have married Christie had he known of her doubtful legitimacy, she leaves him forever, and although he soon repents and begs her to return, she cannot forgive him. The story encodes an explicit statement to white readers that while Native people are more than willing to be equal partners with English Canadians – willing even to adapt to white cultural institutions when led by the heart – Native self-respect will not permit assaults on their cultural integrity. Christie's words when she realizes her husband's contempt for Indian law point to the radical parity at the heart of Johnson's bicultural ideal: 'Why should I recognize the rites of your nation when you do not acknowledge the rites of mine?'[79] Johnson's uncompromisingly bitter ending insists on the swiftness with which love and accommodation can be replaced by enmity and mistrust, resulting in harm to both Aboriginal people and whites.

Pessimism about the future of Native-white relations is even more pronounced in 'As It Was in the Beginning' (1899), one of Johnson's most bitter indictments of colonial violence and Christian hypocrisy. As the title's biblical echo might suggest (Gerson and Strong-Boag note the allusion to the Anglican creed), [80] the narrative is about the 'fall' of a Cree girl, Esther, when she is taken by an Anglican priest, called Father Paul, to a residential school, where no effort is spared to make her a daughter of the church; in order to protect her from 'pagan influences,'[81] she is not allowed to visit her own people, for whom she longs passionately. The experience of adapting to white ways and the Christian faith is difficult for Esther, yet the possibility of a substitute happiness to counterbalance her many losses is suggested by the loving words spoken by Laurence, the priest's nephew. Esther has loved both Father Paul and Laurence from the time she left her family, and marriage to Laurence holds out the possibility of a newborn identity. But her faith and happiness are destroyed when she overhears Father Paul dissuading his nephew from the marriage because of her 'uncertain blood.'[82] Esther leaves the mission, but not before poisoning Laurence with a flint tainted by snake venom.

The priest's malice, the nephew's weakness, and Esther's fury form the melodramatic outline of the by now familiar family configuration, and the story is one of Johnson's bitterest representations of the impact of insensitive Christian missionary activity on a previously coherent people. Taught to renounce her own people's cultural practices but not fully accepted by white society, indoctrinated with a religion that denies her spirituality and leaves only fear rather than Christian love in its place, Esther is deformed rather than reformed by contact with white society. In her final vengeful fury, she becomes the embodiment of white fears and prejudices about the Indian, the implication being that these traits, rather than having been inadequately repressed by white training, have actually been created and nurtured by such teaching. Emphasizing the psychic trauma of Esther's partial accommodation to white culture, Johnson creates both a scathing indictment of the residential school system and a pointed analysis of the process by which white racism creates the very adversary it fears, moulding through discourse and material practices of exclusion a fearful and hating other determined to exact vengeance. Focusing on Esther's transformation from colonial girlhood into a monstrous emblem of rage, the story works on two levels at once: as contemporary social analysis and as a fable of psycho-social rupture. In this and other stories, Johnson's fascination with figures of vengeance suggests that throughout her career she sought to embody not only ideals of loving partnership but also the grim possibility of a rift between whites and Natives, with retaliatory violence enacted by the oppressed.

In all these stories, Johnson employs motifs of intercultural marriage and adoption to stress relationships of intimacy between Aboriginal and Anglo-Canadian peoples even as, in reality, the possibilities for such alliances and intermixing at the social and cultural levels were disappearing. By the early twentieth century, Aboriginal people had been pushed to the margins of Canadian society more fully than at any other time in their history. The need to interpret Aboriginal realities for Anglo-Canadian culture and to stress the possibilities for intercultural partnership was perhaps more urgent than ever before, and at a time when Native advocates were few on the ground, Johnson worked in a number of her most powerful stories to make Aboriginal culture intelligible and attractive to her white audiences.

ESPECIALLY WHEN SHE WROTE about Aboriginal traditions and religious practices, Johnson used the trope of family resemblance to demand and enact a radical empathy. In 'A Pagan in St. Paul's Cathedral' (1906), she argues that the differences between Native and Christian spiritual practices were far less significant than the similarities. She reportedly considered this essay one of the best pieces of prose she ever wrote. It was one of four essays published in the London *Daily Express* during her second tour of the city and was a popular success with a British audience keen to encounter the perspective of a North American Indian. Johnson must have been aware of both the potential to educate a very large audience and the challenge to make herself understood. The final result, in which she casts herself in the role of a traditional Indian warrior struggling to understand a foreign culture, was exotically appealing and also challenging.

The element of challenge is highlighted by Strong-Boag and Gerson, who find that the essay 'asserts the equality of First Nations spirituality with European religion';[83] Francis, on the other hand, while appreciating Johnson's defence of 'the dignity of Native religious practices and beliefs,' argues that the created persona shows Johnson being 'as patronizing towards her own people as any White writer.'[84] The essay would have been much more effective, he believes, if Johnson had defended Aboriginal traditions 'from the perspective of a sophisticated woman with some experience of the world,' rather than as 'a naïve

"Redskin" who seems never to have ventured beyond the edges of the northern forest.'[85] He finds her to be 'clearly pandering to a stereotypical notion of the Indian as an artless, childlike innocent.'[86] Monture agrees, finding the political message of the essay severely compromised by 'the simplistic language ... that only reinforces the idea of England as a colonial father figure to his Iroquoian wards.'[87] The disagreement amongst scholars highlights the complexity of Johnson's rhetorical choices in an essay very much aware of language and difference.

At the beginning of the piece, Johnson's narrator tells us that, having come to England as an ally of the British king, she or he (the gender is unclear) is determined to see all that belongs to the king, including 'the wigwam, known to the palefaces as Buckingham Palace, but to the red man as the "Tepee of the Great White Father."'[88] It is possible that the stereotypical language of the speaker is Johnson's way not of condescending to her people but of alerting her British readers to the particular challenge of cross-cultural reading implicit in all such encounters between white and Native. Applying Native terms to London landmarks, Johnson was not only satisfying her audience's desire for exoticism but suggesting the destabilizing effect produced when one group renames the cultural artefacts and prized institutions of another. Johnson's Red Man in London is not a spectacle to be examined but an exploring visitor who constantly compares present observations with lived experience, to the detriment of neither.

Sitting in St Paul's Cathedral, the narrator is drawn back in memory to the forests, rivers, and lodges of home. Such images counterpoint present observations throughout the short piece to suggest myriad connections and correspondences between them: the 'deep-throated organ and the boys' voices' of St Paul's are replaced in the narrator's mind's ear by 'the melancholy incantations of our own pagan religionists,' while the sight of the 'altar-lights of St. Paul's' are blotted out by visual memories of 'the camp fires of the Onondaga "long-house."'[89] The speaker visualizes an Onondaga White Dog ceremony, at which the sacrifice of a pure white animal expresses worshippers' reverence and aspirations for personal purity. The implication of the comparison is that although the forms of Christian and Aboriginal worship differ, the desire to pay tribute to the Great Spirit is equally heartfelt. Whether Johnson goes so far as to assert 'the equality' of the two religions is impossible to decide, for she refrains from investigating the content of Aboriginal religious beliefs. She confines herself instead to affirming that the impulse to atonement and to communion with God is the same in each group. In the remembered words of the Onondaga fire-keeper, 'The Great Spirit desires no human sacrifice, but we, His children, must give to Him that which is nearest our hearts and nearest our lives.'[90] Although the essay does not undertake any extended comparison between Christian and Aboriginal systems of belief, it asserts that Aboriginal worshippers share with Christians a true yearning for God, and that therefore Christian and Aboriginal beliefs share a family resemblance.

Such family resemblance is also the subject of 'We-hro's Sacrifice' (1907), a story about a boy, son of the Onondaga chief, who gives up the pet he loves dearly for the honour of his people. At first he hides the animal when he learns that a white dog is required as a sacrificial offering at his nation's most important religious ceremony, but when his father requests it of him, he 'crush[es] down his grief.'[91] Stressing the various ways that loving sacrifice underpins Aboriginal spiritual beliefs and practices, Johnson calls upon her readers to notice the correspondence between Christ's teachings and Aboriginal ways.

The story makes central the confrontation between Christian and Native belief in that the occasion of the story is a visit by the Brant-ford Anglican bishop to the Onondaga of the Six Nations Reserve in order to witness their most important ceremony. Again, the specific content of the two religions does not receive analysis, and the story does not condemn the representatives of state and religious authority, presenting both the superintendent of Indian Affairs and the Anglican bishop as well-intentioned men. It merely stresses that Aboriginal traditions deserve respect. The bishop does not understand the Onondaga religion, but he understands enough to honour the faith it embodies: 'It pained his gentle old heart to know that this great tribe of Indians were pagans – savages, as he thought – but when he entered that plain log building that the Onondaga held as their church, he took off his hat with the beautiful reverence all great men pay to other great men's religion.'[92] As he stands inside the ceremonial lodge, the priest's eye is caught by We-hro's suffering face, and when he learns what the boy has done, he blesses him for his greatness of heart, exclaiming, 'Oh, that the white boys of my great city church knew and practised half as much of self-denial as has this little pagan Indian lad.'[93] Suggesting that the young boy's suffering for love of his father is Christlike in nature, Johnson implies that without knowing Christ, the Onondaga enact His message – and even perhaps embody His spirit – in their daily lives.

Consideration of these texts in which Johnson argues for the family resemblance between Christianity and Native religion inevitably raises questions about the role of religious faith in her work as a whole. Not surprisingly, no coherent or consistent statement can be derived from the numerous poems, essays, and stories that address matters of faith. Strong-Boag and Gerson note that, as on every important subject, Johnson's position is a shifting and elusive one, and they hypothesize a development from orthodoxy in early poems to critical distance. A poem such as 'Give Us Barabbas' (1899) and the story 'As It Was in the Beginning,' both of which attack religious hypocrisy and church-sanctioned bigotry, appear to 'chart the public alienation of the formerly "earnest member of the Church of England."'[94] Gray similarly traces a growing scepticism about Christianity in Johnson's development as writer and activist, especially in proportion to her increasing sense of solidarity with Native peoples.

All such teleologies are difficult to confirm, as Lyon argues.[95] Later poems continue to draw lovingly on Christian concepts, as for example in 'Rondeau: Morrow-Land' (1901) when the speaker reflects on how 'This Passion Week of gold and grey / will haunt my heart and bless my way / in Morrow-Land.' A poem about the speaker's decision to return to God's arms reflects on 'a wilderness of thorn and rue' and is suggestively titled 'A Prodigal' (1902). Furthermore, poems of deep devotion occur in the mid-phase of Johnson's career, while notes of criticism and irony are sounded in very early pieces. There could be, for example, no more orthodox expression of loving conviction than the passionate 'Brier' (1893), a devotional poem in which the speaker describes a personal relationship with a tirelessly loving and protective Saviour. In the poem, the speaker addresses Jesus in the second person as friend and protector. Images of Christ's suffering, the thorns, the pierced feet, 'the crown of thorns upon your bleeding brow,' are associated with the speaker's peace and protection, affirming the central Christian belief that Christ paid the full penalty for sin so that erring human beings would not have to. 'Because you walk before and crush the brier, / It does not pierce my feet so much to-night.' Most significantly, perhaps, the speaker desires not to add to Christ's sufferings through sin, acknowledging answered prayers, unmerited grace, and a corresponding desire to know and follow Him:

Because so often you have hearkened to
My selfish prayers, I ask but one thing now,
That these harsh hands of mine add not unto
The crown of thorns upon your bleeding brow.

The earlier 'A Request' (1886), on the other hand, deals provocatively with the meaning of missionary endeavour in the context of national conquest. The speaker sets up an ambiguous contrast between
the British soldiers sent to quell the Northwest Rebellion and the
Christian missionaries preparing to evangelize the Cree and Black-
foot tribes in the Canadian Northwest. Like so many of Johnson's political poems, the text holds up an ideal of national righteousness that
Canada has so far failed to fulfil. Considering that the primary message of British power to the Indians of the Northwest has been with
'cannon, shot, and shell,' she laments British lives lost in a dubious
cause against their fellow countrymen: 'Tis not my place to question
if their laurel wreath still thrives, / If its fragrance is of Indian blood,
its glory Indian lives.' As a counter to the earlier martial advance,
Johnson asks the missionary society to send another band of warriors,
those whose 'strength is not in rank and file, no martial host they
lead, / Their mission is the cross of Christ, their arms the Christian
creed.' A straightforward reading of the poem may view it as a celebration of the missionary enterprise, with its band of workers bringing eternal life rather than martial death, their way to the West lit not
by military fire but by the light of their holiness. Yet in counterpoint-
ing missionaries to soldiers, Johnson also creates a powerful parallelism between the two, suggesting that the missionaries may replace or
substitute for the death-dealing soldiers in conflicting ways: as loving
stewards rather than brutal masters but equally, perhaps, as an army
of empire. While Christian conversion is a positive alternative to
armed conquest, the poem allows for a reading of conversion as another form of conquest, an ambiguity created by Johnson's linking of
spiritual and imperial metaphors, in which the missionaries are both
Christlike with their 'crown of thorns' and regal with a jewelled
crown. Calling upon the language of empire to praise Christian enterprise, Johnson's poem suggests uneasiness about the potential
overlap between state and church power. As in so many of Johnson's
poems, close reading alerts us both to potential ambivalence and to
deliberate ambiguity, a multivalence that denies any simple categori-
zation of the work.

The difficulty of talking about Pauline Johnson is the difficulty of addressing a writer and performer who balanced multiple and conflicting roles, demands, and personae. Speaking as an ambassador in search of common ground and mutual understanding, she crafted a self-presentation that was always at least double, celebrating the potential of Canada's nationalist narrative as she confronted its present-day shortcomings and saluting British cultural institutions while penning sober or angry elegies of Native death and suffering. Praise and blame, reconciliation and challenge, were always carefully overlaid in her complex message as a necessary strategy to both reassure and instruct her listeners. Her ability to use the imperial language to articulate a counter-text of lament and warning justifies Isabel Ecclestone MacKay's assertion, upon Johnson's death: 'Child of the old and new, offspring of Mohawk chief and English gentlewoman, she flashed across the space between.'[96] Hector Charlesworth, writing of the various women writers he had met in his career as a journalist, declared Johnson 'the one who became most famous and certain of a measure of immortality.'[97] Almost exactly one hundred years after her last performance, her vital and compelling persona and challenging texts have renewed debate over her legacy.

4 Gossip, Chit-Chat, and Life Lessons: Kit Coleman's Womanly Persona

Kathleen Blake Coleman belonged to the first generation of Canadian newspaper women and was probably the most famous of them in her day. From 1890 to 1911 she wrote a regular Saturday column in the Toronto *Daily Mail* (from 1895 the *Mail and Empire*) entitled 'Woman's Kingdom.' Her byline, Kit, first appeared in the autumn of 1889, and by early 1890 she was in charge of a syndicated feature of one or more pages, containing an editorial, a 'Pot-pourri' section of observations and short narratives, and one or more columns of 'Correspondence,' in which Kit answered questions from readers writing under pen names. A well-educated but impoverished immigrant from Ireland, Catherine Ferguson had come to Canada in 1884, subtracting eight years from her age and renaming herself Kathleen. She was the widow of Thomas Willis and had had a child who died. After the failure of her second marriage to Edward Watkins, who may have been a bigamist, she adopted the name Blake and began writing newspaper articles to support herself and their two children.[1] She quickly established an attractive and multifaceted public persona with whom many readers felt comfortable, and her column 'became one of the most widely read features in the whole newspaper industry.'[2]

The *Mail* had, by 1892, 'the largest circulation of any paper in Toronto, second only to the Montreal *Star* across the country,'[3] and according to fellow journalist Hector Charlesworth, Kit was 'a real "circulation-getter"'[4] for the paper, a woman in charge of 'the only feminine department ... that was consistently read by men also.'[5] When the paper offered her the chance to travel, Kit was eager to prove her worth, documenting her journeys to California, Jamaica, and London in lively accounts of foreign life and even indulging in some stunt journalism, disguising herself as a man on one occasion to walk the slums of London; ultimately, she established her fame as the first woman war correspondent when she was sent to Cuba to cover the Spanish-American War of 1898. As a founding member of the Canadian Women's Press Club (1904), she was considered by many of her contemporaries to be the queen and mother of them all. Mainly, though, she was known for her advice. Hired by the paper to attract women readers through discussion of feminine subjects, Kit wrote both within and against the parameters of 'Woman's Kingdom,' helping to define a new field for women in journalism that, while limited in certain ways, was remarkable for its range and potential. Over the first ten years of her advice column, she created an alluring public persona famed for her wisdom, humanity, and sharp humour.

IN JULY 1895 KIT MENTIONED to her readers that 'Woman's Kingdom' might become a fashion page rather than the mixture of gossip, observations, travel reports, fashions, recipes, debates, correspondence, and advice that it was at the time. The change was an idea of her editor's, and she asked whether readers would be in favour of it. The letters poured in, some of them published over the following weeks, expressing a near-unanimous no. Readers did not want anyone, especially a male editor who knew nothing about women's interests, to tamper with the Kingdom, and they expressed enthusiastic commitment to Kit's format and content. One reader emphasized the moral good done by Kit's 'heart talks,' in comparison with the frivolity of the usual fashion advice and recipes:

Dear Kit, – Since you ask for the opinion of the girls (and I am one of 'em) about changing our Woman's Kingdom into a fashion page or cook book, let me say no, decidedly no. We want Kit's Gossip and Chit-Chat, her essays, descriptions of her travels, her heart talks which touch the right chord in someone's breast, and make of us better men and women. I say men, because I happen to know of two or three who are as much interested in our Kingdom as we ourselves. We can get fashions elsewhere, and go to cooking schools for our recipes, and I'm sure we might, at least on Saturdays and Sundays, think of other things than our gowns and stomachs. N. of B.[6]

Noting that fashion news could be obtained 'elsewhere,' the writer stressed the uniqueness of Kit's appeal to the emotions and moral

Kathleen Coleman.

character of readers. Another writer emphasized the intellectual pleasures afforded by the column's diverse contents:

> My Dear Kit, – You fill me with horror when you speak of the possibility of our Woman's Kingdom ever becoming a mere fashion column. I love it as it is now, with just a little of everything in it, and am quite sure, should such a change come, the majority of us would cease to enjoy it. I suppose men editors, as a rule, consider that women are not capable of appreciating much else than fashions and receipts, and no doubt that is the reason why a woman's paper edited solely by men seems so flat to the average woman. I have heard men say that a woman's paper cannot, as a general thing, be made to pay, and no wonder, if that is the way men editors seek to please us. I don't at all despise a good fashion column occasionally, and a few good new recipes I consider a real treasure, but I should not care to settle myself comfortably in the shade on a hot Sunday afternoon (as I now do) and carefully read the Woman's page were those its principal contents, and I am not one of the 'clever' women. Devoutly hoping that the vote will prove Canadian women to have more sense than to encourage such a sad change, I remain, yours sincerely, 'ANOTHER KIT.'[7]

These readers' responses, and others like them, are interesting for a number of reasons. They prove the depth of affection many readers felt for Kit's column. She was not for nothing dubbed 'Queen of Hearts' by Jean Blewett, a rival *Globe* journalist turned admirer.[8] The letters confirm the range of reasons – from light entertainment to moral improvement and psychological sustenance – why readers turned so eagerly to her column in the middle section of the Saturday *Mail*. They also suggest the gendered nature of the contract she had created with her readers. Kit had established a feminine space that told women (and men) what they wanted to know and appealed to them on an emotional level. After receiving a deluge of supportive letters, Kit reported with satisfaction that the column would continue unchanged. On 1 August 1896, she was confident enough about her popular support to write in response to a correspondent's praise that she was 'glad that my own idea of a woman's column downs that of the editor. I knew they didn't want fashions and pudding recipes, and how to get rid of ants and cockroaches, all the time.'[9]

Kit had been in charge of 'Woman's Kingdom' at the *Mail* since 1890 and had built up during the intervening five years a significant national and even international following of both women and men. Requests were sent to her advice column from correspondents as far afield as Zurich, Derry, London, California, and Pittsburgh and also from places closer to home, such as Edmonton, Fort Qu'Appelle, Montreal, and Ottawa. People wrote with nearly every conceivable question, problem, or opinion, asking for help in placing quotations, career advice, matters of fact and procedure, philosophical issues, hygiene and beauty problems, and of course decisions regarding love and personal conduct. Kit claimed that 'no letter received by me, whether ill or good, has remained unanswered or unacknowledged one way or another in these columns.'[10] She was inundated with letters, often answering more than fifty per week, revealing knowledge that encompassed stain removal, mathematics, geography, history, theology, and European literature. Her answer to Andrew, whom she informed, 'It is quite true that shepherds and others can by long practice distinguish one sheep's face from another,'[11] was not more unusual than many others.

According to Marjory Lang, women began to be hired by Canadian newspapers in the 1880s because they met an urgent need for advice of all kinds: 'In an era of mobility and rapid change, when generations no longer lived near each other and when mores altered so radically that a mother's advice no longer suited her daughter's dilemma, it would seem that a great many women, and some men too, sought the personal but anonymous counsel of the newspaper oracle.'[12] In their turn, women were attracted to journalism because it was 'respectable, clean, a bit daring, and different' and it afforded them 'a public vehicle for their thoughts.'[13] Brought on staff to boost circulation figures and advertising revenue, women such as Coleman 'carved out new fields of journalism' by addressing 'the minutiae of personality and relationship.'[14] She often characterized herself as a mother to her readers, addressing her correspondents as her 'paper children' and telling them, as on one occasion, 'I would like to mother you for half an hour.'[15]

A glance at any column demonstrates the variety of subjects on which Kit provided counsel, establishing a rapport that ranged in tone from businesslike to intimate. She frequently advised correspondents about religious doubts or fears, quoting Scripture and explaining theological complexities with confidence; though a lapsed Catholic who rejected the strictness of the Roman religion, particularly regarding its Index of forbidden books, she spoke of spiritual matters with an ease and clarity that appealed to readers. She did not hesitate to urge women to leave abusive husbands, telling one that 'I certainly never would live an hour with a man who had struck me'[16] and giving practical advice about legal rights and economic options. Advising men and women about courtship, marriage, sexual morality, and child-rearing, she even fielded a number of marriage offers through the paper; one suitor claimed to have become 'much taken' with Kit because of her 'style' and 'large-heartedness.'[17] Some who wrote were regular correspondents on set subjects: the names Sidney Carton, Philip Wakem, and Fraulein appear frequently, and Kit's answers to them suggest a conversation carried over many letters. Many wrote merely, it seems, to unburden their hearts about loneliness, marital breakdown, failed love affairs, personal disgrace, temptation, and sin.

Kit regularly noted the enormous volume of mail received and the startling geographical range from which the letters were sent. Although occasionally confessing that she could not advise or find the information sought – to Perplexed she groaned, 'My dear, my head is cracked trying to place quotations'[18] – she usually had an answer and was often praised by correspondents for her wide knowledge; her letters revealed her familiarity with French, Italian, and Spanish, as well as some Greek and Latin, and her general knowledge of literature, history, the Bible, mythology, medicine, pharmacy, and the professions. She had a particular talent for remembering the source of quotations. She was also adept at pleasantly and humorously *not* answering a question, as when she responded to Betsy with the query, 'Who on earth could really understand the Manitoba Schools Question? They don't at Ottawa. A politician once began to explain it to me, but he drifted off to other matters. Presently I forgot it.'[19] She also had the saving grace of an irreverent and self-deprecating sense of humour. In the case of one critical reader, she refused to take offence, telling her, 'And so you "don't always approve of me"? Well, Bab, that makes no difference at all, my dear, in our friendship. In fact, I like you the better for your frank way of putting things.'[20]

Curious about Kit herself, correspondents did not always confine their questions to matters of fact or opinion, and she often had to deflect personal queries and requests to meet her. To one writer, Norman, she answered, 'You could not see me if you came to Toronto, Norman. I'm not visible to the naked eye.'[21] And to Nora B she confessed that 'not once have I ever experienced the slightest desire to know any of my correspondents in the flesh. I much prefer them as shadows, and prefer to be a shadow to them.'[22] She told Guinevere that although she felt 'most interested' in her 'paper children,' she preferred not to meet them 'lest both of us should be obliged to smash our ideals.'[23] Rebuffed

in their attempts to know her personally, readers were nonetheless devoted to their elusive adviser, defending Kit's warmth of heart and
kindliness on many occasions. For nearly twenty-five years, even after
leaving the *Mail and Empire* in 1911, she had a remarkably loyal following amongst a notoriously fickle reading public.

What was the source of her popularity? Few scholars have re-
searched the public persona of Kathleen Blake Coleman, despite the
publication by Ted Ferguson of *Kit Coleman: Queen of Hearts* (1978), a
selection of her articles with commentary, designed for a popular audience. In *A Victorian Authority* (1982), which charts the development of
the Canadian newspaper industry, Paul Rutherford places Coleman in
the context of the rise of the mass-circulating newspaper, which sought
to entertain and satisfy the curiosity of the ordinary reader. Douglas
Fetherling similarly identifies, in the last two decades of the nineteenth
century, a new type of 'personal journalism,' which involved 'an eye-
witness approach to news at all levels, a willingness to promote celebrity and a compartmentalizing of the paper, with sections aimed at
particular segments of the total readership.'[24] Columns of personal
commentary and letters were a means of establishing a bond between
the paper and its consumers. Usually distinguished, according to
Rutherford, by a 'casual, chatty style,'[25] an avoidance of polemic, and
an eclectic variety of subjects, the columnist sought above all to intrigue readers with 'a unique blend of news and views'[26] that stamped
the column with a distinctive personality. He mentions Kit as a 'famous' example of this function, discussing her rather dismissively as a
writer who 'furnished a good deal more gossip than argument about
women's affairs – and fashions.'[27] Given the boldness and seriousness
with which Kit expressed herself on many social issues of her day,
Rutherford's summation is inaccurate, but his emphasis on the importance of personality in appealing to a mass audience targets a key
aspect of Kit's popularity.

The one full-length bio-critical study of Coleman is Barbara
Freeman's *Kit's Kingdom* (1989). The result of many years of research,
Freeman's book unearths previously unknown details of Coleman's
shadowy personal life (though she cautions that a 'complete biography is not possible' and 'the real Kathleen remains elusive')[28] and
provides a comprehensive overview of her writing for the *Mail*, paying particular attention to her views about women, her travel writing, and her war correspondence. Freeman is most engaged by the
contradictions she finds in Coleman's ideology of gender. Following

Carroll Smith-Rosenberg's contention that 'the conflict between a woman's real identity and her need to fit into a male milieu – journalism in Kit's case – often results in a literary split personality,'[29] she seeks evidence of such a 'split' in Coleman's self-positioning and, not surprisingly, finds it. Examined from a twentieth-century feminist perspective, Coleman was 'inconsistent in her views on women's rights,'[30] supporting their demand for education and employment opportunities but objecting to 'both birth control and abortion.'[31]

Freeman usefully emphasizes the precarious balance Coleman had to strike between the safe and the unconventional in her column,[32] but her tendency to judge her on the basis of the feminist principles of a later era not only risks anachronism but detracts attention from potentially more fruitful investigation into how Coleman achieved her complex balance between orthodoxy and individuality. The bold and the familiar were engagingly interwoven in a nuanced self-presentation: both the forthright manner in which she addressed her correspondents and the provocative personal subjects she discussed lent an attractive modernity to her column, while her compassion, maternal stance, and Christian framework provided moral authority. Moreover, although fiercely protective of her privacy, Kit allowed her readers to catch glimpses of a private self who suffered and understood, giving an added piquancy and authenticity to her advice.

THE NOVELTY OF A WOMAN'S PAGE – of a woman answering questions, giving advice, and proffering opinions – was a significant part of Kit's draw. As Lang has noted, women journalists succeeded 'by creating literary personae who attracted enormous followings';[33] reportorial anonymity was neither possible for them nor desirable. Readers were intensely curious about Kit's personal life, and she frequently parried questions about her marital status, age, and physical appearance; she also invented a fictionalized version of both her childhood and her present life. In his memoir, Charlesworth relies on Kit's own self-disclosures to conclude, erroneously, that she was a 'writer of aristocratic Irish descent' who grew up in a 'baronial hall,'[34] when in fact her upbringing was much more modest and her marital history murky. In the first year of the column, there was an extended debate about whether Kit was really a woman or not, and the kind of interest generated by readers' speculation was exploited by Kit long after the basic facts about her life became known. Freeman explains her strategy: 'the guessing games served an important purpose – to protect Kathleen's privacy. Her curious readers wanted to know everything about her, including her age and marital circumstances, but she was not about to tell them that she was thirty-four years old, separated from a man who may have been a bigamist, and supporting two children.'[35] As Charlesworth recognized, 'There was always a touch of mystery about "Kit."'[36]

A number of correspondents were convinced either that Kit was a man or that she was married to a man who helped her with her work. 'Is there nothing at all in my writings that suggest the woman?' she once wrote with false plaintiveness to Carro, who raised the gender question. 'What a masculine creature I must be!'[37] Frequently, correspondents claimed to have caught a glimpse of Kit in various public places, and she even had the experience of overhearing people discussing her, often negatively. On one occasion she reported having 'sat for one hour and a quarter in a street car, hearing myself – figuratively – hung, drawn, and quartered' and was amused that her abusers insisted she was a man.[38] At another time Kit heard some ladies identifying a well-dressed woman on the street as Kit of the *Mail*: 'Oh! It's sure to be Kit because she writes the fashions, you know, and is always dressed in the height of them. Look at her dress! My! Ain't that velvet waist pretty?'[39] At the end of the conversation, according to the narrating Kit, the ladies crossed the street, while 'Kit, the real, faded, rather shabby Kit, boarded a Yonge street car and read the evening papers.'[40] The image of Kit passing through the city streets while curious fans argued over her identity and appearance suggests the kind of unsought celebrity that she was adept at promoting. Her sly reference to her 'real, faded, rather shabby' self both confirmed and contradicted her enduring mystery.

Even bad publicity, Kit seems to have discovered, could be turned to good use, and she told one letter writer that 'no woman is worth knowing who is without enemies.'[41] In response to Analon, who passed on some personal gossip about her, Kit protested that she was 'in a chronic state of shocked surprise at the revelations that are made concerning me. Now I am "'a fiend," a "hyena woman," a creature of "violent temper, given to tempests of rage," then a "weird woman, uncanny, and awful-looking"; again, "an artful, calculating, sly person."'[42] With flirtatious ingenuousness, she claimed, 'All these things have been said of me and told to me within the last three weeks, and all about an ordinary, hardworking, elderly person who is about as utterly commonplace as they make 'em.'[43] It was clear, however, that readers did not find Kit commonplace and that her frank responses,

wit, wide learning, and unconventional opinions engaged and provoked them. The fact that some readers disliked her or were offended
by her style and comments merely increased her fame, as she never
shied away from publishing letters critical of her advice, comments, or
appearance. She told readers that 'instead of sending a condemnatory
letter to the waste paper basket, and thereby hiding someone's honest
opinion from the public,' she preferred to 'publish this letter exactly as
it came into my hands.'[44] A few correspondents found her irreligious,
or at least insufficiently reverent or doctrinaire; some were offended by
her comments on alcohol (she was not a teetotaller); and others found
her anti-male. Still others disliked her flippancy or claimed to find her
crude. When Kit published critical letters, readers responded with enthusiastic defences and angry denials.

As one of the first Canadian women to enter the male domain of
journalism, Kit was often solicited for her opinion on the much-
debated Woman Question, a subject about which she was sometimes
bold and never doctrinaire. Her answer to Darwinian, who criticized
her for undertaking, as a woman, to discuss scientific issues, was typical: 'I do not care about the platform, or woman's rights, or that kind of
thing,' she wrote in response to his contention that women disgraced
themselves by stepping into the male sphere, 'but I believe women
have as much intelligence as men, and that as civilization increases, the
women are gradually and naturally coming to the fore.'[45] Here, as so
often, she claimed not to have an opinion on women's rights while asserting their intellectual equality with men. In claiming that women
were 'gradually and naturally coming to the fore,' she suggested that
their rights were evolving with the times; women did not need to engage in agitation or political campaigns, which struck her as unneces-
sarily divisive, because their emancipation was inevitable.

Kit herself was, in her self-presentation, a tough and intelligent
woman who chided female correspondents for making fools of themselves over men. 'Oh you dear girls who are lost in love troubles, what
is the matter with you?' she exclaimed to Madge Lightfoot. 'Can't you
see when a fellow cares and when he doesn't, or are you altogether
blinded by your own affections?'[46] She claimed to be cynical and jaded,
hinting at unhappy experiences that had soured her on men. 'I don't
believe in love,' she said on one occasion, exasperated by women's
gullibility and men's arrogance. 'I did once, but I've outlived it like a
good many other illusions.'[47] At another time, she wrote rather flirta-
tiously to Philip Wakem, 'A man may do all you say without being a

bad man, and a word in your ear, Philip, I like the man who does a little that way best – so do all women.'[48] What exactly did these 'bad'
men do of which Kit saucily approved? She did not say, except to clarify that she was not referring to physical abuse but rather to an indefin-
able masculinity and power of manner: 'Women like a touch of the
master in a man.'[49] She was also sceptical about the power of sisterhood, writing to Jane Eyre, 'Of course I believe in women's friendships
– the love of woman for woman – but these relations are rare, and
where they do exist, they do not often run to generosity.'[50]

Her comments on the women's movement and on relations between
the sexes were frequently a mixture of lively assertion and ambivalence.
She agreed wholeheartedly with one correspondent that far too much
contemporary writing condemned men unfairly, and she apologized
for her part in blaming them: 'If ever I wrote one bitter line, or suggested in any way in any unwomanly manner that marriage and love
were dismal failures, I sincerely regret it.'[51] In another column, though,
she expressed bitter outrage at men's mistreatment of women, noting
women's emotional and social dependence in comparison to men's
fickleness and cruelty. 'God forgive men,' she commented darkly in reference to the many young girls who wrote in despair over illicit preg-
nancies. 'They tempt us past belief, and they are given to much backing
out.'[52] In another letter, though, she lashed out at the New Woman, dismissing feminist claims to equality and independence: 'The fact is, my
dear madam,' she wrote to a correspondent who sought her opinion,
'the new woman movement – a fine one in moderation – has overshot
the mark in the vain effort to equalize the sexes; the chief charm of
which is that they never can be equalized.'[53] Though her column
brought her into contact with the reality of women's powerlessness and
sexual vulnerability, Kit was no consistent ally of feminism.

Freeman argues that such political disengagement and inconsistency
were the result both of editorial pressure at the Conservative *Mail*,
which officially opposed woman suffrage, and of Coleman's inadequately developed feminist consciousness. Wayne Roberts, too, suggests that her decision not to support the suffrage movement until it
was an acceptable cause decades later can be attributed to personal in-
decision and political caution.[54] Yet Coleman's stance may have been
part of a relatively coherent personal philosophy (recognizing injustice
yet holding to female difference, expressing personal anger yet refusing to participate in organized agitation) that happened to coincide
with the paper's rejection of feminist dogmatism. Regardless, Kit

was popular with at least one hard-core feminist. Flora MacDonald Denison forgave her political non-alignment and praised Kit for the humane and literary virtues she brought to her column, stating, 'Kit has not only a brilliant pen but she has a big heart that feels for the underdog.'[55] Ultimately, it is inappropriate to overemphasize either the radicalism of Kit's sympathy for women or the conventionality of her gender ideals. What was remarkable about her was the range of unorthodox subjects she addressed – suicide, abortion, masturbation, marital infidelity, religious melancholia – and her feisty, frank style. There was in Kit's writing an acceptance of the reality of sin and a forthright approach to sexual relations that was distinctly modern and alluring. Yet she was also not an innovator, her role to some extent having been prepared by church-sponsored campaigns for sex education that were increasingly accepted at this time. Responding to readers' requests for moral direction on a variety of vexing issues, she managed to convey both a clear morality and an unflappable tolerance.

MUCH OF KIT'S APPEAL, of course, rested on the quality of the advice she provided and the capacious, though often brisk, sympathy she expressed. She was an exemplary adviser, often providing detailed answers on practical and emotional matters and frequently summoning enormous reserves of patience and empathy. To A.L.S. she wrote at length and kindly on the necessity for assiduous care of perspiring feet, advising twice-daily bathing with 'strong yellow soap' and 'a little powdered bismuth.'[56] To Foolish One she gave a pronunciation list for names such as St John ('Sinjin') and Marjoribanks ('Marchbanks'), nevertheless assuring the writer, 'There is nothing to be ashamed of in pronouncing names as they are spelled.'[57] To Mr Jim she observed with exactitude, 'The best way to produce a thick moustache is to begin by early shaving, and after you have allowed it to grow a little, apply some preparation of cantharides every night before retiring.'[58] To J.Y.G. she apologized for failing to answer in the previous column, giving, as requested, a list of her favourite female names while commenting that doubtless 'by this time you have decided on something pretty for your baby.'[59] To Undone, the victim of a gossipmonger, she wrote with a detailed program of conduct to illustrate her precept: 'Let the gossip say her say, and on no account take any notice ... but quietly, calmly, treat the woman as if she were dead.'[60] Serious attention to readers' problems established her column as a reliable source of prompt and useful advice.

No subject, however obscure or complex, was beneath her notice. Anxious wrote for advice about a parrot who was pecking out her own feathers, about which Kit explained, 'Your Polly is suffering from a mental disease,' and went on to detail the cure for parrot 'melancholia.'[61] To Griselda she advised, 'Take the second man, the one that is truthful, determined, and straightforward,'[62] while to L.M.O. she cautioned that there was 'no such a thing as "odic force." It is an invention of certain spiritualists.'[63] On more serious subjects of personal and social import, she often wrote at length and earnestly. To A Black Canadian she offered encouragement and sympathy: 'You must not call the race that has produced a Fred Douglass "low" or even "downtrodden,"' she argued. 'There are black and coloured men holding high positions in the West Indies. It is all a matter of education. I hold that the black man is as good as his white brother, both being given the same chances. We are all – no matter what colour – of God's making, and made in His image.'[64]

To Little Daisy, who wrote about her abusive husband, Kit showed no hesitation: 'Your experience of marriage has been fearful. You are quite right in acting as you propose to do. No woman could live with such a fiend as you describe,'[65] and she encouraged the same writer just a week later, 'My dear girl, this is a most extraordinary story, and if true your life is not safe for a moment. Never mind "the times being hard." Go to your sister.'[66] To Mater, who wanted advice on how to evangelize the poor, she was blunt: 'How can you expect to do good when you speak in such a high and mighty tone? My dear woman, if you have no kind word to give out of the fullness of your own heart to those who are suffering from crushing sorrows, then you have no use thinking of mission work or district visiting. Your acts should be those of love – not condescension.'[67] In recommending empathy and a response 'out of the fullness of your own heart,' she might have been speaking of her own practice in the column.

The seriousness with which she treated the matters that came to her, from the frivolous to the purely technical to the impossibly personal, demonstrated her humanity and practical sense. Some correspondents wanted Kit to cure their vaguest life discontents, requests that elicited outbursts of annoyance as well as bracing common sense. To Moonshine, for example, she wrote kindly, if brusquely: 'Oh, you small goose! You ask me to teach you how to be happy! Look here, good people, don't you pity me when I'm asked such questions as this one? My dear girl, you are discontented because you are lazy, and won't work ... Turn to your portrait painting – turn to it with a will. I despise women who have no determination; no will power; no application; no endurance. There is the whip for you. Don't be angry, and, listen, don't be proud of your laziness. Get up, do something, and you will be happy. This is, I think, the best advice I can give you.'[68] To S.C.R., who wrote of a 'horrible tendency ... – a recognized aberration of natural instinct' (probably masturbation), she replied, 'Your letter filled me at first reading with horror and loathing; but you are to be so deeply pitied and helped that that first feeling gave way to one of compassion. Lay your case at once before a competent medical man.'[69] She was a master of the pithy response, as when she told Perplexed that 'the man who asks a woman to give up everything, reputation, duty, all for him, and who proves worthy of the sacrifice, has yet to be born';[70] she was equally adept at the indignant rejoinder, as to Sui Generis, to whom she responded, 'You write me an insolent letter about my private affairs. If I were a man I would find you out and thrash you.'[71] To Irene she counselled, 'Never mind his telling you that if you do not marry him his life will be ruined. Better he should ruin one life than two.'[72] Readers were not always happy with the advice Kit gave, as evidenced by arguments within the column, but her reputation for integrity and tough-mindedness meant that they generally did not renounce reading the column or soliciting her views.

The degree of trust that correspondents placed in Kit is demonstrated in the kind of advice sought, much of it concerning highly personal, sometimes life-altering issues, on which her answers were often remarkably frank and detailed. Many wrote for career advice, especially concerning journalism, and although Kit was sometimes irritated by the common assumption that writing was a relatively easy profession accessible to anyone with a pen ('One gets a little weary of reiterating that there is no "short cut" to literary work,' she wrote to Studens),[73] she frequently responded in full about the requirements, practices, physical as well as intellectual demands, and rewards of professional journalism in answers that are fascinating not only for the glimpses they give of Coleman's own approach to writing but also for their evidence of her professional generosity. To O.P. Shaw, for example, she wrote at some length to offer cautious encouragement and advice about subjects and expectations:

Your letter suggests facility in writing. I think I advised not writing on subjects occurring in one's own life but on a subject one was well versed in and which would be, at the same time, bright and interesting and up to date. For instance, when Sandow was astonishing the world with his feats of strength, someone wrote a clever story (I use 'story' in the newspaper sense – we call every article or report a 'story') on the strong men of ancient times. Now that war is raging in Asia, stories about life there are of interest and of value to editors. A writer should be quick to snap up the opportunities of the times. Now, you are ambitious, you say, and discontented with your present work. Listen. All over the world there is a gigantic financial depression. The present war may disperse this, or deepen it. Wise men and women are holding close to what they've got, and it will be a foolhardy person who just now will throw up a security for an uncertainty. And take this well to heart. There is no profession more precarious and less successful financially than literature. First of all, you will have to serve your apprenticeship, and write steadily and carefully in the hope of getting into type. Simply that. You will be well repaid if you are printed, and after a year or so paid a little. Like every other market, the literary one is glutted. And with men and women of brains – of genius. Unless you are a very clever, quick, and original writer you will find it hard to get a footing. Not that all writers are all of these, or even one of them, but they got in when the market was not so full, by some special bit of work, or brilliant story; and possession is nine parts of the law, is it not? I do not want to discourage you utterly, but I do ask you to be very careful, and remember the days of 'dashing off' things are done (I doubt they ever existed), and that newspaper and other work of the kind is real, hard, wearing, laborious work, which steadily robs one of a certain amount – a large amount – of vitality. I would advise you, since you ask my advice, to remain in your present position, devoting your spare time to acquiring such ease and facility in writing as will secure you a good position one day. If you get your stories printed be thankful. After a while when people are looking for your name, you may expect remuneration. Remember, in justice to yourself and to myself, I am putting things in their grayest dress for you. Yet I leave you the silver lining. It is always there. Remember this, too (it is one of the serio-comic phases of newspaper work), that no matter how good your journalistic work may turn out to be, your best stories will be lost in the columns of the daily papers; so lost, indeed, that, like the old parson with his sermons, you might turn to what you had written last year and present it again to your readers without finding it – save by a few – recognized. So much for newspaper 'fame.'[74]

The mixture of professional advice, friendly concern, and saving humour are typical of Kit's careful yet forthright style, which helped to make her reputation as a tough-minded woman of the world with, nonetheless, a mother's heart and a democratic spirit. As in all her long answers, she provides enough detail that the response makes sense to her readership without the specific questions and commentary that inspired it, but not so much detail that the correspondent loses the gratification of a personal dialogue. The passage is structured by a series of imperative clauses, with a particular stress on personal pronouns, the 'I' of Kit the newspaperwoman and the 'you' of the correspondent, the would-be writer, brought together at key points to stress the relationship being established in the passage. Moreover, the frequent use of sentence fragments, tag questions, and especially direct address creates the humane, colloquially arresting note that Kit could so often strike. On other occasions she responded with greater brevity but also gave encouragement and practical advice, telling Peas Blossom that she wrote well but needed to 'avoid stilts ... don't polish too much,'[75] while informing Gretchen how to go about submitting material to a magazine.[76] Her willingness to mentor beginning writers foreshadowed her later leadership of the Canadian Women's Press Club.

On other occasions she was confronted with questions about moral conduct of a deeply personal nature, and again she responded with precision, directness, and sensitivity in a personal register that was striking given the conditions under which she worked. To Perplexed, who evidently inquired whether she should tell her husband about an infidelity, Kit wrote without dogmatism:

> Ought you to tell your husband? That is your question. Ought he to be told? He is happy now; but your story will bring him lifelong shame and misery. Do not expect ever to be quite the same woman to him again if you tell him. There is no hope of that. If you keep your story to yourself, there is happiness for him, and perhaps by and by, forgetfulness for you. Tell it, and everything is uncertain. And yet ought it not be told? Is not candour best? Can your sin be properly punished until it has brought upon you the degradation and humility of confession, not to an unknown friend such as I am, but to your husband? Sin is sometimes inexorable. It exacts payment to the uttermost mite. What shall I say to you? The uttermost mite in your case is confession to your husband; but is it necessary? It is a horrible ordeal, and unless he is a wide-minded man, a fatal one for you. Yet, constituted as you are, you will know no peace until you confess. Try him. Be brave. After all, truth is best.[77]

The series of rhetorical questions with which Kit punctuated her response conveys her sense of the emotional gravity and complexity of
the situation. Her determination to do justice to such complexity is
demonstrated in the deliberate parallelism of many of her structures.
She emphasizes the contrast between a peace that rests on lies and a
justice that will likely destroy peace; her sensitivity to the emotional
paradoxes of the issue is an effective preamble to a conclusion favour-
ing truth and confession. As she often did, Kit complicates the moral
framework of her answer by overlaying her Christian emphasis on sin
and confession with a psychological parable about mental peace.

Kit was often gentle in telling correspondents that they were 'in the
wrong,' as in the following case, a detailed response to a woman who
had quarrelled with her sister and felt unable to forgive her. The keen
insight with which Kit sketches her correspondent's state of mind and
the determined pathos of the future she imagines, in which the sister is
dead and beyond the reach of forgiveness, creates the kind of urgency
and intimacy for which Kit was both adored and criticized:

Johanna. – That is a most unhappy state of affairs, and if you don't mind
my saying so, I think, my dear, you are in the wrong. You are very proud
and reserved, but yours is not the right kind of pride; it only generates
misery for yourself and those around you, and don't you think our little
span of life is too short for such foolish actions? You know you love your
sister and she loves you, but your pride will not let you break down the
barrier between you. It is such a pity and so foolish. Do you ever think that
perhaps one day you may look upon her dead face, and your very heart
will wither because you will know that never, never can you recall that one
year in which you held her aloof and would not speak to her, all for a petty
bit of gossip. I tell you if such an unhappy day ever comes to you – which I
pray it will not – you will suffer such agony in your proud soul, such absolute physical torture, that the very devils in hell would turn aside and refrain from looking on your shrinking soul. Remember, time flies ever
onward, and you can never get that year back. Make up for it now. Believe
me, you never felt such happiness as you will feel in the moment of your
self-humiliation. What if she never came back from those holidays, when
you refused her proffered good-bye! What if death, or worse, shame and
misery overtook her. Of what use are your prayers for her, when you shut
your mouth and will neither speak to nor look at her all and every day!
You love her in your secret heart, and she is anxious to 'make it up.' Will
you not do it, and let me know about it? I shall be so glad.[78]

The passage is notable for its combination of sympathetic solidarity and instruction. Emphasizing her correspondent's mistaken pride, Kit softens her criticism by acknowledging the real love for her sister with which it is intermingled. At the point of her harshest judgment on Johanna, when she tells her that her pride 'is not the right kind of pride,' she switches from second-person direct address to first-person plural to soften the remark, addressing 'our little span of life' as 'too short,' to suggest the universality of her correspondent's error. Twice she calls Johanna's actions 'foolish' (and also 'a pity'), rather than vindictive or selfish. In fact, Kit deliberately refrains from targeting her correspondent's selfishness, representing her stubbornness as a struggle between a mistaken and self-destructive pride and the better self who loves and suffers. The major part of the passage focuses on the correspondent's love for her sister and the burden she would bear if the rift between them were to become permanent. When Kit ends by urging Johanna to do the right thing 'and let me know about it,' it seems certain that her warm-hearted appeal will have its effect. A few weeks later, however, the same correspondent had written again, irritated at Kit's advice and humiliated by what she saw as public exposure. 'So you are angry because I gave you a bit of sensible advice, and told you to make up with your sister,' Kit responded in frustration. 'Why did you write to a newspaper if you didn't want an answer? You are proud, vain, and conceited; you "imagined every person knew" who my answer was directed to! You poor unit!'[79] Clearly, all stories did not end happily.

Kit must often have felt that the problems of her letter writers, involving intense loneliness and mental anguish, were far beyond her powers to help, yet she rarely declined to give an opinion or advice both spiritual and practical. In some of the worst cases, as in response to Despair below, she advised medical assistance while also offering the human sympathy and practical guidance the correspondent sought:

> You must 'take hold of yourself.' Your letter almost frightened me. You are in an extremely nervous condition, and ought to put yourself at once under medical care. Now listen to me, and be brave. You are an old woman, your sufferings have driven you almost to distraction, and you are giving in to your nervousness. Stop it at once. You talk of trust in God, but are you trusting Him? I wish I could talk to you. Go at once to the very best doctor you can find. If you are poor, go to an hospital. See some one, and save yourself from insanity. You are suffering from hysteria and

a craving for sympathy, which is the worst possible thing for you. Try to forget yourself, my woman; remember the dreadful misery other women get through bravely and calmly. Take hold of yourself, and steady your soul. Let.your religion come to your help, and stop this wild giving way to all unreason and nervous fears. Write to me often, it will maybe take you out of yourself. Now mind, go to a doctor, say your prayers, and think about other people.[80]

Kit's focus on her female correspondent's suffering, which evidently *did* frighten her, is reflected in her alternation between imperative clauses and descriptive statements that detail the causes and symptoms of her misery. Combining diagnosis, advice, and empathy, Kit sought both to affirm and to alleviate the sufferer's pain. Her contention that self-absorption caused depression and that thinking of others and writing to a sympathetic other could assuage it not only reflected contemporary popular psychology but also articulated in a nutshell the rationale for 'Woman's Kingdom' as a whole. In response to Norma, who praised Kit for helping her 'to know the uses of adversity, and the dignity of suffering,'[81] she responded with satisfaction that her purpose in the column was 'to touch some one suffering heart, and relieve it of the too great burden of human sorrow.'[82] Sympathizing with her letter writers' 'craving for sympathy,'[83] she was sensitive to audience suffering and need.

Frequently, Kit was forced to improvise practical psychiatric advice on matters about which contemporary medical science had little or nothing to offer. To Mrs T.W.B., fretting over a son who insisted on wearing girls' clothes, she counselled firmness in what she confessed was a 'peculiar' case, nonetheless offering a clear rationale and plan of conduct for a mother at her wits' end: 'Keep the boy in girls' clothes – you can do nothing else with him. Exaggerate the affair, and mock and laugh him out of it. Tell him that if he insists on doing it, you will tell all his young friends, boys and girls, and I think perhaps you will cure him. Is his brain at all weak? Consult a good physician. And be sure to punish the girl, his elder sister, who aids and abets him. I would have no such nonsense. Of course you won't be cruel; only firmness is necessary. If possible, send the boy away where he will mix with lads of his own age. Yours is a peculiar case. Be firm.'[84] Kit's own firmness, practicality, and unflappability over such perplexing matters must have reassured readers that, no matter how bizarre, their problems were not beyond help or alleviation. Her own psychological burden in striving to answer so many questions and share so many troubles must at times have been tremendous, but her insistence on the power of kind and encouraging words was unvarying.

KIT WAS ALSO DELUGED with questions of a religious nature from correspondents curious about details of Scripture, worried about biblical interpretation and its implications for belief, or confused about how to live their lives in accordance with Christian doctrine. Some of the issues were, for her, relatively simple ones: 'You can dance your heels off, my little girl,' she advised Another of Kit's Girls, 'and still be a very good Christian indeed.'[85] To a correspondent with questions about Jesus' brothers, she gave a detailed answer with many scriptural references,[86] revealing familiarity with and confidence in the biblical record. To Fearless she gave an extensive list of texts on both sides of the argument about the veracity of Scripture,[87] and with Didactic she undertook to negotiate the troubled waters of scriptural literalism:

> You ask a strange question, 'Could God have really made the world in six of our days, and did He?' We cannot discover, and it is useless to discuss what God could have done, but we know tolerably well what has been done. It is, for instance, as much of a certainty as anything can be that the world was not created in six days, but that it has come to its present state by gradual changes extending over enormous periods of time. There are thousands of facts to prove this, and not one (fact) to disprove it. You base your question entirely on the poetic expression 'days.' If you read the chapter in the Revised Version, you will find the term is used much more indefinitely than in the Old Version. In the second account of the creation (chap. ii), Jehovah is said to have made the earth and the heaven in one day (verse 4), not in six. The first account speaks of man having been created after the other animals. The second account creates man first and the animals afterwards. These are small points, but they show how rash people are who hang beliefs on a few words. You say that 'if science is accepted, simple faith will soon go to the wall.' If it is 'simple faith' in an untruth, then the sooner the better. Religion does not depend upon the wholesale and credulous acceptance of the poetical licenses of writers whose very names have perished off the face of the earth. The story of this old world is written on her rocks more plainly than it is told in any book. There are fossils in old Sidney mine, to go no farther, computed by geologists to be upwards of two million years old.[88]

Such an answer demonstrates Kit's accommodation of scientific knowledge and faith: her approach to Scripture was neither literalist nor skeptical: she prided herself on a 'liberal' position on social and religious controversies that did not slip into apostasy. 'I have always tried to conduct these columns with reasonable liberality – nor shall I change my course,' she answered a critic who charged her with expressing 'objectionable sentiments.'[89] For her position, she frequently had to defend herself. A few weeks after the discussion about the Genesis account of creation, for example, she wrote to Religion, 'I did not say the "Mosaic" account of the creation of the world was fabulous. What I said was that it is a poetical account of the way the world was evolved.'[90] Kit's willingness to argue with readers about scriptural authority, a fraught subject for anyone but especially for a woman, signalled her refusal to limit the intellectual territory encompassed by 'Woman's Kingdom.'

And indeed, her column was often a forum for discussing the great questions of the day. While proclaiming herself a 'reverent believer in Jesus Christ and His exquisite teachings,'[91] she frequently acknowledged the reasonableness of doubt and uncertainty, advising Marcus against anxious reflection on the great religious mysteries: 'I don't think you need be in such a terrible state of doubt and anxiety. Even the Apostles asked Christ what He meant. Why do you pin your faith on the exact words of the Bible when you know that the Pope gives one reading from it and the Protestant Church another?'[92] Often she stressed the need for a greater faith, not in the exact words of Scripture, but in the good news of redemption through Christ and the necessity of brotherly love. 'Surely if you collect from the Bible all that Christ thought necessary for His disciples, you will see how little dogma there is. "Pure religion and undefiled is this, to visit the fatherless and widows in their affliction, and to keep himself unspotted from the world." There is as a rule too much mind and too little heart in religion nowadays,'[93] she wrote to Clerico. Clerico, in fact, was a frequent correspondent, plagued by worries about doctrinal differences and details of religious observance, against which Kit occasionally had to scold and reassure in equal measure: 'This is not the place for discussion on auricular confession,' she wrote a few months after the exchange on dogma. 'You are wrong to read such books, as I think I told you before. Keep by your prayer book in its entirety and its simplicity, and try to be less bigoted. Christ died to save all, not you and those of your faith alone.'[94] She even did not hesitate to contradict a preacher whose theology she found wrong: 'Change your place of worship for a time,' she advised S.G., who worried that he had committed the unpardonable sin, 'and remember that though a fierce and energetic pastor may insist that certain sins are past pardon, a sweet religion of pity and love tells you otherwise.'[95] Kit's confidence and clear answers offered much-sought guidance and reassurance at a time of mounting religious doubt and continuing doctrinal dispute.

Assurance of God's love and infinite mercy, in fact, was a keynote of Kit's correspondence column. To Sorrowful she stressed the compassion of Jesus: 'You will, I know, repair your sin by earnest industry and purity of life. You erred through warmth of heart, and you must remember how much was forgiven one who loved much, and how gentle God is.'[96] To Troubled in Soul, fretting over the condition of the dead, she stressed the need for confidence in divine mercy:

> Dismiss all such melancholy thoughts from your mind. Have no fear for the fate of the departed. To my mind such views are impious. The Creator is assuredly maligned when He is represented as taking pleasure in the misery of His creatures. You and I – mere human units, unfeeling, cruel, heartless as we are, more or less – would surely not condemn our greatest enemy to the torments of fire everlasting, and exult in his sufferings. Why then insult the great God by supposing Him capable of cruelty from which our limited and human sense of sympathy and compassion recoils? The whole teaching of the Bible, of Christianity, is involved in the few words, 'Love one another' – and there is no room in the Gospel of Love for cruelty of any kind, much less the hideous torture you suppose. There are no dead – they are sleeping, waiting the great time of the second coming of Christ. You suffer agony, you say, thinking of your beloved in the horror of 'eternal fire.' There is no need for you to suffer. The dead are at rest. It is we who are distracted with the griefs and worries – we who live and can feel. Take peace to yourself and help the weary, living ones.[97]

While this answer may have comforted the letter writer, it no doubt enraged those who read in it a glib denial of the doctrine of damnation.

The other side of such comfort, though, was a stress on the reality of sin and the need for amendment of life. Kit wrote to A Little Friend, 'I would comfort you if I could in the way you mean, but I want you to take Christ's comfort first. What would it avail you to do this heavy wrong to your husband, to your own soul, for the short time permitted. You must do right, my dear, hard as it is, and now more than ever.'[98]

She also did not hesitate to rebuke those who persisted in wrongdoing. To A Sinner, who wrote for her advice about a young woman he had made pregnant, she stressed the urgency of atonement: 'If there is a spark of honour left in your breast you will marry the girl at once ... Heavens! That anyone calling himself a man should for a moment hesitate in such a case!'[99] Two months later she wrote even more strongly to the same correspondent: 'You write me that you are in the "same case when last I heard from you, and you want my advice." No, you don't. If you did you would have taken it when you got it, and have married the mother of your child ... Go down on your knees and ask your God what you should do.'[100] To Joan, tempted by a forbidden love, she urged purity and self-denial: 'If all your life is blighted and your hopes smashed – they must go – you must do the right, and loving him is not right.'[101] Whether the strict orthodoxy of such answers reflected Kit's own beliefs and conduct – biographical evidence, though cloudy, suggests otherwise – her moral certainty was an essential prop for the humour and daring that also characterized her column.

That so many correspondents wrote to Kit about their emotional distress suggests that her column met a need. Psychiatry was in its very early stages during this period, a time also when concern about social breakdown, mental deficiency, sexual irregularity, and the proliferation of urban vice was increasingly widespread.[102] Mainstream Protestant churches were in spiritual disarray, their ministers unsure of such fundamental elements of doctrine as the reliability of Scripture and the reality of conversion and salvation;[103] traditional moral guidance was crumbling at the very time it seemed to be most needed. Correspondents were keen to take advantage of the opportunity to write under cover of anonymity to a figure who was motherly but difficult to shock, morally confident but full of sympathy and reassurance.

IF KIT'S APPEAL WAS BASED on the quality and moral framework of her answers, it also owed a good deal to her individuality and whimsy. Her tone of voice altered depending on her perception of the personality with whom she was dealing, reinforcing readers' sense of the intimacy of her response: in a single column she might express jovial cheer, maternal tenderness, sisterly sympathy, moral asperity, or saucy rebuke. To Clementine the Crank, she wished 'every crank sent me as good-natured a letter as yours.'[104] One correspondent's praise of the column stirred her to flirtatious pleasure: 'I feel,' she wrote to Hippodadle, 'like a cat that has been rubbed along her ears, and I would purr, if I only knew how.'[105] To Rema she joked, 'You really must not say such nice things about me. You will make my bonnets so very small.'[106] On a more serious note, she stressed to Hazel Eyes how much she had benefited from the correspondent's words, asking, 'What can I say in answer to your magnificent and most womanly letter but that it has lifted me to higher things and helped me?'[107]

Readers must have felt curious about what might or might not provoke Kit to strong emotion, either in sympathy or in annoyance. She responded to a despairing letter from Jack that 'it seems a poor thing to send you only a few hollow words, but you asked for a kind line and a touch of sympathy, and I offer them to you from my heart.'[108] But she was also prone to irritation and impatience. To A Troubled Wife she advised, 'You are one of those awful, tearful, good women who drive more men to drink than do all the viragoes in the world. Stop whimpering for pity and be thankful you are so well off as to have the love of a kindly, manly chap whom you are treating shamefully.'[109] She responded tartly to G.S., who wrote asking 'how to become an early riser' with the brief, 'Get up early, my friend.'[110] To Wamba she wrote merely, 'Your letter was too stupid to bother with. I sent it to Mahoud.'[111] Kit had a variety of devilish names for her wastepaper basket, where she liked to send unpleasant mail.

That some correspondents were frightened by her cross words and sarcastic quips is evident from her apologies and justifications. To Little Dorrit she confessed, 'I suppose I'm a cross old bear sometimes, and then I growl, but truly I should never think of growling at you, my shadowy little friend.'[112] She apologized to Nancy Lee, 'I am sorry that an occasional sharp answer (which I assure you is merited) to some correspondents should make genuine inquirers like yourself timid in referring to this column.'[113] Much as she might apologize for growling, though, she kept it up, and it seemed not to diminish but rather to sustain the volume of her mail. Perhaps her severe rebukes and sarcastic outbursts strengthened readers' faith in her integrity; they certainly added piquancy to the column, which nearly always contained at least one sharp retort to a writer judged by Kit to be unreasonable, importunate, or immoral. Of Desperate she asked sarcastically, 'My dear young man, couldn't you have managed to tell me in less than thirty-two pages that you were "desperate" because the young lady you are engaged to dances with other men?'[114] In response to one Kingston Youth, who chastised her laxness about wine drinking, quoting Scripture to reinforce the prohibition on alcohol, she retorted, 'Go home, friend, and instead of shouting Scriptural texts at a very busy woman, sit down and learn from them a little more charity.'[115] To Harriet, who 'has a few things to find fault with' in the Woman's Kingdom 'but does not care to do so lest our correspondence should suddenly cease,' she responded, 'By all means let it cease, "Harriet." I have more than I can manage on my hands now, and the only place for cranks who cannot or will not bring forward substantial charges is the waste basket. Therefore, in you go, my dear, and there is an end of you.'[116] Her ability to be irritated or revolted likely heightened the value of the patience and sympathy she more often expressed.

A frequent source of frustration for her, as it had been for Sara Jeannette Duncan in the previous decade, was the intense Mrs Grundyism she detected in many of her correspondents, which seemed to her a feature of the Toronto public generally. 'Mrs. Grundy,' to whom Duncan had dedicated her first book, was the nineteenth-century symbol of prudish propriety. An excessive concern for correct appearance and the rules of moral conduct was an irritant to the breezy, occasionally irreverent writer, who detested cant. To one correspondent Kit wrote, 'I hate Mrs. Grundy – always did, and so one day long ago – I don't really care to think how long – I slipped from under her unlovely yoke.'[117] Grundyism she defined as 'the terrible trembling of conventionality, that truckling which kills charity and generous impulses, which makes us at once proud, vain, and narrow-minded; which destroys liberality of thought and action, and makes of us prim puppets that can be set dancing to any tune or any measure.'[118] It meant thinking according to social convention rather than honest personal morality. Correspondents regularly chastised Kit for flippancy or impropriety, and she responded with irritated sarcasm: 'I reply to you out of your turn,' she wrote sarcastically to Miles Standish, 'because of the intense interest you take in my spiritual welfare';[119] she mocked him as a 'delightful Pharisee'[120] intent on pointing out others' failings while ignoring his own. To Mrs J.M. Teartop she responded, 'Oh, you delightful moral censor, you dear, patient, and punctilious follower of Mrs. Grundy, why don't you mind your own business and let me alone?'[121]

Perhaps Kit's wittiest attack on Grundyism came in a long answer she gave to the self-styled Prunes and Prism, who had complained about the naked figure of Cupid adorning the 'Woman's Kingdom' page the previous week. Any avid nineteenth-century reader would have recognized 'Prunes and Prism' to be a reference to training in proper deportment given to little girls in Charles Dickens's *Little Dorritt*; in the novel the governess, Mrs General, insists that her girls repeat 'papa, potatoes, poultry, prunes, and prism' for the training these words provide for pretty lips. With a metaphorical roll of her eyes, Kit addressed another such Dickensian prude:

> Prunes and Prism. – What a capital pseudonym for one of your delicate sensibilities. Well, THE MAIL artist and myself had a long discussion about that very same Cupid. 'I'm afraid they won't like him in Toronto,' said I, in reference to fat little Dan. 'Don't you think you could manage to put a small pair of trousers on him and a little coat, or drape him with a sash of some sort?' The artist looked at me with murder in his eye. 'Make a John-nie of him!' said he sarcastically. 'Put a jacket on him! Why, what do you think I'm going to do with his wings? Everyone would think if I dressed him up like that, that he was a Toronto newsboy. "Drape him with a sash," went on the artist scathingly; "Hide all his pretty dimples." Upon my word, Kit, you may be able to scribble off a lot of tarradiddles and nonsense, but you know nothing whatever of art.' And, upon reflection, I agreed with him. I was only trying not to shock the goodly people *for once*, and the artist wouldn't let me. So my dear, that's why you had Cupid in all his chubby nudity in last week's paper, and if you're going to kick up a fuss about a baby-boy, why, I advise you to pack up your traps, hire a Mrs. General (you'll get plenty of her in Toronto at a moment's notice) and set off for Europe.[122]

On the subject of impropriety, Kit was often at the end of her patience. Mainly, though, she was unpretentious and quick to sympathize, and even her anger probably impressed readers as proof of her insight. As she phrased it to Oakley, who must have written complaining about her sharpness, 'Because a correspondent writes and explains his or her trouble is not in itself a reason for sympathy. One must be fair; and sometimes those who ask advice do not prove their right to sympathetic consideration.'[123]

More often, she showed herself deeply affected by the letters sent to her: 'Latterly the shadows' letters seem to hurt so much. There seems so much more weariness, and grief and pain everywhere.'[124] She complained to Mrs A., 'I have so many letters from girls and women who are poor and out of health, and I am of such little use to help them, that I often feel I carry a certain share of their sorrows with my own.'[125] To Adrienne she stressed her sense of shared grief: 'You will say I am preaching, and call me a bore and an old crank, and maybe I am, but

my heart is full of your trouble, and my own, and all our little commonplace troubles, as I write to you.'[126] Tart as she might often be, Kit
demonstrated empathy and solidarity with her correspondents.

It required a careful balancing act to maintain personal privacy
while also establishing an accessible public persona, and Kit's ability
to do both was another aspect of her appeal. She had a talent for self-
deprecating humour and was skilled at turning ordinary experiences
into amusing vignettes, with herself in the starring role as a lovable in-
competent or comic victim of fate. Answering letters while she was
staying in California to cover the 1894 Mid-Winter Fair, she responded
gleefully to Bugaboo, who wrote of insect troubles, about her own bug
encounters, revelling in the colloquial language and high-spirited hyperbole that such a frivolous subject invited: 'You ask for a word of
sympathy, and say that your trouble will sound "tame" to me but is
very real to yourself. Not it. I've had five months of the California flea.
I've become an adept at catching native sons. I've seen decorous old
ladies pounce on them in the middle of the sermon, and hold fast to
them till the anthem was over; and whole rivers of sympathy have
flowed from my understanding heart. Now that no longer the airy flea
disports himself among my underwear, I am devoured by flies and
snapped at by spiders, and I can wail out my purest sympathy to you,
my bug-ridden friend. Have courage.'[127] On another occasion, while
staying in Jamaica, she described killing two cockroaches and watching their bodies quickly borne away by an army of ants that appeared
as if from nowhere. The roaches were carried off, violently fought over,
and quickly consumed, leaving only 'a regiment of gorged ants, swol-
len to a disreputable degree, and lying about in West Indian *dolce far
niente.*'[128] Kit's skill with language could turn the most banal incident
into broad comedy.

The self-ridiculing tendency that encouraged readers' affection was
on full display in a detailed account of her first lesson in bicycle-riding,
when she described herself being led around the cycling arena by a
young man to whom she was attached by a leather lead. Kit had commented frequently on the bicycle craze in earlier columns, mentioning
her annoyance at aggressive riders and her uncertainty about undertaking the exercise herself. Finally, after watching a young woman who
'ambled around so easily and gracefully,' she thought she would try,
but quickly found herself defeated by the terrible machine:

I had mounted with a sort of smiling contempt, but when the thing began
to go, and I forgot to pedal and lost my feet, so to speak, and had them

crunched by the wheel, and shrieked dismally to the agreeable young man not to let me go on any account; and lastly when the silk under-flounce of my skirt went rip and the cold perspiration broke out upon my face and crept down my shoulders – what a dreadful ordeal it was! What a wiggling, fiendish, desperate thing a wheel is! With a mind of its own that beats an ass for obstinacy or a mule for temper! It ran into the wall and barked my shins; it raced madly after the fat gentleman, who nearly shied into the elevator in a frantic effort to escape; it dashed round curves, and shot me forward and shot me backward, and nearly shot me into the insane asylum.[129]

The frequent rhetorical parallelism, anaphora, and exaggerated contrasts – as between her 'smiling contempt' and dismal shrieks – demonstrate the skill with which Kit could turn her own humiliation into humorous copy. Refusing to take herself too seriously, she demonstrated that religious principles and self-respect could coexist with an Irish gift for mockery.

But melancholy and vulnerability were also elements of Kit's self-image that probably increased readers' sympathy and interest. Often she complained of being tired and overworked, confessing to readers in tones that varied from high-spirited to depressed of the piles of letters waiting to be answered and her inability to summon the energy to work properly. To Romona, who questioned whether real letters were the basis of the correspondence section, she described her desperate plight using jaunty rhythm and rhyme: 'Letters in front of me, letters all round me, letters in tatters and letters in rags. Stormed at with pen and ink – often I sadly shrink from the fell task – to think what's best to say.'[130] Frequently she thanked readers for encouraging her, revealing to them the 'grey' times when she believed her work was no good and her life meaningless. After J.B.R. had written words of encouragement, she responded, 'If you knew what a sense of courage your letter – coming in a grey moment – gave me, you would be glad, I think, for you are a kindly person. So often there is a sense of failure, of hopelessness, and sadness, and then cheery words are God's own messages.'[131] Returning to work after a period of illness, she wrote that 'the cheery letters of "welcome back" have heartened and encouraged a woman who lately was pressed down by illness, and who is often – in the old human way – "blue" and depressed.'[132] To Ring Mahone she confided that 'sometimes it is so hard to live; and there are nights – we all know them, must know them, it seems to me – when we would not be sorry to think there would be no more getting up in the morning, but a blessed rest for always.'[133]

And she was endearingly frank about her aspiration to be a 'real' writer, confiding to Em'ly, 'I have in my desk a drawer, which is labelled "Disappointed Ambition," and which is packed full with returned MSS. I tell you, I look at some of the effusions and wonder who on earth wrote such twaddle and expected to get it printed, but the small poor signature "Kit" in one corner reminds me that I was the foolish one, and must do better – must and will do better.'[134] On being encouraged by her readers to publish a collection of her travel sketches, she confessed her dread of rejection: 'If I were in any degree confident of the success of the venture, I would gladly revise the letters and publish them in a little book, but I fear the hopelessness that failure would bring.'[135] Unashamed to tell readers of her own disappointments and difficulties, Kit appealed to them as a fellow traveller on an often discouraging road.

She hinted, too, at personal heartbreak, the death of children, and marital tragedy. To Hope Fairfax she confessed, 'My dear, I know what it all means, and my heart aches for you when I think of those lost babies of yours. Ah! If you only knew how just now you have touched me upon a most tender point!'[136] To Rosalie, whom she had earlier advised to give up all thought of marrying an alcoholic whom she hoped to reform, Kit suggested that she had known the same grief: 'No matter what you suffer, you have done what is right. If only I could tell you what I know has happened through marriage with one suffering from a like disease.'[137] To V.D. she asserted that 'when one has known acute suffering, has been buffeted pretty well all over the world, has had life end at 20, there is little left except to help others,' and then she added teasingly, 'Of course I'm not alluding to myself. I'm talking of, let us say, Mrs. Harris.'[138] In her response to Abbie, she confessed, 'Your letter affected me, it is such a bitter letter for a girl to write, but I know how you feel – unfortunately for myself. Do you understand?'[139] To Helped she wrote in detail to show 'how deeply I feel with you, because I suffered the same way,' telling a pathetic tale about how she had always longed to publish something to make her father proud but that he had died just at the time her first piece was printed.[140] Stressing her identity as a woman who had experienced most of what women suffered – unrequited love, a bad marriage to an unreliable husband, the loss of a child, the humiliations and loneliness of approaching old age – she highlighted her ability to give advice from personal knowledge.

Vulnerability and self-exposure, then, balanced Kit's brusqueness and superior knowledge. As often as she angered readers with a sharp or unorthodox remark, she must have disarmed them with tenderness or a glimpse of personal pain. Perhaps one of her wisest decisions in this respect was to publish letters critical of her column – rebukes from offended prudes and denunciations of her advice or physical appearance from readers who believed they could conduct the column more effectively. One letter to the editor by an annoyed reader found her un-ladylike, objecting to both the style and the content of her columns as follows: 'She spoke once of someone pursuing her like the "devil on two sticks"; such language might be heard in a barroom, but looks singular, to say the least, in the Woman's Kingdom. It is not long since she informed us that it had been hinted to her that she disliked bloomers because her own lower extremities were not beautiful. I am not giving her exact words, but that was her meaning. How could any well-bred woman discuss such a thing in the columns of a newspaper?'[141] On another occasion, she was criticized for an unattractive appearance and shabby clothing by someone who addressed her as 'Madame Kit' and was irritated by her fashion analysis:

> You profess to pose as a critic of society and the gowns women wear at the Horse Shows, Races, and other functions which you visit as a paid servant of the press – therefore of the public. You are unsparing in your criticism. Would you like a critique of your own appearance as it struck the eyes of those so unmercifully 'criticized' by you?
>
> Here is what we saw: – A tall, gaunt, passe woman, nearer to fifty than forty, gowned shabbily in an old black silk that smelled of ammonia (we passed close to you, Madam), and wearing a hat – a dusty, faded old chip hat, laden with ancient feathers, which matched your air of shabby gentility; old black kid gloves, printers'-inked at the fingertips, and large feet, encased in merely passable shoes; a face like a mask, powdered heavily, impassive, hard, cruel. That's what you looked like, Madam. Yet here you are with your 'clever' criticism of people whose shoes you would not be permitted to blacken. You may find this a hard letter, but it is only holding up the mirror to you, to show you yourself as others see you. MRS. GRUNDY.[142]

Kit also did not escape condemnation for impertinence, flippancy, and bad advice, as in the following letter, which she published 'in that spirit of justice to the public'[143] on which she prided herself. Identifying herself as 'A READER' (whom Kit later revealed to be a woman), the writer attacked her for giving bad advice to someone who wanted to break into the field of literature and went on to criticize her generally for bad writing and impudence:

> We have good-naturedly tolerated your gush for eight or nine years, and if you would confine your effusions to the parading of your family affairs, your much-regretted lost youth, your absurd repetitions of Dickens gush, and even your harmless plagiarisms, we could tolerate you eight or nine years longer, but when you use a great journal to give flippant, untruthful answers to earnest enquiries through its columns, you need a 'pull up.' If you were a young writer, your sometimes impudent answers would be amusing, but being a person of ripe years, and also a woman of the world, your flippancy is impertinent, and an insult to the average intellect. Pray remember that apart from the 'smart set,' you cater to a great, watchful majority, who frequently weigh you in the balance and find you wanting.[144]

The response to these criticisms was swift, as letters defending Kit flooded in. She printed some of them and made grateful mention of many others, noting how cheered she was to receive such testimonials. In response to the criticism that Kit's language and ideas were unwomanly, one reader remarked scornfully, 'Mary E. is one of those persons who, being left a legacy from a great aunt, would, with pursed-up lips, inform her acquaintances – she never has friends – that she had been left a "limb-acy," the other word "having a tendency to demoralize."'[145] A gallant defender of Kit's fashion critique wrote a satirical poem about her attacker, Mrs Grundy, ending with the following tribute:

> You are gaunt, we are told,
> And you also look old –
> Don't mind Mrs. Grundy – you know it's her way;
> With your heart young and kind,
> And your clear brilliant mind,
> Your name will be honored for many a day.[146]

By far the greatest number of defenders, however, arose in response to the criticisms alleged by 'A READER,' and Kit filled her column of 11 February 1899, with their rebuttals. Robert Addison wrote dismissing the 'malicious letter' to say, 'We all know how original, clever, and bright you make the Kingdom, and what interesting information we derive from its perusal, and can only very inadequately thank you for the cheery messages you send the weary ones.'[147] C.G. commended Kit for having 'the broadness of a man – the mental breadth – and generosity, coupled with the sensitiveness of a true woman.'[148] And Katie Ireland wrote an indignant rejoinder, claiming, 'The creature ... did not reckon on your army of loyal hearts and true.'[149] She ended with a wish expressive of the sentiments of many of Kit's readers: 'Long may you reign in the Kingdom for your loving paper children.'[150] Buoyed by such 'splendid backing' from her shadows, Kit announced at the end of the column that letters attacking her work in the Kingdom would be, for the present at least, cheerfully ignored. 'You are good to me, my dolls,'[151] she wrote gratefully.

Kathleen Coleman was to continue to write for the *Mail* for another decade, secure in her position as the undisputed champion of the lonely-hearted, the confused, and the curious. Opinionated, feisty, sympathetic, and droll, she charmed many, enraged a few, and fascinated a wide reading audience over many years. Part of her enduring popularity seems to have stemmed from her ability to fashion a persona unconventional enough to interest readers but not so unconventional as to turn away those seeking her moral wisdom and practical advice. She was unafraid to tackle issues that were deeply controversial in her day – wife abuse, marital infidelity, religious doubt – without compromising her respectability or womanliness, and her many-sided personality, which could be playful, sombre, and bitingly satirical in a single column, kept readers interested in what she had to say. Most importantly, perhaps, she made them feel they knew her and were intimately known by her, though she remained protective of her dignity and mystery. To make correspondents feel individually loved and supported while insisting that she did not care to meet them was in itself an achievement. In the range of subjects she wrote about and the frankness, wit, and occasional audacity with which she expressed herself, her columns are a valuable record not only of the everyday preoccupations of late Victorian Canadians but of the forms of self-fashioning available to their public confessor.

5 Heroines and Martyrs in the Cause: Suffrage as Holy War in the Journalism of Flora MacDonald Denison

Known today as the mother of the pioneering playwright Merrill Denison, Flora MacDonald Denison was a columnist for the Toronto Sunday *World* from 1909 to 1913 and a leading activist in the Canadian suffrage movement. Deborah Gorham considers her one of the few radical feminists in the suffrage struggle, distinct from the middle-class social reformers who made up the majority of members of the movement. Such a distinction is also made by Alison Prentice and her co-authors, who note that she was 'one of the few Canadian women to identify herself publicly as a suffragette,'[1] rather than the more moderate 'suffragist.' According to Catherine Cleverdon, Denison was the most influential Ontario leader during the crucial period from 1906 to 1914, and her Sunday *World* page 'was of great propaganda value.'[2] Suffrage was not her only passion: her wide-ranging and unorthodox interests included spiritualism, parapsychology, the free thought of Earl G. Ingersoll, the syncretic Eastern religion theosophy, vegetarianism, and the poetic philosophy of Walt Whitman.[3] In the final years of her life, she ran a nature retreat at Bon Echo, north of Belleville, where Canadian and American artists and free spirits gathered to discuss socialism and to commune with Whitman in seances. For the four years she wrote her weekly column at the *World*, however, suffrage was her main public focus and she was its tireless champion.

A close friend of suffragist Emily Howard Stowe and her daughter, Augusta Stowe-Gullen, Denison also had ties to the international women's movement, which included the American leader Anna Howard Shaw and the British suffragette Emmeline Pankhurst. It was after attending the International Suffrage Alliance Conference in Copenhagen in 1906 that Denison became an organizer in the Canadian Suffrage Association, eventually serving as its president from 1911 to 1914. The Sunday *World* was a vehicle to promote the cause and an opportunity to articulate her feminist philosophy. In the pages of her column, she developed a revolutionary language that envisioned the women's movement as a spiritual solution to the world's ills. Rejecting the Christian framework and middle-class emphasis of Canadian moderates, Denison articulated an alternative perspective in which suffrage was neither a basic right nor a means to other ends but a cosmic assault on injustice. Within this framework, suffrage workers were not merely political activists but glorious martyrs whose example and self-sacrifice would usher in a new world order. Her spiritual emphasis and transformative vision made her a compelling voice for the feminist revolution.

IN THE LATE FALL OF 1909 Denison, then vice-president of the Canadian Suffrage Association, was instrumental in bringing Emmeline Pankhurst to Toronto to give a speech at Massey Hall. Leaders in both the American and the British suffrage movements regularly made visits to Canada, seeking to promote a cause that had always been strongly international in flavour. According to Cleverdon, Emily Howard Stowe had brought 'both Dr. Anna Howard Shaw and Susan B. Anthony to Toronto in 1889,'[4] and Canadian women had been attending suffrage conventions abroad for decades. But Pankhurst was a different order of activist. She was the leader of the Women's Social and Political Union (WSPU) in England, an organization that had distinguished itself by its militant tactics, including mass protests, the heckling of politicians, hunger strikes, acts of vandalism and arson, and demonstrations that often turned violent; members of the WSPU regularly spent time in jail for disturbing the peace or destroying property. Moreover, British authorities' decision to force-feed the hunger strikers while they were in jail brought their cause unparalleled attention – and notoriety. Many suffragists in Canada found the suffragettes' tactics shocking and indecent, but Denison was an admirer of Pankhurst, declaring that 'those who connect her with hysteria and fanaticism will be greatly surprised when they see and hear her.'[5] She was delighted to announce Pankhurst's upcoming visit to Massey Hall, predicting, 'A woman willing to give her freedom or her life for the sake of principle ... will be one we will all want to see and hear.'[6] Her championing of Pankhurst was both an affirmation of solidarity and a declaration of her own radicalism.

Flora MacDonald Denison.

Just prior to Pankhurst's arrival, Denison went to New York 'to welcome her for Canada,' and after Pankhurst's Toronto address, she wrote about the visit in rapturous terms, stressing the emotional impact Pankhurst had made on all who heard her:

> I feel very kindly this morning toward everybody. I am very new at weekly newspaper work, and I am still more modern as regards entertaining celebrities, but I want to say that I hope I shall have plenty of newspaper work to do and an occasional celebrity to entertain for the rest of my life.
>
> Of course, there is only one Mrs. Pankhurst and there is little to be added now to what the public already know about her. As in other places, so here, 'She came, she saw, she conquered.' Prejudices have been removed, malice fled before her kindly presence, and she left us crowned with the admiration of everyone who heard her and loved by everyone who was privileged to know her.[7]

Denison was not alone in being favourably impressed by Pankhurst's speaking abilities. Even the 'staid and dignified *Canadian Annual Review*,' according to Cleverdon, reported on her 'bright, intelligent, gracious and feminine personality' as well as her 'effective and eloquent' speech.[8] For Denison, though, Pankhurst was more than an effective speaker: she was a guiding spirit whose triumphant address buttressed Denison's conviction that passionate words could change lives.

As so often in her column, Denison strikes a personal note here in a comment combining diffidence and pride; she points to her inexperience as a writer and activist, but also revels in and is buoyed by her contact with the renowned Pankhurst, happily imagining a future in which she will meet and interact with other inspiring women. Manifest in her description is a delighted consciousness of having participated in a signal moment in the Canadian women's movement; in bringing Pankhurst to Toronto, she knew she had helped to make feminist history. Over the next few years, Pankhurst was to be her guide and ultimate standard of commitment and fervour.

The breathless enthusiasm created by her parallel phrasing and unapologetic use of cliché in the above passage are characteristic of the style and personality of Denison's suffrage column. Always spontaneous, unpretentious, and emotionally engaged, Denison embodied the popular face of the suffrage movement, even as she established her credentials as a leader with significant international connections. She developed a mode of expression and an approach to her subject that was neither original nor analytical and expressed a complete and passionate identification with the suffrage cause that was unparalleled in Canada. The quasi-religious overtones to her conviction are evident in a statement she made early on in the column, when she explained, 'To the questions of an interested admirer, "Are you a socialist, a Christian, a spiritualist, a freethinker, an Ibsenite," I would simply reply: "I am a suffragist."'[9] For Denison, suffrage was not only a social and political cause but an all-consuming identity and faith. The particular force of her column stemmed from her ability to articulate that identification through personal anecdotes, romantic tributes, and rousing exhortations.

Denison's purpose in writing for the *World* between 1909 and 1911 was to convince other women to make suffrage their primary source of identification too, encouraging them to join 'the greatest movement along reform lines that the world has yet seen.'[10] Her first column was published on 12 September 1909, under the romantic-sounding header 'Under the Pines: What Women Are Doing for the Advancement of Civilization – Suffrage News.' In it she issued a rallying cry with a substantial list of answers to the question 'Why should women want to vote?' The *World*'s editor informed readers in his introduction to the new column that Denison, as organizer of the Canadian Suffrage Association as well as 'a talented speaker and writer,' would supply 'official news of the suffrage movement throughout Canada and other parts of the world.' He added that it was 'a subject in which womankind is believed to be generally interested.' Seventeen months later, on 5 February 1911, Denison announced that the character of her column, having achieved its goal of raising the consciousness of Torontonians about the movement, would change; it would become a 'human interest' column with a wider focus on social betterment under the title 'The Open Road towards Democracy.' It remained a regular column until 1913. For a year and a half, however, suffrage was her only subject; she published reports from the national president, described suffrage and related reform conventions, published suffrage poems and songs, recommended books on the subject, and shared her thoughts on all matters related to justice for women. As a recognized organ of the movement, Denison's column provides an illuminating example of popular suffrage ideology.

FLORA MACDONALD DENISON'S particular genius seems to have been her understanding of the practical and psychological challenges of galvanizing a mass of people to work for a long-term political objective. On one occasion in her column, she outlined the psycho-history of reform movements, noting that they began in their early days in 'altruistic ardor' during a period of confidence that a nation's leaders would want what was best for the people and that the people would want the best for themselves. Such movements then invariably ran up against 'custom and prejudice, precedent and ignorance';[11] difficulties and unexpected delays caused adherents to fall away and disillusionment to set in. The pioneers in the cause experienced social opprobrium and even persecution, while a self-protective majority stood back from the struggle. Yet the true disciples worked diligently, converting a few individuals gradually over a long period. At last, their idea became accepted among the general populace, and the reform was implemented. Denison did not doubt that the time for suffrage in Ontario would come: it was necessary only 'to agitate and educate until selfish ignorance is overthrown.'[12] To combat apathy and selfishness, she understood the need to keep people focused on immediate goals ('to have some definite object for which to work') while also firing their enthusiasm and ardour for the greater objective, and it was this office – providing short-term objectives while keeping zeal and commitment alive – for which Denison designed her column.

The Sunday *World* was Toronto's largest illustrated weekly, a mass-circulation 'people's paper' that favoured eye-catching headlines and human-interest stories rather than sober, detailed analysis.[13] Its sympathies were democratic, its focus local, and its style often sensational. In keeping with the paper's populist stance as well as her own writing strengths, Denison focused on storytelling, stating as her belief: 'A little personal sketch will often drive home a point more readily than any amount of abstract reasoning.'[14] The column was characterized by extended anecdotes, autobiographical reflections, and rhapsodic expressions of admiration and hope, as when she sent out a Christmas greeting 'to all women of whatever race or creed or calling, and especially to our English sisters fighting in the storm centre,'[15] and hoped that 'something would strike Canada to show that we too have buried metal [sic] awaiting development in our women.'[16] Sprinkled with sentence fragments, digressions, incomplete observations, and abrupt transitions, the column established Denison's identity as a busy activist campaigning for women's advancement, finding personal fulfilment in the cause, and calling other women to share in the work. She was less concerned to develop detailed arguments or a polished style than she was to foster devotion to an ideal, seeking to create a revolutionary sisterhood of 'public-spirited' women, working and sacrificing themselves 'for the common good of all.'[17]

Unlike the other writers in this study, Denison's interests and abilities were not primarily literary, and she had extensive experience of the business world. A native of Belleville, Ontario, she was educated at the Picton Collegiate and graduated at age fifteen; she was then employed briefly as a teacher, an occupation she did not enjoy. After giving up teaching, she worked in Toronto and in Detroit, Michigan, where she married and did some newspaper writing before taking up long-term residence in Toronto, supporting herself and her son as a skilled seamstress, first for Simpson's department store and then in a self-owned business.[18] She published one novel, Mary Melville, The Psychic, in 1900, described generously by Ramsay Cook as 'filled, appropriately, with revelations.'[19] It was a thinly disguised biography of her late sister, Mary, a mathematical prodigy thought to have had psychic and telekinetic powers. It also contained a denunciation of Christian orthodoxy and a statement of belief in a non-personal, supernatural force for good. Reviews were lukewarm at best (a number noted crudeness of style), and there is no evidence of a significant readership.

Another novel, left unfinished at Denison's death, with the unpromising title 'L'il Sue,' is of interest only for its advocacy of women's economic and emotional self-sufficiency.[20] It is possible that, with fuller training and without the pressure to support herself and her son, Merrill (her husband seems not to have provided financial support and eventually they separated), Denison might have developed her writing talents more fully. Gorham finds her journalism politically significant but intellectually and aesthetically undistinguished: 'Denison was not an original thinker and the writing of popular pieces for a "people's" journal encouraged her to blunt and simplify her thoughts rather than to refine and develop them.'[21] Andrea Williams views her writing more favourably, emphasizing her inclusivity and ability to popularize complex ideas, a crucial component in any successful revolution. However one assesses her prose style, Denison was undoubtedly a successful journalist during her years with the Sunday World. Her weekly column not only communicated suffrage news and arguments but also effectively captured the tremendous passion and enthusiasm she felt for the cause and particularly for the women, whom she called 'noble pioneers' and 'Great Ones,' those who were clearing the way for women's freedom.[22]

In turning to journalism, Denison chose a literary medium closely identified with political advocacy. As Marjory Lang has demonstrated in her study of the first generations of female journalists, many newspapers in the early twentieth century began to feature columns on club activities, which gave politically oriented writers the opportunity to comment extensively on clubs dedicated to reform causes or the advancement of women. Cleverdon notes that, in addition to 'Women's organizations, farm and labour groups [and] a substantial number of the Protestant clergy,' the support of 'the most influential sections of the press'[23] was central to the success of the suffrage movement. 'Had it not been for this journalistic assistance,' she argues, 'the road to political emancipation would have been much harder.'[24] Long before suffrage initiatives had either political support or widespread popular appeal, a number of newspapers, including Denison's *World* and the Toronto *Globe*, went out of their way to champion suffrage. As Cleverdon reports, such papers 'not only gave suffrage bills and activities complete coverage in their news columns but often extended strong editorial support.'[25] The newspaper's role in educating the public and popularizing the cause was thus of inestimable importance.

Historians of the Canadian women's movement have tended to place Denison's radical politics in clear opposition to the maternal focus of most reformers. According to Carol Bacchi, Denison 'fell firmly within the feminist tradition established by Dr. Stowe,'[26] a minority tradition that stressed women's equal rights, rather than their special interests, and rejected the sexual division of labour. For Gorham, Denison's feminism rested on her analysis of women's economic dependency within the modern family.[27] Denison's feminist philosophy did include these elements, but it was an eclectic mix of platforms and approaches. In a column intended to interest a mass audience, she was not concerned to advocate a consistent ideology; she filled the column with aphoristic assertions and ringing calls to arms, and she did not eschew the effective and time-worn tropes that many more moderate activists employed. Thus she too claimed political rights for women based on the maternal virtues and concerns they brought to politics, their 'mother-hearted' concern for children, the poor, and other mothers. As she explained it, 'The mother heart and the mother love, the mother instinct and the mother judgment are needed in every place,' not just in the home.[28] In memorializing Dr Emily Howard Stowe after her death, Denison stressed that her activism expressed her womanhood and had not in any way detracted from it: Stowe was no less 'a devoted wife because she took an interest in others; no less a home-maker because she wanted it possible that other women might have homes; no less a mother because she wanted every child protected.'[29] In this now-familiar line of reasoning, social activism was an extension rather than a diversion of women's innate motherly energies.

In addition, Denison stressed that women had a lived understanding of the need for various social improvements, such as systems to improve sanitation or promote water purity, decent conditions of work for labourers, and protection for girls from sexual predators. Whether married or single, mothers or childless, women had a natural desire to care not only for family but also for neighbours and fellow citizens; their pursuit of the vote was an expression of that desire: 'Instead of any thought of deserting home and children,' Denison reassured the doubtful, 'they want the weapon of power in their hands to protect both home and children.'[30] Accordingly, she drew heavily on the image of the home to emphasize that even the most conservative and domestic women had a duty to become politically involved: 'Politics comes into the home through the drain-pipe, through the water supply, through the milk, through the food the children consume, [and] through the air they breathe.'[31] Thus, she asked rhetorically, 'Has any mother a right to neglect politics? Contagion may claim her beautiful child just because she has no time for politics.'[32] These kinds of arguments placed Denison in the mainstream of suffrage rhetoric.

She also moved into more radical territory, criticizing traditional ideas about the family and the role of women within it. In particular, she scorned the church's concern with 'race suicide' (a coded reference to birth control) and suggested that women should have the power to control reproduction for the betterment of themselves and their children. Concern about the declining birth rate was widespread in Canada in the early twentieth century among reformers and social conservatives alike.[33] 'The church and the state pretend great alarm at race suicide,' Denison wrote bitterly, 'and yet neglected, half-fed and half-clothed children swarm like bees in our cities. Better to look after the children that are here than fuss too much about the ones that will never exist.'[34] She recounted stories of deserted mothers struggling to care for their children alone and unassisted by either church or government: 'The church that told her "To bear many children," the state that wants increased population – she gave eight well-born children to them and what did they do for her? Let her scrub a bar-room on Xmas day to keep these children from starving.'[35] In giving these and other examples of religious hypocrisy, Denison presented suffrage as the only solution, emphasizing that 'If I did not honestly believe that woman suffrage would be a strong factor in rectifying many crimes against childhood and be instrumental in doing away with the white slave traffic, I would not work another day for it.'[36] Suffrage was never merely about rights for Denison; it was about putting an end to the misery of the oppressed.

Yet human rights, representative democracy, and basic justice were also first-order considerations. In her first column, when she appended a list of statements answering the question 'Why should women want to vote?' maternal and rights arguments reinforced one another. The right to vote was 'the foundation of all political liberty,' according to the principle that 'those who obey the law should be able to have a voice in choosing those who make the law.'[37] Parliament should reflect the will of the people, and it could not do so 'when the wishes of the women are without any direct representation.'[38] Such appeals to democratic principle were coupled with assertions about women's particular concerns and contributions to society, including the fact that 'laws affecting children should be regarded from woman's point of view as well as man.'[39] For Denison, women's right to representation was intimately connected, without conflict, to their social role in caring for and educating the next generation. She coupled her contention that 'the possession of the vote would increase the sense of responsibility among women towards questions of public importance' with an assertion that 'public-spirited mothers make public-spirited sons.'[40] As Veronica Strong-Boag has noted of Denison's contemporary Nellie McClung, 'the distinction between maternal and egalitarian arguments'[41] was often blurred in the rhetoric of these pragmatic activists.

In stressing the domestic concerns that inspired women's political involvement, Denison also wanted to counter the notion that suffrage activism was underpinned by antipathy to men. On the contrary, she asserted, 'women wanting the vote are on the very best terms with the men and want an opportunity of assisting them in making this world the best possible of worlds.'[42] She delighted in reporting male support for suffrage and stressing how women's public involvement strengthened ties between the sexes. Home and world were inseparable: 'Men need women in politics; women need men in the home.'[43] Her column for 7 November 1909 included a moral fable asserting the mutual benefit to men and women when women would be 'the companions of men, not their door-mats, their servants, nor their playthings.' In the same column she responded to a slur against political women by reporting that the leader of the International Suffrage Alliance, Carrie Chapman Catt, had always been ardently supported by her husband, who had left her a legacy of a million dollars at his death to carry forward 'a work so near the hearts of both.' Closer to home, Denison took every opportunity to thank male supporters of the cause. Discovering that the members of the Dickens fellowship of Toronto had postponed their dramatic evening in order to attend Pankhurst's talk, she praised a leading club member and supporter: 'We are indeed glad to have Mr. Bell-Smith with us, for no more public-spirited man lives in our Province today than he.'[44] She stressed the broad-mindedness of suffrage activists, who cared not only about the vote but also about mother's pensions, child welfare, employment rights, tree conservation, and an end to war.

What distinguished Denison from other Canadian leaders in the suffrage movement was her greater commitment to cross-class alliances and her particularly intense concern for poor women. Her greatest hope for the suffrage movement was that it would inspire public-spirited women to improve the conditions of life for the poor, especially poor mothers. She believed that a commission of women was needed 'to agitate and bring pressure to bear on our governing bodies to see to it that mothers are paid to look after their own children instead of separating mother and child.'[45] To this end, she strongly supported state-funded daycare and mother's pensions as well as collectivized laundry, communal living arrangements, and cooperative daycare – a kind of socialism for mothers (though she would not have called herself a socialist at this time) – in recognition of the crucial importance of mothering in society. Many of the stories in her columns focused on the burdens borne by poor mothers and the degrading work they did to support themselves and their children. Middle-class and upper-class women needed to be shaken from their complacency, she believed, by confronting the situation of their sisters. In fact, one of the many splendid effects of the suffrage cause was the breaking down of 'caste' barriers; Denison observed with delight that 'women are meeting on a different basis than that made by the positions their husbands occupy or the locality they live in or the size of their bank accounts.'[46] At last women were beginning to understand that their ethics 'must be the ethics of solidarity and mutual aid,'[47] regardless of class position or status. She was delighted to report of a strike by 30,000 shirtwaist workers in New York, 'Never before has such common cause been made between the rich woman and the working woman.'[48] Repeated expressions of cross-class solidarity and of concern for the poor sprang from Denison's awareness of her own humble origins and her hope that a revolutionary movement such as suffrage would transform the social order.

Because she believed that people had the greatest power for good in the places they knew, Denison called on middle-class readers to interest themselves in the struggles of the women and men they employed in their homes and passed on the streets. She had been horrified to learn from the International Council of Women, she mentioned, that prostitutes most commonly began as domestic servants, a fact she attributed to their degrading treatment by upper-middle-class women, and she commanded each reader to 'ask yourself if you are treating the girl who is making your home comfortable for you as you would like to be treated.'[49] She reported with sympathy on labour actions in Toronto, particularly a strike of overall makers in February 1910, and made a point of emphasizing her personal contact with the striking women as well as their intelligence and capability: 'As I chatted with them and watched their earnest, anxious faces and listened to their intelligent discussion of their situation, I mentally compared them with groups of afternoon tea in many of our handsome homes ... and I do not hesitate to say they compared most favourably.'[50] Denison also embarked on a rhetorical rehabilitation of the word 'work' itself, insisting that cross-class respect could flourish only when the dignity of all labour was properly recognized. The time when a woman's claim to social superiority was that she did no physical work was long past, she declared, for in a world 'where every necessity, comfort, and luxury denotes somebody's work, it is high time we got over a lot of silly nonsense in connection with "working people." We should all be working people.'[51] The naïveté of such expressions did not cancel their moral force. On 13 February 1910 she called explicitly for the end of class distinctions: 'We are obsessed with the idea that to be a clerk in a bank or to slave in a great department store is more honorable and respectable than to be a mechanic or a farmer. The great labour movement of the world ... is breaking down these silly notions, and the dignity of labour will increase as the make-believe character of all other dignities is exposed.' In telling stories that emphasized the dignity of labour and in outlining ways that women from all social ranks could make common cause, Denison hoped to inspire her readers to cross-class unity and political action. As she liked to assert, 'There is neither race, color, caste or creed in woman's suffrage.'[52]

BECAUSE DENISON SAW her purpose to be that of creating, through the printed word, a real and imagined community of heroic activists, she found inspiration – and hoped to share it – in stories of solidarity and sisterhood, and she reported many examples of selfless devotion to the cause. She praised Barbara Leigh-Smith Bodichon, renowned British artist and feminist, co-founder of Girton College, Cambridge, and an activist for the reform of marriage laws, as a woman who 'sacrificed her ambition for the sake of other women';[53] she commended Augusta Stowe-Gullen for having 'given her very self' for the suffrage cause;[54] and she paid tribute, at her death, to Florence Nightingale for pursuing noble work despite considerable opposition.[55] Denison's highest ideal was a 'woman willing to give her freedom or her life for the sake of principle.'[56] The Christian underpinning to metaphors of sacrifice and self-giving emphasized her belief in the holiness of the cause. Affirmations of sisterhood filled her column, as when she was able to report the contributions of American activists to the Canadian cause,[57] acknowledge the dedication of suffrage workers at the Toronto office,[58] or commend the contributions of other journalists, praising Kit Coleman, for example, for publicizing women's unfair treatment under Canadian laws.[59] She seems not to have missed an opportunity to rally suffrage fighters and to report the ever-increasing surge towards victory, with many of her columns structured as a series of brief updates emphasizing the political gains and growing strength of the movement, often punctuated with assertions of exhilaration: 'Never in the history of the movement has there been so much activity as at the present time.'[60] Always she worked to summon the shared emotion and principled commitment that would unite women and men in a noble struggle.

Denison also sought to inform women of local issues around which they could organize. A scandalous Ontario court case that awakened her indignation involved Annie Robinson, a rural woman sentenced to death for smothering two babies born to her daughters, both of whom had been sexually abused by their father over many years. This story, featuring a violent and sexually depraved man and multiple female victims, galvanized feminist journalists across Ontario, a number of whom felt, as did Denison, that although Mrs Robinson was undoubtedly guilty of two capital offences, her situation as the helpless wife of a brutal man cried out for leniency.[61] Over a number of weeks, Denison reported the agitation surrounding the case in an attempt to convince readers of the need for action. She also praised Coleman's contribution to the cause, stating that she had 'told the story with such touching pathos last week that anyone reading her account would be willing to join a general uprising of protest should an attempt be made to carry out the sentence of hanging.'[62]

A week later Denison reported on the 'white heat of indignant protest' felt by those who had followed the case, urging readers to sign a petition for pardon being organized by the Canadian Suffrage Association in coordination with other provincial women's organizations. She related how a very elderly lady had come to sign, 'saying with tears in her eyes as she wrote her name: "Ontario could never wipe out the disgrace if this woman is allowed to hang."'[63] A month later Denison expressed impatience; despite a province-wide outcry, pardon had not yet been granted: 'If the voice of the whole people of Ontario has been ignored by the powers that be, what is the use of anybody doing anything?'[64] Ultimately, she had the satisfaction of learning that the popular agitation she had helped to nurture had played a role in the commuting of Mrs Robinson's sentence of death to imprisonment for ten years.

As was appropriate to her anti-elitist message and stirring calls to arms, Denison's style was direct and personal, emphasizing lived experience, practical knowledge, and emotional commitment. Personal integrity became the standard to which she held the many feminist writers and speakers on whom she reported in the column. Speaking well was not enough: she looked for total personal commitment. Commenting on the rhetorical abilities of her heroine Emmeline Pankhurst, Denison made clear her preference for an unstudied manner that expressed experience rather than trained skills: 'Why does Mrs. Pankhurst outclass women and men who have had ten times the educational advantages she has had?'[65] she asked in one column. Her answer was Pankhurst's embodiment of purposeful suffering: 'Simply because she has for the background of her speech her own experiences; she has lived the story she tells, while most speakers tell you what someone else has written.'[66] A powerful style, Denison implied, was inseparable from bodily and emotional authenticity, from words that articulated lived feeling. She was fascinated to discover, in conversation with Pankhurst, that many of the suffrage speakers in England were entirely untrained. Pankhurst had told her that in talking about their work and their suffering to an audience, 'they would get so in earnest that before they realized it, they had made a very acceptable and often a very eloquent speech.'[67] Just over a year later, Denison reported on the sensation being caused by Sylvia Pankhurst, Emmeline's daughter, and once again she emphasized a rhetoric of lived experience, asking her audience to imagine 'a little slip of a girl, only twenty and looking far younger, entertaining to the point of wild enthusiasm a Carnegie Hall audience ... To have suffered, to have been imprisoned, for a cause, is indeed to have made that cause a very part of one, and when to this is added extraordinary ability, there is a force felt by all.'[68]

On another occasion, in contrast, Denison was disappointed to attend a learned talk on ancient architecture at which the woman speaker failed to reveal her experience, relying on a practised manner and carefully trained voice to deliver a polished lecture. Denison would have preferred, she told readers, the woman's own story:

> Mrs. Cutter would not need to say where she was trained, for the Emerson School of Expression was in her pronunciation and gestures and voice tones. The lecture was carefully prepared, and a verbatim report would read smoothly and its similes would leave one rested, but someday Mrs. Cutter will get a modern inspiration, a social betterment idea, perhaps, and then she will forget her training, forget her gracefully posed hands, arms and body, forget to carefully pronounce each word, and then we will see some of the real metal [sic] of the woman who supported her child while educating herself. This in itself was a big thing to do, and this is a story Mrs. Cutter could tell in a big way, and her audience would feel grief and joy and ambition as she talked of battles fought and won – her own battles.[69]

Sara Jeannette Duncan would have writhed in detestation over this levelling preference for the woman's story, the note of pathos, over analysis of Greek and Egyptian art. 'The Greeks and the Egyptians were great, but we, too, are great,' declared Denison irreverently. Her romantic elevation of personal suffering in a cause led, in this instance, to a devaluation of intellectual and aesthetic achievement in favour of personal martyrdom.

Ultimately, style – like everything else about the women she admired – acquired a mystical quality in Denison's conception; it came to signify the powerful essence communicated from speaker to listener, a transforming enthusiasm beyond words or actions. In a discussion of two suffrage speakers recently in Toronto – Emmeline Pankhurst and Ethel Snowden – Denison was fascinated by their contrasting rhetorical styles and effects:

> Mrs. Pankhurst had the saddest tone in her voice I have ever heard, brought there by grief, hardship, misunderstanding and cruel misrepresentation,

but through it all not one hint of bitterness – nothing but sweetness and kindness. While our sympathies were all with Mrs. Pankhurst, while all the pathos in our natures was touched, Mrs. Snowden – bright, beautiful, brilliant Mrs. Snowden – came along to cheer us up.

Not less cultured, not less refined, equally logical, more militant in manner if less in method, than her illustrious co-worker, Ethel Snowden made a splendid complement to Emmeline Pankhurst.[70]

Rhetorical power was, for Denison, less a question of word choice, structure, and metaphor than of personal substance, the whole character and emotional force a woman revealed along with her message. It was as much the communication of personality as of message that brought converts to the cause, and thus her own column devoted much of its space to describing people and emotions, summoning the passionate devotion of great female martyrs.

Tributes to activists filled the column. After attending a meeting of the Canadian Suffrage Association, Denison was struck by the dedication of an Englishwoman who 'had bought no new clothes for four years, preferring to devote every penny to the cause.'[71] After encountering another woman who was working to establish a cooperative apartment complex to provide child care for the working poor, Denison celebrated her selfless dedication: 'Here was a woman with the true suffragette spirit – here was a woman consecrated to work for a reform so badly needed, and willing to give her last speck of vitality and energy.'[72] Learning of Elizabeth Fry's work in prison reform, she rhapsodized, 'Generations will come and go, nations will rise, grow old and die, kings and rulers will be forgotten, but as long as love kisses the white lips of pain, will men remember the name of Elizabeth Fry – friend of humanity.'[73] She also commented on a biography of Susan B. Anthony that had inspired her anew concerning the self-sacrifice that Anthony had made in service to the cause, exclaiming, 'The story of such an exceptional woman will be read with moistened eyes by generations yet unborn.'[74] Promoting a fund to build a commemorative bust of the late Dr Emily Stowe, she eulogized Stowe's public-spiritedness and wrote of her own connection: 'I had the privilege and honour of being Dr. Stowe's friend. I held her hand when she died and stood beside her coffin while hundreds came to pay their tribute or respect.'[75] These fervent testimonials gave personal evidence of the women's cause on many different fronts and were clearly intended to provide models of dedication for the column's readers.

In line with this emphasis on the personal, Denison's column frequently contained extended autobiographical reflections. When reporting on the reception given to Pankhurst in New York City, where 'Beautiful girls crushed to touch her hand' and 'Old women ... hailed her as a great savior,'[76] Denison was prompted to recount small sacrifices and triumphs that she too had known in the service of the cause and to record the awe and humility that overwhelmed her in the presence of the leader:

> I have been told I would lose friends, turn my husband against me, and leave my child homeless on the street, if I persisted in fighting for woman's suffrage. Instead, I have made friends of women and men whose names are honored the wide world over and whom I would never have had an opportunity to meet had I not been fighting for woman's suffrage. As for my husband, he is willing always to make up the deficit on what the conservative members of my family call 'fool fads,' and my son paid his last five dollars to have a VOTES FOR WOMEN advertisement put in the Jarvis Collegiate official paper. But after seeing and hearing Mrs. Pankhurst, after shaking her hand and giving her Canada's greetings before that great audience in Carnegie Hall last Monday night, I felt that I had never done anything for suffrage, I felt that undeserved honours were heaped upon me when she thanked me. I have had a long schooling in self-control, I know something of values, I do not cry when Desdemona is killed by Othello, nor do I shout when a Toronto man wins the Marathon, but I cried and shouted when Mrs. Pankhurst told her story. I have seen audiences thrilled, but never thrilled as Mrs. Pankhurst thrilled that vast audience, where thousands had been turned away.[77]

The series of parallel clauses expresses the excitement and pleasure that Denison associated with the mass gathering. She was proud to count herself an activist alongside other noble women and also humbled by the superior dedication and powers of a 'savior' such as Pankhurst.

On another occasion, she used a personal anecdote to emphasize how suffrage activism had overtaken her earlier commitment to creative writing:

> Why have I called this department Under the Pines? Well, I will tell you. I wrote a story of a beautiful Indian girl – who had been deceived by a white man – and I called it 'Under the Pines' because it was under four beautiful pines back near my log shanty in the Highlands of Ontario

where I wrote it. I would much rather write Indian romances than suffrage news, but the call came. The story is not of an Indian girl being deceived by a white man, but of white women being deceived and of white men being deceived; and of wrongs that can only be righted by an enfranchised womanhood. So I will write suffrage news and tell what women are doing till Ontario gives her women the vote, and then I will go back under the pines and write more Indian stories or, better still, I will write the history of how women got the vote in Ontario.[78]

The 'call' to activism, she affirmed, had transformed her life, and the hope she expressed throughout her column was that other women would be similarly changed. Always emphasizing the urgency and excitement of suffrage work, she called on her sisters not to be left behind by the great movement of emancipation. 'Holidays are here,' she wrote at the start of the summer season, when Torontonians began to leave the city for their cottages, 'but there is no time for holidays in a movement that has reached such a critical point in its history that victory is staring us in the face.'[79] She was always enthusiastic in welcoming converts to the struggle (she was pleased when Margaret E. Sangster became 'an ardent suffragist')[80] and forthright in chastizing the apathetic and the arrogant. Announcing herself irritated by 'the excuses some women will make for not working even after they admit themselves to be ardent suffragists,' and appalled at the complacency of many Ontario women, she hoped fervently, 'Surely Ontario women as a whole are anxious to lead in this great international movement,'[81] and 'Surely the decade will not see Canada a laggard in this race.'[82] She quoted the words of Pankhurst in order 'to enthuse us to undertake extra responsibility and work for a cause that is evolving martyrs in the old land.'[83]

Indeed, though, the situation in Canada was different from that in Great Britain, where mass rallies, petitions, and demonstrations had given consistent evidence of British women's commitment. In Canada, as Cleverdon has noted, suffragists had to deal with 'the apathy, if not outright hostility,'[84] of other women. Even at the height of the campaign, 'suffrage forces constituted but a small minority of Canadian women.'[85] Bacchi avers, 'At its height in 1914, the movement probably had a total membership of ten thousand men and women, only 0.2 per cent of the adult population at that time.'[86] A front-page editorial by the Toronto *World* on 23 October 1909 endorsed the cause but warned suffrage workers that one of their major obstacles was the indifference of those on whose behalf they were campaigning. Denison's wistful glance at the martyrs in the 'old land' betrays her awareness of the problem.

In the midst of enthusiastic reports of suffrage triumphs across the globe and of the international network of women carrying them through, then, Denison frequently sounded a note of concern that so few Canadian agitators of equal stature and dedication had yet emerged. She raised the question 'with all this energy and work and self-sacrifice on the part of our English sisters, what are we in Canada doing? This war is ours just as it is theirs.'[87] She referred to the brutal backlash against the suffragettes in England and reflected that the backlash had, after all, produced women such as Pankhurst and Mrs. Snowden: 'I wish something would strike Canada to show that we too have buried metal [sic] awaiting development in our women,' she ruefully concluded.[88] She even ventured to suggest, 'Possibly the worst thing about the movement here is that there is no opposition.'[89] The complacency of Canadian women was a problem greater than the political obstacles in their way, one she hoped to overcome through the infectious force of her own example and by sharing stories to create a common front, for 'Canada should have stories to tell and women to tell them as well as any other country under the sun.'[90]

When, in March of 1910, an Englishwoman named Olivia Smith caused a commotion in the Ontario legislature by protesting the injustice of its laws, Denison gloried in her courage. Smith had stood up in the Legislative Assembly and, before stunned legislators, addressed herself to the lieutenant-governor. 'There is just one thing you have forgotten,' she is reported to have said. 'I object to this Parliament closing without doing justice to women.'[91] Here was another woman who showed up the selfish complacency of Canadians. 'We have no women who are anxious to be martyrs or desirous of sacrificing decorum for unpleasant notoriety,' Denison wrote with a touch of acerbity, 'but when a woman modest, refined, and capable comes amongst us and does what we would do if we had the courage, it is up to us to take her by the hand and say "Sister, well done."'[92] Too often, though, brave women were left to work alone, unrecognized and misunderstood. Denison reported with dismay the conservatism of a number of women attending a Women's Institute conference in Toronto. Some expressed concern that attending the conference might link them to the suffragettes, with whom they dreaded to be associated, and Denison's scorn for their timidity was apparent in her reported reply: 'I assured them that there

were only two "suffragettes" in Canada, and these we had to import
from England. To be a suffragette, you have to abandon self and work
for the emancipation of your sex. I have been trying to attain to this distinction ever since I had the honor and privilege of hearing that master
woman Mrs. Pankhurst, but I am miles down the mountain side yet.'[93]
Furthermore, when she learned in May 1910 that the Hamilton Local
Council of Women had gone on record as opposed to the National
Council of Women resolution for suffrage, Denison was flabbergasted:
'When women cling to the chains that bind them,' she fulminated, 'they
make a sorry picture against the great army of progressive women who
are bound to be free.'[94] Uninterested in the complexities and ambigui-
ties of women's political allegiances and self-identification, she painted
a dramatic picture of a righteous war, with heroes and martyrs on one
side and cowards and collaborators on the other.

Denison wanted nothing less than to inspire a legion whose dedication to the cause would be absolute. Her metaphors were frequently
martial and religious, depicting the suffrage struggle as a holy war
with a venerable roster of prophets, saints, and martyrs. Of the group
of young women closely associated with Pankhurst, Denison noted,
'They are fired with the enthusiasm of the early martyrs and are in this
fight to win or die.'[95] She went so far as to state that the wartime hero-
ics of men paled in comparison to the actions of the suffragettes, who,
in 'fighting and sacrificing,' were 'displaying more heroism than was
ever displayed in any war that was ever waged.'[96] Describing a series
of mass protests by the WSPU, she characterized them as war rallies,
declaring her confidence that the women's forces would prevail: 'Each
of the five great meetings held there has had its distinctive note –
warlike, indignant, expectant, welcoming. The last meeting was a combination of all these, with a louder note than all – the note of triumph,
the confidence of assured victory.'[97] When one of the young militants,
Miss Mackenzie, visited Toronto, Denison recounted the ordeal of her
hunger strike as if describing the spiritual struggles of a religious dev-
otee, a member of a holy order so strict that even to be tempted was to
sin. Ill in her cell while on her hunger strike, Mackenzie had had a jug
of milk brought to sway her: 'The temptation, the terrible temptation,
to sip the soothing, refreshing milk was almost too much for her. She
took up the jug in her hands and then she rose in all her fine heroism,
put it down and was not tempted again. She blamed herself as a coward for even lifting the jug.'[98] The Canadian suffrage movement
needed advocates similarly committed in body and spirit, Denison

wrote: 'We now want workers who will be willing to be devotees, the same as our English sisters.'[99]

The intensity of Denison's response to women such as Miss Mackenzie, her celebration of willing self-sacrifice, and her frequent use of expressions such as martyr, sacrifice, leader, and saviour emphasize the religiosity of her conception of the movement. She concluded her account of Miss MacKenzie's martyrdom by recording an exchange between them: 'I said to her, "But you might have killed yourself." Her face lit up as she said, "What matter – could one die in a better cause?"'[100] For Denison, the suffragettes were Christlike in their willingness to give their lives so that others might be free, and she saw herself as an apostle of the good news. Talking of the spread of militancy to the United States, she predicted that Canada could not for long remain unaffected, and her reference to 'the spirit' of the struggle suggests not only an ideological or political movement but also a spiritual awakening that would spread from nation to nation, just as the gospel of Christ was spread by the early Christians: 'The spirit is spreading, and there is no telling how soon Canada will join her spectacular sisters of England and the United States and do something to rouse our friends in the park.'[101] With orthodox Christianity on the wane, as she imagined, Denison saw movements for social uplift, of which suffrage was, for her, the most important, as the natural heir of humankind's spiritual hunger and longing for right. The suffrage movement was not concerned only with women's rights but also with truth, love, and social righteousness, and her language was frequently near-apocalyptic in discussing its historical implications. Suffrage was 'a human movement, a great race war, where the cosmic urge for justice is asserting itself in all men and women of all nations. It is the greater part of the Great Spirit of the age fighting for a real democracy, a real brotherhood.'[102] Her intensely utopian and spiritual language demonstrated her expectation that woman suffrage would renew the world.

Devotion to the English suffragettes (she admitted once that she was 'apt to be a hero worshipper')[103] led Denison to defend the justice and effectiveness of militant tactics on numerous occasions. On one occasion she expressed her belief that the suffragettes had been 'driven' to extremes by the violent suppression of their peaceful protests by authorities. On another occasion, she warned her readers that English news reports of militant violence were distorted by bias and that the activists were suffering under police brutality: 'The cablegrams about the militant doings must always be taken with a grain of salt ... It is clear that it was the police who handled the women with extraordinary roughness and brutality.'[104] Pointing to the agitation preceding the Reform Acts of 1832 and 1867, she reminded her readers that 'militant methods have been used to clear the way for every step that British liberty has taken,'[105] and ultimately she dwelt on the success of the suffragettes to contradict those who believed their strategies lost them support. 'If money talks,' she exulted on one occasion, 'the growing revenue of the W.S.P.U. speaks clearly on the much-discussed question whether the militant methods are repelling public sympathy.'[106] A year later she reported with satisfaction, 'The Woman's Social and Political Union stands today before the world as an active factor in the practical politics of England, and few are now apologizing for their methods or their tactics.'[107] Ultimately, she predicted, no opposition could stand against the militants' boldness, self-sacrifice, and righteousness, as new soldiers were daily being recruited to the cause as a result of the repression they experienced. 'The injustice of our laws makes me strong to fight in this battle of women's emancipation,' one woman reportedly told Denison,[108] and Sylvia Pankhurst was quoted as saying, 'I would gladly let a chariot run over my neck if it would help the cause of woman's suffrage.'[109] Exhilarated by the fervour that led privileged women to embrace deprivation and incarceration, Denison used her column to counter the disapproval for militancy issuing from other Canadian newspaper sources.

The spiritual intensity of her devotion to the cause left no room for any other faith, and her language makes it clear that woman suffrage became the future salvation to which Denison looked forward with longing. Associating the Christian church with repression, fear, and hypocrisy, she posited woman power as the true Messiah inaugurating new life, freedom, and abundance, even referring at one point to the 'gospel of sisterhood.'[110] In that longed-for day of suffrage fulfilment, there would be a new heaven and a new earth, and she caught a glimpse of what the transformation would bring when she reported, 'In Colorado, where women vote, there is a town with a golden name and golden morals, Eldorado, where for three years there has not been a single arrest nor a person in jail.'[111] Dismissing the established church, she applauded instead all 'signs and portents of a new renaissance of the social Christ' and called for new evangelists of industrial, social, and political freedom.[112] Suffrage was, as she stressed, a 'holy war'[113] for which the suffragettes and others had made themselves 'martyrs,'[114] suffering in prison in the manner of the apostle Paul.

Eulogizing the late Victor Gilpin, a renegade Methodist minister forced to leave the church because of his unorthodox views, Denison imagined him a dishonoured prophet of a higher truth than the church could tolerate. 'Had he been less progressive,' she commented, 'he would have remained in the Methodist Church.'[115] Suffrage enthusiasm was for her a kind of Holy Spirit manifestation, convicting adherents and making them into one body united in ardour for a common cause – she frequently spoke of how 'the spirit was spreading'[116] – while heaven, she imagined, was composed of souls that vibrated strongly in sympathy with a mighty cause of collective liberation. She imagined, for example, her excommunicated Methodist pastor being welcomed 'across the divide' by 'Emerson, Whitman, Thoreau and Ingersoll.'[117] Denison's summing-up of the woman's movement was on one occasion even more than ordinarily fervent, describing the movement as a social embodiment of the 'Great Spirit,' her impersonal god of justice and right: 'One idea that we have to get out of our heads is that it is an exclusive women's movement. It is a human movement, a great race war, where the cosmic urge for justice is asserting itself in all men and women of all nations.'[118]

Denison's commitment to the coming revolution led her to criticize those who appeared to act in bad faith and, increasingly, to proclaim forthrightly her heterodox beliefs. She was blunt in assessing the timidity of the National Council of Women, noting that the 'policy of this organization seems to be to endorse measures after it is quite sure it is the popular thing to do.'[119] She scorned those who stayed quiet for fear of social disapproval: 'There are a whole lot of people who are "scared stiff" over the other fellow's opinion,' she wrote from bitter experience, 'It is easy to conform: it is easy to avoid criticism: just be nothing, do nothing, say nothing: but there will be whole worlds that you will never enter and exquisite joys that you will never know the meaning of.'[120] Perhaps her greatest scorn was reserved for Christian belief about God, sin, judgment, and salvation, which she held responsible for most of the misery in the world: 'When people believed in a literal hell fire, it was easy for them to act the part of devils,' she quipped.[121] But such superstitions were quickly dying out, she asserted, to be replaced by scientific truth and a more appropriately modern conception of God as a benevolent cosmic force alive in every individual. 'Education based on truth as it is known, mixed with a reasonable amount of common sense, is the salvation that saves. Emerson's self-reliance has been a greater blessing than the doctrine of the

Vicarious Atonement, and no blood has been shed to establish its truthfulness.'[122] Only the true religion of woman suffrage, justice, and democracy could 'bring the long lost Eden back again to this twisted old world.'[123]

Flora MacDonald Denison's own refusal to avoid criticism, her refusal to 'be nothing, do nothing, say nothing,' led to a position of increased leadership in the Canadian Suffrage Association and then, ultimately, to a break with the movement she had helped to build and inspire. Having supported suffrage with her pen, actions, and finances for the crucial years from 1906 to 1914 she found herself at odds with the majority of more conservative members on such issues as religious orthodoxy, birth control, and the militant tactics of the WSPU.[124] In 1914 she resigned as leader of the Canadian Suffrage Association, and although she worked in New York as part of the state suffrage campaign in 1916, she largely turned her attention to other issues thereafter, including theosophy; the Whitmanite Fellowship, which she helped to found; socialism; spiritualism; anti-war propaganda (publishing a pamphlet called *War and Women*); and her nature retreat at Bon Echo. Here she became, in the words of Michèle Lacombe, an 'ecofeminist' offering visitors 'an accessible wilderness interlude compensating for the material, ideological and other pollutants'[125] in the city. She continued to write, publishing a number of issues of *The Sunset of Bon Echo*, a newsletter founded in 1916 and dedicated to exploring the ideas of Walt Whitman, the restorative effects of outdoor life, and the reality of spirit communication. By 1918, when Canadian women finally won the federal vote, Denison's suffrage enthusiasm seemed spent, and she wrote bitterly during the war of Emmeline Pankhurst's support for the Allied cause.[126] Focused as she was on rejecting orthodoxy and embracing new ideas, especially ideas concerning spirituality and social relations, it is probably not surprising that she lost faith in suffrage just at the time that it ceased to be a visionary cause and became a working reality compromised by practical politics. However, her journalism remains a significant legacy of the movement, demonstrating how one zealous spokesperson for the cause imagined the role of women in a revolutionary world order. Her rhetorical framing of suffrage in spiritual as well as social and political terms enabled her to communicate its urgency and potential in an emotionally compelling way.

6 Nellie McClung and the Rhetoric of the Fair Deal

In the late spring of 1914, newspapers were exclaiming over the exploits of Nellie McClung, forty-year-old prairie author and 'great woman orator.'[1] In May and early June of that year, just a few months before the beginning of the First World War, she was on a speaking tour of her home province that would involve as many as one hundred political addresses to Manitoba audiences large and small. Her goal was to help defeat the provincial Conservative party, which was on record as opposing woman suffrage and other reforms, including temperance legislation, that were dear to her heart. Already a beloved platform speaker and popular novelist, McClung was lionized in the press as 'the apostle of truth and justice in the politics of Manitoba,'[2] with her speeches reported in detail and her magnetic personality celebrated in superlatives. Reporters gave her credit for turning the tide of public opinion against the Conservative government under Premier Rodmond Roblin and paving the way for profound changes in the status of women.

Sometimes called 'the Canadian Joan of Arc'[3] and 'the platform Nemesis of Premier Roblin,'[4] McClung was so feared by opponents that she was even burnt in effigy by members of the Conservative party machine in Brandon, Manitoba.[5] According to a reporter for the Brandon *News*, she was such a persuasive speaker that in every town 'strong attempts were made to keep the people away from her meetings.'[6] Her winning personality and command of descriptive detail, narrative pacing, memorable aphorisms, and rhetorical emphasis all guaranteed that phrases she had coined or popularized (her famous 'fatty degeneration of the conscience'[7] and 'criminal contentment')[8] gained widespread recognition and often entered the public lexicon.

A year later, in 1915, McClung published a version of her speeches as *In Times Like These* (1915), a collection of essays that she dedicated to 'men and women everywhere who love a fair deal, and are willing to give it to everyone, even women.'[9] Confident, forthright, and humane, yet also piquant and at times audacious, the essays demonstrate McClung's ability to frame an argument in a memorable and decisive manner and to make divisive, complex issues clear and urgent. At once sermon and political argument, *In Times Like These* has been called by Veronica Strong-Boag 'a classic formulation of the feminist position,[10] and by Carol Hancock 'McClung's most consistently witty and politically combative written work,' in which 'she pinned the oppressive domination of women to the wall for all to see.'[11] However, with a few exceptions,[12] there has been little detailed rhetorical analysis of the published essays and almost no analysis, apart from Mary Hallett and Marilyn Davis's biography,[13] of her tactics as a public speaker. McClung's speeches and published essays demonstrate her ability to craft a revolutionary program of emancipation from the restrictive domestic sphere established in conservative discourse.

It is important to state from the outset that McClung was working within a well-established tradition of feminist rhetoric and that there was nothing particularly original in the substance of her arguments. As a number of scholars, including Strong-Boag,[14] Warne,[15] and Dean,[16] have demonstrated, she was effective in challenging conventional ideas from within, using conservative clichés about women's 'nature' – as mothers and as housekeepers – to call for a greatly expanded social role for them as the nation's housekeepers and as mothers of the race. This trail had been blazed by a generation of activists before her. The temperance advocate Letitia Youmans had used the phrase 'home defence' in the 1870s to link domesticity with feminist activism,[17] and many of McClung's contemporaries in the suffrage campaign, including Flora MacDonald Denison, as we have seen, Francis Marion Beynon, Lillian Beynon Thomas, and E. Cora Hind, associated women's housekeeping and mothering roles with their ability to 'clean up' the nation, 'purify' politics, and 'mother' the race – challenges that the men, they pointed out, had so far failed to meet. It is worth considering, then, the particular power of McClung's language. What made *In Times Like These* such a landmark publication? How was it that, at a time of unprecedented women's activism in Canada, Nellie McClung became '*the* woman in Canadian politics'?[18]

Nellie L. McClung.

The question cannot be definitively answered, but one element that made her writing and speeches so consistently effective was the unequalled adroitness with which she deployed familiar turns of phrase and lines of attack. She had a remarkable ability to revitalize well-known figures of speech, associations, and analogies, appealing to what was familiar in social discourse while creating fresh humour or relevance through a shift in emphasis, a redefinition, or a new perspective. Her particular ability to puncture clichés made her a formidable critic and enabled her to manipulate the familiar language of anti-suffrage rhetoric, transforming standard images and aphorisms to make their progressive or subversive meanings seem obvious and undeniable. She could turn anti-feminist clichés into feminist aphorisms with such ease that the feminist message seemed always to have resided within the anti-feminist assertion. Newspaper reports of her 1914 speeches, as well as the text of *In Times Like These*, reveal how McClung employed parody, aphorisms, and witty rebuttal to revivify suffrage rhetoric.

BORN IN 1873 IN GREY COUNTY, Ontario, Nellie Letitia Mooney moved with her family to a homestead farm in Manitou, Manitoba, where she grew up longing to do some good in the world and wanting to be, like Charles Dickens, a 'voice for the voiceless.'[19] She would claim that she fell in love with Wesley McClung, a pharmacist (with whom she eventually had a happy marriage and five children), because she was so taken by his mother, a feminist and temperance activist whose social commitment and fearlessness called forth Nellie's admiration.[20] After moving to Winnipeg with Wes in 1911, McClung herself became politically active, galvanized by the wretchedness she observed in the city's slums and sweated industries and by the apathy of the premier, Sir Rodmond Roblin, who seemed not to care about the workers' suffering and who informed McClung, when she and other activists tried to interest him in factory reform, that women had no business involving themselves with such matters. Convinced that only the power of the ballot would help them to effect the changes they believed necessary, McClung and others began to campaign for woman suffrage, using the coming provincial election as their springboard.

By the late spring of 1914, McClung was engaged in a whirlwind speaking tour that included 'at least a hundred meetings'[21] across Manitoba. 'The great woman orator,'[22] as the newspapers referred to her, was credited with seriously damaging the credibility of Premier

Roblin. Her 'sincerity and fearlessness,' wrote one commentator, 'contributed largely to the success of the drive against Roblinism.'[23] As late as 1935, she was remembered in the Toronto *Mail and Empire* for her role 'in bringing the Roblin government to destruction.'[24] Manitoba papers reported extensively on her enthusiastic receptions, telling how thousands packed auditoriums to hear her speak while hundreds more were turned away: 'The greatest auditorium in Winnipeg is too small for the crowd that would like to hear Mrs. McClung,' reported the Winnipeg *Free Press* just prior to her last election speech, when she participated in a 'monster mass meeting'[25] at the Walker Theatre. According to Hallett and Davis, 'Every [Liberal] candidate was anxious to have her in his riding so that he could make his appeal to the largest possible assembly. People flocked to hear Nellie because they expected to be entertained, and they were not disappointed.'[26]

It is impossible to recapture the experience of hearing McClung speak, and she does not seem to have written detailed drafts of all the speeches, preferring instead to speak from notes or extemporaneously. Fortunately, detailed newspaper reports, many of which quote her verbatim or paraphrase her talks in detail, enable us to reconstruct with some accuracy the qualities of organization, expression, and development that made these speeches so powerful. The reports, preserved in McClung's scrapbooks (now held at the Provincial Archives of British Columbia), reveal the effective combination of humour, anecdotes, aphorisms, irony, emotional appeal, and logic that caused reporters to marvel, and they enable us to see how McClung developed and refined her strategies of persuasion throughout the course of the campaign, polishing and shaping the talks that would become *In Times Like These*.

McClung's involvement in the provincial election in Manitoba is a story in itself. It was rooted in her anger at the Manitoba premier's complicity in the liquor trade and his opposition to woman suffrage. Dependent on the political support of those businessmen who profited from the sale of alcohol, Roblin had, in the past, given lip service to temperance legislation, a popular cause in the early years of the new century, but had made no move to implement it; in addition, he liked to flaunt his preference for chivalrous regard over suffrage rights for women. In January 1914 McClung and other members of the Political Equality League, a social reform organization dedicated to suffrage and factory reform, petitioned Roblin in the Manitoba legislature to make votes for women an election promise. An overconfident Roblin responded that he respected women too much to involve them in the corrupt world of politics. When the Liberals, led by T.C. Norris, made suffrage a campaign platform and pledged to hold a prohibition plebiscite if they were elected, McClung joined them in working to defeat the premier.

To that end, she began to speak out against the corruption of the Conservative government, highlighting its long record of financial scandals and unprincipled deal-making, becoming in the process, according to the Hamilton *Herald*, 'the platform Nemesis of Premier Roblin.'[27] Her strategy was to shadow the premier on the campaign trail: when he spoke in a particular town, McClung spoke there a few days later, ridiculing his arguments and advancing the causes of temperance and democracy. A brilliant mimic from childhood, she delighted audiences by mocking the premier's verbal mannerisms and argumentative tactics. One reporter noted her technique of 'chasing Premier Roblin all over the province, holding meetings close upon his heels, at which the keen shafts of her wit were brought to play upon his public utterances, riddling his somewhat bombastic speeches by her keen satire and polished invective.'[28] The result, reported the Montreal *Herald*, was that all Manitoba 'has been made to laugh at Sir Rodmond Roblin.'[29] Moreover, she won audience respect and sympathy with her personality, wit, and logic. The Killarney *Guide* reported approvingly that 'her ladylike manner on the platform, coupled with a winning personality and a keen and incisive wit, soon had her hearers intensely interested in her arguments.'[30] Although she was never officially a part of the Liberal campaign team and insisted on paying her own travel expenses, defraying costs by charging admission to her talks, she became the most feared opponent of the Conservative machine.

That she could charge admission for a political speech and still turn people away at the door indicates the depth of affection McClung had already secured in her home province. Her first novel, *Sowing Seeds in Danny* (1908), had been an immediate best-seller, rivalled only by L.M. Montgomery's *Anne of Green Gables*, published in the same year. Enthusiastic reviews of the book and of the author established them as sweet, wholesome products of the Canadian West. 'Sound and sweet and wholesome as a big red apple' was the phrase repeatedly cited in connection to *Danny*.[31] Rural simplicity and practical wisdom were the keynotes struck again and again in descriptions of the author as, for example, in the Toronto *Globe* in 1910: a 'happy, contented little woman who writes novels, loves her family, and understands beefsteak frying better than she does Browning.'[32] McClung built on her reputation by publishing an acclaimed sequel in 1910 (*The Second Chance*) and a collection of short stories two years later (*The Black-Creek Stopping House*); she also embarked on a series of recitals of her work, earning high praise in the Kenora *Examiner* for her 'easy, winning manner' and 'expressive sweet face.'[33]

Recitals gradually broadened to include inspirational talks promoting McClung's ideals of social service, temperance, and Christian compassion, often given under the auspices of the WCTU, the Women's Missionary Society, or the Social Service Council. By the time she took to the campaign platform in 1914, she was already, as the *Canadian Thresherman and Farmer* dubbed her, 'a woman for the people and loved by the people,'[34] widely admired for her progressive ideas and powers of expression. As the premier discovered to his chagrin, she was so popular that his attempts to defend himself from her charges backfired, for when he mentioned her name in connection with the attacks, reported the *Globe* in July 1914, 'there was a spontaneous outburst of applause which lasted for a full three minutes, while the Premier was obliged to stand glumly and wait for the storm to subside.'[35]

McClung was an effective orator who used gestures, modulations of voice, and a blend of humour, denunciation, and pathos to engage her audience emotionally and intellectually. The Winnipeg *Free Press* noted her careful balancing of '[d]eeply earnest passages' with 'swift flashes of wit' and summed up the powerful effect of her physical presence: 'The magnetic personality of the speaker, her poise of body, the movement of the arms in bringing out a point, [and] the inflections of the voice were all used toward the achievement of a magnificent address.'[36] The *Free Press* commended McClung's presentation in Stonewall, Manitoba, on 30 June 1914 as 'sparkling, forceful and convincing.'[37] In Neepawa, where over one-third of the town's population turned out to hear her, her talk had 'alternate flashes of satire, humor and pathos.'[38] Her address at Brandon, where she was greeted 'with almost wild applause' by three thousand people in a packed auditorium, was commended for her 'native wit, her effective points, her cutting irony, and her apt stories.'[39] A reporter for a British paper on a visit to Manitoba gave an admiring account of the impression created by McClung's effective tactics: 'Scorching sarcasm (hurled not at people for hatred's sake, or for the sake of any party, but straight at the head of vice and drink and evil and those who protect these), masterful reasoning, vehement condemnation of the liquor interests, exposure of unequal laws on the Statute Books of the Province, all blending perfectly into an unbroken whole, rich with poetic fervour and ringing with fearlessness and righteous wrath, softened at times into pleading earnestness.'[40]

According to the accounts, a typical address during the campaign lasted for about an hour and a half. McClung spoke, rather than read, in a calm, natural manner that led one observer in the Toronto *Daily News* to commend her 'absolute lack of self-consciousness or stage manners.'[41] She must occasionally have been heckled by unruly members of the audience, but the newspapers report predominantly respectful listeners whose main response was laughter and applause. While the content of the speeches varied, one can discern a general structural pattern, a plan designed first to disarm, then to engage and convince, and finally to inspire to action.

Frequently, McClung began with a few humorous remarks, sometimes with a tongue-in-cheek allusion to attacks on her character by Conservative opponents, who often portrayed her as a neglectful mother or unmanageable wife. A reporter for the Winnipeg *Free Press* noted that at the start of a number of meetings in small-town Manitoba she had 'made a decided hit by assuring those who were reputed to be in great solicitude about her children, that she had just telephoned to Winnipeg and had learned that they were all right and in good hands.'[42] At a Brandon meeting, according to the local *Sun*, 'She proudly told her audience that she had a husband and five children and was proud of them, and that she had been married eighteen years and liked her husband more every day.'[43] In response to misrepresentations that she was being paid by the Liberals to defame Premier Roblin, she informed listeners that she had 'declined having one cent of her expenses paid from the campaign fund of the Liberal party'[44] and was freelance in the fight. Setting her audience at ease, she sought to establish herself as trustworthy and unthreatening with these light-hearted comments.

Having warmed up listeners and quashed damaging rumours, she began to address her subject, using homey examples and common-sense logic. Often she began by addressing some of the most common objections to woman suffrage, employing humour and mockery to point out logical inconsistencies in an amusing, memorable manner. 'Men tell us with a fine air of chivalry that women should not be given the vote, because women don't want it, the inference being that women get nothing unless they want it,' she would note incisively, proceeding to play havoc with flabby reasoning by reminding her audience that individual desires were irrelevant to political justice. In fact, 'Women get a lot of things they do not want – the liquor traffic, the lower pay for equal work, and so on,' she reminded her listeners. And she went on to point out that one woman's lack of interest in political matters should not disqualify others: ' Surely you would not want the irresponsible women to set the pace for the rest of us? Surely no irresponsible woman has any right to force her votelessness on us!'[45] Some men said that women must not sully themselves in political life because they were 'angels' and too pure to mix in public affairs. McClung did not think women were angels, she said, but supposing for a minute that they were, wouldn't it be marvellous if a few did get involved in political life, 'for there seemed to be a little scarcity of angels just at present.'[46] Some men claimed to put women on a pedestal in order to worship them, she said, but women themselves preferred to be with their menfolk, and besides, it was embarrassing 'to have to come down from their pedestal and cut wood.'[47] Bursts of laughter demonstrated the audience's approval of McClung's ability to puncture the false claims of chivalry; her humorous responses to anti-suffrage clichés exposed objections to woman suffrage as illogical and exaggerated.

McClung supported her arguments with facts, statistics, and causal reasoning to reinforce her position that public affairs needed the woman's influence. If the hand that rocked the cradle truly ruled the world, she frequently asked, then why were property crimes punished so much more severely than sexual crimes against young girls? She pointed out, for example, that the abduction and sexual abuse of a girl was punishable by five years' imprisonment, while the stealing of a cow was liable to a fourteen-year sentence; such a bald fact enabled McClung to conclude, 'Property has ever been held dearer than flesh and blood when the flesh and blood are women's.'[48] The law was not so chivalrous in regard to women. Was it right that a woman who had worked all her life to support her husband's farm should have no share in the ownership of that farm after her husband's death? Was it right that a mother had sole responsibility for an illegitimate child but could make no claim to legitimate children in the case of divorce? Statistics could be particularly compelling in attacks on social injustice and iniquity. 'One boy out of every fifth family becomes a drunkard to support the legalized liquor traffic,' she informed her audiences, and then asked, 'Have you a boy to spare to keep up the revenue?'[49] McClung collected such statistics to prepare an inevitable-seeming conclusion: 'Eighty thousand young girls are trapped every year into a life of shame through the crime of seduction. Hundreds and thousands of young girls and women are employed in sweated industries, where a living wage is not paid them, while rich men grow richer as a result of their unpaid toil.'[50] Indirect influence was insufficient when the laws were wrong. Women's direct influence was needed, she affirmed, to legislate an end to such cruelty.

Speeches were brought to an end with a charged emotional appeal to traditional ideals of motherhood, chivalry, and endangered innocence. On one occasion, McClung referred to women as the mothers of the race who risked their lives in childbirth, and she exhorted men not to deny them any weapon necessary for their children's defence: 'Have men any right to withhold any weapon whereby a mother can defend her children?'[51] According to the reporter, 'her audience needed no urging, for then and there they unanimously passed a resolution voicing the sentiment of the men present as in favor of and prepared to work side by side with women for the ballot.'[52] A frequent refrain was the following appeal to old-fashioned values: 'I appeal to you men in the name of your manhood that you protect our homes and our children, and I tell you women that if there ever was a time when you should be roused, it is now.'[53] McClung summoned pitiful images for a pathetic appeal, asking male voters on election day, when they were 'alone with [their] God and [their] thoughts,' to imagine 'that long line of 6,000 little boys as sweet and fresh as any of your own going to the bar for the first time' and to see 'that long line of mothers, with eyes reddened with weeping and faces dreary and haggard, waiting in the night for the footsteps of the drunken fathers.'[54] She ended with the prospect of failure intolerable: 'If you ballot against them, I won't know what to think of you.'[55] As journalist Gertrude Richardson described the effect of such rhetoric, 'But when she speaks! It is not easy to do justice to her power.'[56]

When her speech was finished, McClung invited questions from her audience, readying herself to parry sceptical or hostile opponents and to explain the particulars of political platforms, liquor laws, and women's legal status. Here she needed all her wit and ingenuity to persuade the wary and answer challengers capably. At one meeting in Winnipeg a man asked whether, in view of the huge financial resources of the Roblin government, the Liberals stood any chance of victory. McClung's response made a lasting impression on the reporter at the meeting. 'You don't,' she said, 'have to pay men money to do right. It is only necessary to urge them to do right. But it is necessary to pay them to do wrong, and that is why the Roblin government requires for this election campaign a great amount of money, which, nevertheless, may not save them.'[57] A reporter for the Cartwright *Review* also noted her adroit handling of a challenger who sought to overturn her appeal by declaring that the majority of women had voted against local option in a certain district. The description of the exchange suggests something of McClung's formidable quickness on her feet. '"How do you know?" asked Mrs. McClung; "is not the ballot secret?" The interrupter confessed that he did not know. Mrs. McClung followed this up with the query: "If women are not opposed to local option, why are the liquor interests opposed to extending the franchise to women?" And there was silence.'[58] The exercise of wit necessary to respond to questions and objections must have been exhausting at times, but McClung seems always to have been equal to the challenge.

THE REPORTS OF MCCLUNG'S SPEECHES not only demonstrate the native humour, narrative ability, and concise wit that kept people entertained for an hour and a half in a stuffy town hall, but also enable us to observe a first-rate orator in action as she refined her approach and learned how to present her material most effectively and strikingly. Over the course of the election campaign, McClung was trying out various lines of argument, honing her details, and polishing her satirical technique. Observing the changes she made to examples, structure, details, and expression, we can speculate about some of the principles that guided her rhetorical choices.

McClung was gifted with the ability to satirize the platitudes of her opponents, and mimicry was an effective vehicle of ridicule. In the town of Carman it was reported, 'Her good natured mimicries of the premier were especially popular with the crowd.'[59] Yet she seems to have relied on mimicry sparingly, perhaps recognizing the danger of causing offence, and the description of her manner as 'good natured' was a significant part of her appeal. Reliable sources of humour were amusing personal anecdotes, well paced and rich in descriptive detail. The following story in the Winnipeg *Free Press* of McClung's description of the premier's response to suffrage delegates, probably including some mimicry and interspersed with ironic reflections, became a well-known anecdote to which McClung frequently returned:

We asked the government for the vote in order that we might be recognized as citizens, as human beings, as individuals, and you know what our chivalrous premier said? He told us that he did not believe in women's suffrage personally, that he had always been brought up to lift his hat to the ladies, and that he always gave up his seat in street cars to the ladies, etc. That, of course, should help a good deal but it was hardly an answer to our questions. We went there asking for plain, common justice, an old-fashioned, square deal, and in reply to that we got hat-lifting.[60]

This anecdote is approvingly mentioned by a number of writers for different small-town papers as an effective vehicle of satire. Interesting to note is that while Roblin sought to present his position as one of old-fashioned, and by implication unimpeachable, chivalry, McClung was quick to claim the ground of equally 'old-fashioned' justice.

Aphorisms were another rhetorical strength of McClung's; some papers published lists of them from her speeches, and she obviously created them with care and delivered them effectively. When she found an aphoristic assertion that worked well, she used it frequently, often embellishing the anecdote or discussion preceding the aphorism to increase the rhetorical impact. At an address in Gladstone on the campaign trail, McClung gave a pithy summation of women's twofold duty, reported by the paper as follows: 'She said she did not apologize to anyone for daring to be interested in public affairs. Every mother had two duties to her home: one was to train her children to be good citizens of the world and the other was to try and make the world a fit place for her child to live.'[61] McClung used the same formulation in a later speech, in the Walker Theatre in Winnipeg at one of the final meetings before the election. This time she employed an expanded version. A longer narrative buildup created anticipation for her punchy assertion, and the discussion was enriched by satirical humour: 'Perhaps it may seem somewhat strange to some of you to hear a woman speak on political matters. For a long time we have been taught that women and children should be seen but not heard; that it was woman's place to be sweet, just like charity, bearing all things, enduring all things, and believing all things. We have been told that men must work and women must weep – that is if they do it quietly, for loud weeping is called hysteria and is very bad form. I believe women have two duties. One is to make their children fit citizens of the world and the other is to make the world a fit place for their children to live.'[62] In the second version, McClung not only delayed the concluding aphorism to create emphasis but also strengthened the parallelism of her phrasing, repeating 'make … fit' to heighten rhythm and memorability.

In another example, we can see how she came to expand a key assertion about women's role in purifying political life. In one of her talks on 'The New Chivalry,' she argued against the adage that politics were too corrupt for women. 'Men are willing to admit that politics are in such a bad mess that women should not touch it,' she began, 'but when they do so they are also admitting that they have failed to keep politics clean, and I want to tell you that politics never will be clean until women are allowed to give a helping hand in the game of national house-keeping.'[63] There were a number of key themes here that McClung was to expand over the course of her many addresses: that one of men's most common objections to woman suffrage was actually an admission of need; that women sought to enter political life to help men improve it, not to claim privileges; and that women, as tested housekeepers, had a natural gift for cleaning up politics.

In its final form in her *In Times Like These*, McClung's initial assertion was modified to increase its effectiveness. It became, in effect, a central thesis of the sixth chapter. 'Any man who is actively engaged in politics, and declares that politics are too corrupt for women, admits one of two things, either that he is a party to this corruption, or that he is unable to prevent it – and in either case something should be done.'[64] In this version, McClung no longer accepted, as she had done implicitly in her speech, that political affairs were, in fact, corrupt, changing the verb 'admit' to 'declares.' The assertion about politics, she suggested, was a contention to keep women out rather than a statement of truth, enabling her to make the argument that there was nothing 'inherently vicious' in politics. [65] She strengthened her attack by suggesting that any man who used the excuse admitted one of two things, either his own corruption or his own ineffectuality. Two unpalatable admissions, she must have reasoned, were more effective than one. Moreover, she created a rhetorical delay between the claim of corruption in politics and her rejoinder that women should have the opportunity to clean the political house; the rejoinder came, in a much expanded version, some paragraphs later, in a famous sentence beginning, 'Women have cleaned up things since time began.'[66] The delay gave her a chance to elaborate on the various useful implications of the initial compact statement. This example shows how McClung worked to develop and refine the wit, logic, and rhetorical effectiveness of her arguments.

McClung's speeches were carefully structured to appeal to listeners on a variety of levels. Frequently, her examples combined several causal arguments with an emotional invocation of shared values and a stirring ethical justification for action. Speaking to a large audience in West Kildonan under the auspices of the Kildonan Liberal Club, for example, McClung began by evoking well-established arguments linking alcohol consumption with systemic poverty, physical degeneration, and domestic violence in a single pithy reference to the rights of a child to life and opportunity. She ended by demonstrating how commitment to children was the motive for her public campaign, powerfully reinforcing the maternal justification for her action while creating a strong appeal to shared values of child protection and social responsibility. The liquor trade, she asserted, 'strikes at the hearts of children, robbing them of their chance in life. It takes the shoes off their feet and gives them blows instead of caresses, and if any word of mine can save one child from blows or curses I shall feel well repaid for being here.'[67] After clarifying the urgency of the present problem, she used simple language to undermine the policy defences and claims to integrity of the Conservative leader on the issue, pointing out the hypocrisy of his current support for the very legislation his government had failed to uphold. 'Sir Rodmond claimed that the Conservative party had put on the statute books a prohibition act that served as a model for other provinces, and this was true. He omitted, however, to add one little thing – it was never enforced. It was considered too good to live and so they killed it.'[68] And she ended by expressing confidence in the ability of her audience to make political choices based on conscience, predicting that 'the independent Conservative, who is not bought and owned by the government, is the man who will save the country in this election. To him will belong the honor of having made a sacrifice of party for the sake of principle.'[69] With a few words, McClung attacked her opponent, strengthened her own case, bolstered her image, and established goodwill with Conservative audience members.

Perhaps her greatest strength was the projection of her forthright, high-minded character as the 'heroine on the campaign,'[70] a woman of earnestness, kind heart, generosity, and integrity. As one reporter phrased it, her denunciation of Roblin's government 'was done in a way that could hurt the feelings of no one, unless they were unusually thin-skinned.'[71] Another reporter described her attacks on the Roblin government as conducted more 'in pity than in anger or disgust.'[72] On the occasion of speaking in Roblin's home town, she gave a personal invitation to his supporters to criticize or deny anything she said that was wrong, and her candidness and lack of malice showcased her ethical character: 'She explained that she was going to hit the premier pretty hard, and hated to do it in his home town without giving him a chance to reply. In his absence she was giving his supporters every opportunity to speak for him.'[73] Perhaps not surprisingly, no one accepted her invitation.

McClung was often described as someone who made her attacks without malice, as a woman angry at injustice but not prejudiced against any individual, group, or party; this reputation for fairness was a key factor in her ethical appeal. She was well aware that her opponents tried to paint her as an unnatural and disgruntled woman who neglected her children, disliked men, and sought to usurp male power; she was vulnerable if she made any statement that could be interpreted as a blanket condemnation of men or as betraying a desire to reverse a social hierarchy to women's advantage. Sometimes she was even willing to bend truth so as to emphasize her faith in male fairness, as on the occasion when, speaking in Weston, she claimed that 'man was not to blame for women never having had the franchise' because women had only recently begun to ask for their rights in the matter. 'Men, she said, are not opposed to granting the franchise to the opposite sex, and anyone who thought the men of Canada would refuse women the right to vote appraised them lower than she does.'[74]

Yet on another occasion, speaking at Portage la Prairie, she did blame men, asserting that women had stepped out of their proper sphere because men had failed in theirs. It was a variation on a familiar theme – that women were entering public life to defend their homes – but in this case it carried an aggressive edge normally absent from McClung's explanations: 'if the men had defended the home the way they should have done, perhaps the women would have stayed within the four walls. Men had allowed the liquor traffic to invade the home, and women had been forced to go out and fight it!'[75] Although the newspaper reported that this assertion was greeted by 'cheers' and there is no evidence the statement provoked backlash, McClung seems not to have repeated the assertion, probably preferring to target individual and legislative perfidy rather than attack men as a group. As she would write later in In Times Like These, it was always better to make a friend of one's opponent than to defeat him.[76]

In light of her concern not to cause offence, it is interesting to speculate about a humorous comparison that McClung appears not to have developed during the campaign. An undated clipping reports that at one meeting, 'the speaker caused great amusement when she stated that women had as political peers the idiot, the lunatic, the convict and the Indian. The condition of women with regard to enfranchisement was worse than any of these.'[77] It was reported that McClung developed the contrast by noting that convicts, lunatics, and idiots could resume voting when they returned to society – with a sly reference to the release of convicts at election time – while women had no such future hope. Her explanation, which turned misfortune, illness, and criminality into comedy, is noteworthy for its silence about the position of the Indian in the list of legal exclusions. In her writing, McClung was sympathetic on the occasions she addressed Native people and issues, but their situation never aroused her sustained indignation in the way that other cases of disempowerment did. It is not clear, then, whether she originally intended in her speech to articulate a rationale for Native disenfranchisement in order to contrast a justified with an unjustified exclusion. Given the rarity of miscalculation in her speeches, one can only speculate whether the incompleteness of the parallel suggests discomfort on McClung's part, mere forgetfulness, or the assumption that the contrast needed no explanation.

Such speculation is heightened when we consider that McClung employed a similar line of reasoning in an address at Binscarth, this time dropping the reference to Indians altogether. 'The election act debarred idiots, lunatics, and criminals from voting,' she stated on this occasion; 'A woman was even in a worse position than any of these.'[78] The revision may indicate that casual references to idiots ('one who could never have the use of his reason')[79] and lunatics ('one who had temporarily lost the use of his reason')[80] were appropriate in a discussion of the franchise, while Indians made a more complex and rhetorically awkward parallel. Perhaps McClung recognized but did not wish to pursue the similarity between the situation of women and that of Aboriginal people. Or perhaps she considered the Native situation too ambiguous to be placed alongside that of criminals and lunatics. Whatever the reason, Indian (non)voters do not appear again in the surviving newspaper reports, and the entire discussion of the justly disenfranchised was not carried over into *In Times Like These*. Perhaps McClung felt it raised too many discomfiting questions and associations to aid her cause.

Care not to offend was also needed in the question period that she encouraged after her speeches, for here an off-the-cuff statement might easily become cause for regret. On one occasion, after discussing the injustice of existing property laws in Portage la Prairie, McClung was challenged by a man who remarked sceptically that, according to her representation, 'there must be a lot of bad men in the world.' She answered with a decided negative, pointing out that 'the laws were not made for the good men, but for the bad, and that while the average man did not know that such things occurred, it was because the ninety-nine lived above the law, unable to believe the meanness and criminality of the one hundredth.'[81] Here McClung was careful to make clear that her attacks on legal discrimination did not indict all men for gender bias. At another talk a woman noted that the vote of 'ignorant' men should be taken from them and granted to intelligent, responsible women, a suggestion rife with race-based implications about corruptible foreign immigrants who did not understand Canadian laws. Such comparisons between foreign men and disenfranchised white women were often the occasion for racist pronouncements by angry suffragists. Not so McClung. In a statement she was to use repeatedly in other speeches (and that was to find its way into *In Times Like These*), she asserted that she did not want to take away any men's vote, but that she would like 'to take away their ignorance,'[82] expressing her faith both in the men's capacity to learn and in Canada's role in providing a lesson in democracy. Although some commentators did find McClung to be biased against men or offensively extreme in her ideas, she worked hard in her speeches to prevent such perceptions and to promote her public image as fair-minded and optimistic.

Perhaps buoyed by McClung's moral fervour and confidence, many newspapers predicted that the Conservative party under Roblin would be soundly defeated on election day. They must have been surprised when the Conservatives held on to power with a reduced majority. One year later, however, under the cloud of yet another scandal, Roblin was forced to the polls again, and McClung, now living in Alberta, returned to Manitoba to see him defeated. Under the Liberal government, the provincial franchise was granted to women on 28 January 1916. Despite the historical untidiness, the 1914 campaign is the one that has been preserved in public memory as a decisive moment for Canadian politics and for McClung, establishing her on the national and international stages as an invaluable political ally and a formidable opponent. Hallett and Davis state, 'There can be no doubt that in the Manitoba election campaigns Nellie McClung reached the pinnacle of her public career.'[83] Furthermore, amidst the near-constant travel and fatiguing yet exhilarating work, she forged the core arguments of her best volume, *In Times Like These*. The reports of her speeches make possible an exercise in historical reconstruction that provides tantalizing glimpses of her considerable rhetorical powers and political acumen.

MCCLUNG UNDOUBTEDLY HAD unusual abilities as a speaker. Yet as I suggested at the beginning of this chapter, the most important source of her rhetorical power lay not in the originality of her arguments nor in the effectiveness of her delivery, but rather in the unparalleled skill with which she manipulated familiar phrases, images, and metaphors. Using language with which her audience was intimately familiar, she adroitly freshened and reshaped it, revitalizing clichés, redefining overused words, and enlivening standard phrases with her wit, humour, and command of anecdote. This strategy, which is evident in her speeches and particularly so in her essay collection, was brilliant in its simplicity. Throughout *In Times Like These*, she was able to manipulate the words of her opponents with such dexterity that anti-feminist assertions were not only rebutted and decisively undermined but actually transformed and rehabilitated for her own purposes. She was thus able to deprive opponents of their very language by appropriating and recasting their favourite maxims and arguments.

McClung was formidable in argument because of her ability to ridicule platitudes and false sentiment. She frequently warned her listeners against men who praised 'the fair sex,' referring to such men as dealers in 'dope,' and her campaign speeches sought to inoculate against its soporific effects. Speaking in Brandon just before the Manitoba election, McClung evoked the shopworn phrasing of Roblin's chivalrous concern for women to make it ridiculous. Simply by taking the clichéd phrases of gentlemanly regard – references to, for example, respect for womanhood, reverence for purity, and protection for the weak, the sonorous platitudes with which the premier was indelibly associated – and linking them to the depredations of alcoholism, McClung could suggest the hollowness of the premier's vaunted respect for women. By supporting the liquor trade, she asserted, he proved himself no defender of the family or of the sanctity of the home. She began by asking the women in the audience what they thought of the liquor traffic, reminding them that the premier and the minister of education 'had declared it to be a good thing,' and she followed this query with a stinging denunciation of governmental duplicity:

'Speak up, ladies,' said Mrs. McClung. 'Tell us what you think of it. You've had some experience with it. Has it been a friend to you or your children? Has it gladdened your hearts or brightened your homes; has it helped you in the battle of life; has it made your life sweeter and better and more noble for you or any of your family? Come forward and tell us, ladies. Has it respected your womanhood; has it reverenced the purity of your children;

has it protected you from insult and wrong; has it listened to your plead-
ings; has it ever spared the widow's son out of pity for his mother? Well,
then, what do you owe to the liquor traffic, and the government which pro-
tects and defends it? We owe the liquor traffic our unchangeable bitterest
hatred, and for the men, self-styled chivalrous men, who defend this greatest enemy of our home, we can have nothing but scorn.'[84]

McClung's consistent attacks on the premier were so effective because
she not only challenged his policies and leadership but struck at the
very heart of his self-presentation and public image, ridiculing the way
he expressed his ideas, tainting with her satire the characteristic turns
of phrase he employed on the campaign trail. That Roblin would never
agree to a public debate with McClung is not surprising in this regard;
he recognized how disabling her satire was, for it threatened to deprive him of words altogether.

McClung's assault on Roblin's pious language did not prevent her
from making use of metaphors just as well worn and descriptive language just as familiar and sentimental, but her language, in voicing
women's righteous anger on behalf of the innocent and the powerless,
was much more difficult to satirize. Following her denunciation of
Roblin, McClung appropriated the rhetoric of defensive warfare to describe her own and other women's participation in the political sphere.
She spoke of an 'army of women' engaging in a 'great struggle' that
they did not initiate but had no choice but to enter in order to 'defend
their home and their children.'[85] Claiming the high ground of chivalry
for courageous women, she evoked the mythic register of the heroic
epic. Using parallelism and balanced structures to create ringing ca-
dences and emotional impact, she characterized women's involvement
in the election campaign as a noble response to intolerable provocation, an action in an ancient tradition of courageous motherhood that
could be traced back to those rugged prehistoric ancestors who fought
off marauding beasts of prey. The beasts of prey in this case were the
corrupt politicians whose legislative policy was guided by economic
interests, rather than the health of mother's sons. Claiming that she
spoke not for herself but for all women whose families had been
harmed by the liquor trade, McClung delivered the following defence
of the women's crusade, mobilizing her most emotive language:

I feel that I'm speaking for an innumerable army of women whose lives
have been blackened, whose hopes have been defeated, whose homes
have been ruined by the open bar room, and if I seem to speak boldly on

these matters it is because I cannot forget the injury that has been and is being done to the women and children in this province, and I feel that I am speaking for them. Some say a woman should not take part in politics, some say women are invading politics. It is not so. Politics have invaded our sphere. We are acting on the defensive. It is not a new thing for women to defend their home and their children. The cave dwelling women fought the wild beasts that prowled about at night, and though through luxury and ease and the softening effect of civilization some of us may have lost the courage of our grandmothers, still the throb of the old blood is in us yet, and in the great struggle which concerns the happiness of our children, it will not be said of us that we showed the white feather. What do we care for criticism or slander or ridicule from our opponents? We expect it and welcome it. It convinces us that we are doing something and we will not cease from our political activities until the last poll is closed on the 10th of July. We may win, and we may lose, but in either case we must work, and if it is so appointed that we will go down to defeat, let us be found in the last ditch.[86]

By casting women as the heroic defenders of the home against the 'wild beasts' of the liquor interests, McClung severely impaired the effectiveness of the premier's discourse of chivalry. No wonder, as one reporter declared, 'Sir Rodmond would have great pleasure in escorting this modern Joan to the stake, where the Conservative party could be safely depended upon to furnish cheerfully the wood for the burnt offering.'[87] The damage she did to the premier's ability to defend himself and his government's record was immense.

Despite her many attacks on the language of male chivalry, McClung was not ready to discard chivalry as merely an old-fashioned adjunct to prejudice and injustice, though she became famous for her assertion 'Chivalry is like a line of credit. You can get plenty of it when you do not need it.'[88] In 'The New Chivalry,' one of her most popular public talks in the spring of 1914, she gave the term a vigorous redefinition, linking it with such progressive themes as partnership, fairness, and good citizenship. Speaking to the men of the Young Men's Christian Association in Regina, McClung tailored her discussion to the organization she addressed, linking chivalry to Christian social principles and men's civic identity. She began by noting that the YMCA stood now 'for a great many things which could not have been associated with Christianity as our fathers interpreted it forty years ago.'[89] Such change did not mean a falling away but a renewal; Christian institutions were changing for the better as they embraced progressive social ideals and enlightened attitudes towards women. In doing so, they were helping to create the more abundant life that Jesus had heralded. Chivalry too, she asserted, was changing: it no longer needed women's weakness as the condition for generous assistance; modern chivalry involved the understanding that men and women were meant by God to work together for each other's good, and that both partners needed all their strength to fulfil their roles. The conclusion to her speech tied the movement for woman suffrage with a newly emerging progressive Christian masculinity, thus affirming that a changing social order did not mean loss for men; on the contrary, the new chivalry had given men an expanded field of action. '"This, then," said Mrs. McClung, "is the new chivalry. The women are holding out their hands and asking to be taken as partners in the task of making a national home, and their place is just as important in national home making as in the family circle. Men and women were meant to take up the business of life together. It is the Lord's own plan, and you can't beat it."'[90] Whether or not all the men in the audience accepted the radical implications of her call for partnership, the reporter noted that the course of McClung's address was 'constantly interrupted by vigorous applause.'[91] On another occasion she neatly reversed the accepted definition of chivalry as the code of brave men and fair women, claiming, 'I point to a better day, which will reverse the old order, a day of brave women and fair men.'[92]

In her role as a platform speaker and social leader, McClung had taken as one of her tasks the close scrutiny of social discourse in the cause of justice. In her published essays she made that mission explicit, opening *In Times Like These* with a statement about the need to resist conventional thinking in order to overcome indifference and spiritual sloth. 'People like not only to travel the easy way, but to think along the beaten path,' she warned, 'which is so safe and comfortable, where the thoughts have been worked over so often that the very words are ready made, and come easily.'[93] Ready-made words, she suggested in a formulation George Orwell would have approved, were a form of intellectual capitulation, of refusal to think clearly. In a demonstration of how she intended to unsettle conventional thinking, McClung attacked the spirit of resignation signified in the clause 'Thy will be done.' The expression, from the opening lines of the Lord's Prayer, had been misused and misrepresented in order to suggest that limitation, pain, and injustice were aspects of God's will to be endured rather than resisted. Such was, McClung asserted, a misconception of God. People once accepted plague and disease as God's will, 'resigned when they should have been cleaning up'[94] and ascribing to God what was due to unsanitary conditions. But as the Scriptures made clear, 'It is never God's will that any should perish!'[95] McClung then proposed an activist reinterpretation of Christian submission:

> 'Thy will be done!' should ever be the prayer of our hearts, but it does not let us out of any responsibility. It is not a weak acceptance of misfortune, or sickness, or injustice or wrong, for these things are not God's will.
>
> 'Thy will be done' is a call to fight – to fight for better conditions, for moral and physical health, for sweeter manners, cleaner laws, for a fair chance for everyone, even women![96]

This adroit redefinition fulfilled a number of aims. Most fundamentally, it proved McClung's ability to balance the spiritual and social dimensions of her subject. She demonstrated her serious allegiance to the Christian faith, rebutting conservative objections to her suffrage activism while asserting her own biblically faithful Christian commitment and piety. Just as importantly, though, in deflecting a standard criticism of woman's rights agitation as ungodly, she transformed a phrase associated with religious resignation into a powerful and irreproachable rallying cry for her cause. This manoeuvre, which McClung accomplished with such ease, is a hallmark of her exuberant challenge to outworn thinking and social complacency. She heightened the resonance of familiar phrases and well-known ideas by redefining and thus revitalizing orthodox imagery, allusions, and metaphors.

In another example, astute redefinition revealed the subtlety of McClung's thought and the radicalism of her social vision. Describing the impact of the First World War, which had brought devastation and despair to so many nations, she found reason for thankfulness in the clarity with which the conflict had revealed the failure of civilization and the need to rebuild nations on a Christian basis:

> In the first days of panic, pessimism broke out among us, and we cried in our despair that our civilization had failed, that Christianity had broken down, and that God had forgotten the world. It seemed like it at first. But now a wiser and better vision has come to us, and we know that Christianity has not failed, for it is not fair to impute failure to something which has never been tried. Civilization has failed. Art, music, and culture have failed, and we know now that underneath the thin veneer of civilization,

unregenerate man is still a savage; and we see now, what some have never seen before, that unless a civilization is built upon love, and mutual trust, it must always end in disaster, such as this. Up to August fourth, we often said that war was impossible between Christian nations. We still say so, but we know more now than we did then. We know now that there are no Christian nations.[97]

Examining the oft-repeated assertion of Christianity's failure enabled McClung to articulate, in a statement of compelling conviction and clarity, how nations had instead failed Christianity, which remained vital. Once again, the adroitness of her refashioning of familiar assertions underpinned a memorable and moving statement of hope at a time of crisis.

Charity, too, was a word McClung worked to revitalize. Although charity lay at the heart of Christian doctrine, the word had been so layered over with convention as to have lost its meaning; it had come to refer to a social custom, a show of respectability that covered over, and even made possible, a profound social irresponsibility. In the following description, McClung's emphasis on the superficiality of women's and men's customary charities reveals, through ironic contrast, how such false charity is inseparable from a system of economic and moral injustice. She begins by listing four exemplary female occupations that have led women to contemplate the underlying causes of social conditions. The first of these is 'embroidering altar cloths,' and although church work is not mentioned in the rest of the discussion, it is likely that McClung chose this as her first example precisely to suggest the connection between the degeneration of the word 'charity' from the meaning the apostle Paul had given it and the necessity for a religiously inspired reawakening of social conscience:

Custom and conventionality recommend many and varied occupations for women, social functions intermixed with kindly deeds of charity, embroidering altar cloths, making strong and durable garments for the poor, visiting the sick, comforting the sad, all of which women have faithfully done, but while they have been doing these things, they have been wondering about the underlying causes of poverty, sadness and sin. They notice that when the unemployed are fed on Christmas day, they are just as hungry as ever on December the twenty-sixth, or at least on December the twenty-seventh; they have been led to inquire into the causes for little children being left in the care of the state, and they find that in over half of the cases, the liquor traffic has contributed to the poverty and unworthiness of the parents. The state which licenses the traffic steps in and takes care, or tries to, of the victims; the rich brewer whose business it is to encourage drinking, is usually the largest giver to the work of the Children's Aid Society, and is often extolled for his lavish generosity: and sometimes when women think about these things they are struck by the absurdity of a system which allows one man or a body of men to rob a child of his father's love and care all year, and then gives him a stuffed dog and a little red sleigh at Christmas and calls it charity![98]

This illustration of the ironic interconnectedness of conventional charity and social corruption leads to a much longer discussion of 'root causes' that becomes the focal point of McClung's call for a radical social responsibility. In it she develops vivid anecdotes and memorable analogies to illustrate her point that real charity must address the sources of suffering and injustice. A charity that 'merely smoothes things over'[99] is like the kindly gentleman who places a sick dog in the cool of the shade cast by his carriage before driving away, satisfied with his own benevolence. '"Lie there, my poor fellow!" he said. "Lie there, in the cool shade, where the sun's rays may not smite you!" Then he got into his carriage and drove away.'[100] This analogy, adapted from public speeches because it always evoked appreciative chuckles, buttresses McClung's central discussion of how a responsible society must develop durable forms of charitable intervention.

Another analogy about root causes became one of her most effective redefinitions of women's social role; in the analogy, a surface charity unable to address causes is like a woman forbidden by her husband to clean her dirty house. In this witty and memorable parable, a woman is brought to a new house by her husband, but warned by him that she must not attempt to clean it: 'This house to which I am bringing you to live is very dirty and unsanitary, but I will not allow you – the dear wife whom I have sworn to protect – to touch it. It is too dirty for your precious little white hands! You must stay upstairs, dear. Of course the odor from below may come up to you, but use your smelling salts and think no evil. I do not hope to ever be able to clean it up, but certainly you must never think of trying.'[101] The application of this delightfully ludicrous narrative is clear: with false chivalry, men forbid women to attemp to clean up the mess of the world, yet the men themselves can do nothing to prevent the 'odor from below,' the degradation and corruption of the world, from affecting the women's lives. What true-hearted woman could accept such a living situation? There could be no pleasure in living amidst a rankness and disorder that one had no power to combat. The 'odor from below' would be made worse for the woman by the knowledge that she might eradicate it with her own cleaning energies but is forbidden to do so. With such pithy and humorous analogies, McClung makes clear how unfair it is for women to be encouraged to care for the sick and the distressed but not to seek to eradicate the disease and poverty that cause sickness and despair: 'If women would only be content to snip away at the symptoms of poverty and distress ... they would be much commended for their kindness of heart; but when they begin to inquire into causes, they find themselves in the sacred realm of politics where prejudice says no women must enter.'[102]

Women have no choice but to enter politics, McClung makes clear, for all women and all families are affected by public affairs, all homes threatened by the existence of unjust laws, infectious disease, alcohol, prostitution, and crime. In one of her boldest and most memorable redefinitions, McClung recasts the meaning of housekeeping so that it encompasses the whole territory, domestic and public, in which a mother's sons and daughters are likely to venture. Concluding her parable, she quotes the response of the woman brought by her husband to the unsanitary home:

Do you think any woman would stand for that? She would say: 'John, you are all right in your way, but there are some places where your brain skids. Perhaps you had better stay downtown today for lunch. But on your way down please call at the grocer's, and send me a scrubbing brush and a package of Dutch Cleanser, and some chloride of lime, and now hurry.' Women have cleaned up things since time began; and if women ever get into politics there will be a cleaning-out of pigeon-holes and forgotten corners, on which the dust of years has fallen, and the sound of the political carpet-beater will be heard in the land.[103]

In this brilliant formulation, McClung ensured that references to home and clean-up could no longer be separated from politics, that the imagery of the domestic and of women's sphere had been decisively, perhaps even irrevocably, expanded. The 'sound of the political carpet-beater' would be associated not only with women's struggle for the suffrage but with any attempt by anti-suffragists to evoke the traditional womanly sphere.

The reference to women 'embroidering altar cloths' in the conventional definition of charity, above, is expanded in a later chapter of *In Times Like These* entitled 'Women and the Church,' another chapter in which reformulation of traditional associations underpins an argument for radical change. In earlier chapters, McClung's Christianity is explicit but undeveloped. Bible stories form a significant number of her examples, and references to God and Jesus Christ indicate the broad theological framework within which her thinking had developed. McClung did not doubt that social reform was a Christian duty as much as a civic responsibility. However, in this chapter she focuses in a much more pointed way on the church as an institution, calling for a radical redefinition of the relationship between women and the church family. As in her other essays, the cause of her ire was dishonest language and tired prejudice: she attacked church leaders' cant about feminine service and self-sacrifice, which had led to passivity about women's social situation and resistance to change within the church. The traditional position of the church towards women reflected, she believed, an unthinking prejudice, an attitude of 'mild contempt,'[104] that had no basis in Scripture; the prejudice was yet another example of human beings' tendency to 'think along the beaten path,' with unjust – and, in this case, spiritually dangerous – consequences for women and for Christian mission work generally. Once again, McClung developed her argument for a radical shift in perspective through humorous analogy and unorthodox redefinition.

'Women and the Church' is perhaps the weakest essay from *In Times Like These*. McClung's usual sustained witty analysis, wealth of detail, and complex satire are absent, and the structure is diffuse and repetitive, rather than focused and logical. Perhaps because criticism of the church was a more emotionally fraught subject than criticism of society, she was unable to provide the specific examples and detailed analysis that made her other chapters so effective. Questioning the accepted doctrine that Christ's disciples were all men, she could marshall nothing more compelling as evidence against the tradition than that male scribes might 'naturally ignore the woman's part of it.'[105] Her promising claim that 'the church has been dominated by men and so religion has been given a masculine interpretation' is developed with little more than vague references to sex prejudice in ministers' sermons; Paul's injunctions against marriage and women's speech in church are cited without any pointed rejoinders, and church dignitaries' objections to women's preaching provide no occasions for wit. This master of parody and incisive rebuttal is reduced to stating, 'The antagonism of the church to receiving women preachers has its basis in sex jealousy. I make this statement with deliberation. The smaller the man, the more disposed he is to be jealous.'[106] The flat language and flabbiness of assertion illustrate, by contrast, just how masterful McClung's other essays are. Yet despite these weaknesses, she does present a compelling case for the threat posed by church passivity to its ongoing life and spiritual mission.

There was little doubt that women would eventually win their civic and human rights in full, McClung asserted, and yet the damage to the church that had not aided them could be incalculable. Women's sense of alienation was almost inevitable, for 'when all is over, the battle fought and won ... many women will remember with bitterness that in the day of our struggle, the church stood off, aloof and dignified, and let us fight alone.'[107] In the meantime, the church was already profoundly weakened, crippled by its choice not to benefit from the full abilities, talents, and energies of half its body. It was not the agent of social purity and revival that it might be because of such self-amputation. With characteristic wit, McClung cites a fable to illuminate the consequences of this short-sightedness. The absurdity of the story, with its comic image of an elegant but toothless dog unable to defend its master, lightens her otherwise grim prediction of the decay of the church as a moral force in modern society: 'There is one of Aesop's fables which tells about a man who purchased for himself a beautiful dog, but being a timid man, he was beset with the fear that some day the dog might turn on him and bite him, and to prevent this, he drew all the dog's teeth. One day a wolf attacked the man. He called on his beautiful dog to protect him, but the poor dog had no teeth, and so the wolf ate them both. The church fails to be effective because it has not the use of one wing of its army, and it has no one to blame but itself.'[108] It is not exactly clear how we are to interpret all the elements of this story: does the dog represent women? the evangelical 'army'? woman suffrage? What exactly is the church afraid of? Who or what is the wolf? Nonetheless, McClung's general message is clear: the church was morally compromised and in danger of social irrelevance if it abandoned the very people who were its vital power base. When it most needed them, they would not be able to do its work.

Even more serious, though, were the spiritual dimensions of the contemporary crisis, for in hindering the social advancement of women and failing to take a positive stand on woman suffrage and other issues, the church was in various ways blocking women's work as disciples and evangelists and hindering the spread of the gospel. To illustrate her contention, McClung told a melodramatic story of a 'fallen woman,' a Scottish girl who had immigrated to Canada after her mother's death. The story resonates with her earlier account in the chapter of Jesus and the woman taken in adultery, in which Jesus offers forgiveness and humanity rather than moral condemnation. In McClung's story, the girl, upon arriving in the new country at age thirteen, had been abducted and raped, and the experience had destroyed her faith. That God had not answered her prayers for protection seemed to the young woman a proof that He did not exist. Unlike Jesus, the modern church was silent on the issue of sexual crime, 'fold[ing] its plump hands over its broad waistcoat and mak[ing] no protest'[109] against the weakness of the law to protect young girls from male predators. What were social workers to say to this girl, McClung asked, given the utter indifference of the church regarding the legal status of women? How could church leaders explain their failure to challenge 'the white slave evil'?[110] And if the church would not help women in their efforts to change the laws of the land, how could it claim to represent God's love on earth? McClung castigated the church for a fundamental failure of commitment to its divine mission: 'The demand for votes is a spiritual movement and the bitter cry of that little Scotch girl and of the many like her who have no reason to believe in God, sounds a challenge to every woman who ever names the name of God in prayer. We know there is a God of love and justice, who hears the cry of the smallest child in agony, and will in His own good time bind up every broken heart, and wipe away every tear. But how can we demonstrate God to the world!'[111]

In McClung's assessment, the church's stance on the Woman Question had become a measure of its ability to carry the gospel into the twentieth century, and the forecast was not promising. A church that did not pastor its members and had lost its ability to spread the good news of salvation through its own benevolent actions was clearly a church in trouble. It had even, according to an audacious reversal of terms by McClung, made 'fallen women' out of its members, instructing them in a 'narrow-gauge religion,' rather than 'the larger citizenship' to which all were called. 'Inasmuch as we have sat in our comfortable respectable pews enjoying our own little narrow-gauge religion, unmoved by the call of the larger citizenship, and making no effort to reach out and save those who are in temptation, and making no effort to better the conditions under which other women must live – inasmuch as we have left undone the things we might have done – in God's sight – we are fallen women!'[112] This was a harsh condemnation for a faithful Christian to make. But McClung would not have been the inspirational speaker she was if her message was one of pessimism. Firm in her belief in 'a God of love and justice,'[113] she did not really doubt that women and men of purpose would transform the church from within. Not unlike Agnes Machar before her, McClung made a passionate appeal for a renewed understanding of the Christian mission, not by suggesting that the church existed only to pursue social goals, but by demonstrating how the social and the spiritual were implicated in one another. Her challenge to the church to fulfil its social responsibility towards women was also an invitation to a renewed evangelism, a vision of how the church could once again, like the apostles, 'demonstrate God to the world.'[114]

These various redefinitions – of an evangelical church demonstrating the love of God by protecting the weak and fallen, of motherly women cleaning up the public sphere, of chivalrous men working by their side – were central to McClung's vision of a renewed social order. This vision was at once radically transformative, involving the complete abolition of gender hierarchy and of divisions based on race, creed, and religious denomination, and deeply conservative, built on traditional conceptions of Christian duty and self-sacrifice, social purity, and maternal love. The interdependence of radical and conservative elements, which gave it such wide-reaching appeal, also makes this vision very complex for twenty-first-century scholars to assess. It achieved its fullest expression in what is probably McClung's most significant chapter, entitled 'The Land of the Fair Deal.'

This chapter represents McClung's most thoroughgoing intervention into the future of her country, for it was an attempt to define the national myth itself, to answer the question 'what will be our [Canada's] distinguishing feature in the years to come?'[115] In present-day jargon, it was an attempt to intervene in the discourse of the nation. Canada's youthfulness meant that the country was still malleable and potential, with 'no precedents to guide us,'[116] and therefore McClung believed the time had come to imagine 'what we would like our character to be,'[117] to create a national ideal. The ideal was not of her own making: it had been growing up around her for some time, in the encomiums lavished on the western spirit that breathed in her fiction, in the narratives of her pioneer experience and the virtues it had nurtured, in her own cherished personal myths of prairie community and egalitarian western Canadian values. McClung's contribution was to blend such foundational ideas into a memorable and evocative metaphor. She imagined that the new country in the twentieth century might become known as 'the land of the Fair Deal, where every race, color and creed will be given exactly the same chance.'[118] Her ideal country of fairness, tolerance, and love, holding out to immigrants the promise of a new beginning for all, was rooted in a poetic conception of the qualities of prairie geography, in which expansive space and an open horizon were the physical equivalents of generosity and open-mindedness. In McClung's optimistic view, geography was both metaphor and shaping destiny, offering assurance that Canada would be a land of forgiveness, peace, and welcome:

> Look out upon our rolling prairies, carpeted with wild flowers, and clotted over with poplar groves, where wild birds sing and chatter, and it does not seem too ideal or visionary that these broad sunlit spaces may be the homes of countless thousands of happy and contented people. The great wide uncultivated prairie seems to open its welcoming arms to the land-hungry, homeless dwellers of the cities, saying: 'Come and try me. Forget the past, if it makes you sad. Come to me, for I am the Land of the Second Chance. I am the Land of Beginning Again. I will not ask who your ancestors were. I want you – nothing matters now but just you and me, and we will make good together.'[119]

Here the land itself becomes a subject, calling to those in search of freedom and a second chance. Like many other prairie reformers, McClung understood rural life to be morally and physically superior to city life, believing that one of the keys to Canada's prosperity was a return to the countryside. She saw the prairies as the locus of the great social experiment of the twentieth century, offering literal and metaphorical vistas of sunlight 'to the discouraged and weary ones of the older lands.'[120]

For its time, this was a remarkably inclusive, utopian vision, though all utopian visions rest upon exclusions of one kind or another. Critics of McClung note that her compassionate welcome 'to the discouraged and weary ones of the older lands'[121] was directed to the immigrants of 'Middle Europe,'[122] rather than to all immigrants, an emphasis not surprising given the prominence of the war with Germany in the contemporary Canadian imagination. Canada's racial exclusions – against Aboriginal people in a nation of immigrants, against dark-skinned people considered unassimilable (the South Asians of the *Komagata Maru* incident) – are unaddressed, and even perhaps reinforced, in McClung's national prescription for social justice, though racism is repudiated in other writings. Moreover, she was quite explicit in excluding the 'unfit' – the mentally and physically disabled – from her images of productive community and service, emphasizing the need for physical strength and moral acumen in building a peaceful and productive community. While awareness of such exclusions is necessary for a full assessment of McClung's politics, the impression left from reading *In Times Like These* is one of generosity and openness rather than suspicion: her overriding faith was that differences could be overcome in the new country of vast territory and seemingly endless natural resources; British civilization was superior to others, she believed, not because it was British but because it was 'the cradle of liberty,'[123] having developed a commitment to education, liberty, and the rule of law that was in theory open to all. The paramount importance of inclusivity as a principle in a country with 'room for everyone'[124] created a foundation for future accommodations and redefinitions of national citizenship.

McClung's national ideal meant freedom and 'equality of opportunity,'[125] but not absolute freedom or opportunity, and her concern for a state-fostered moral order is one aspect of her vision that may sit uneasily alongside present-day ideals of individuality and self-determination. She believed that her own generation was destined to carve out the paths for others to follow, that they must shoulder a responsibility 'to lay them [the paths] broad and straight and safe so that many feet may be saved from falling.'[126] Although not straight and *narrow*, the broad path had to be 'straight and safe,' an imperative that made necessary certain restrictions on individual freedom for the good of all, including the prohibition of alcohol. In the paragraph with which she ended her essay on Canada's future, McClung declared her commitment to moral reform in response to the common objection that human goodness cannot be legislated:

> But there are people who cry out against prohibition that you cannot make men moral, or sober, by law. But that is exactly what you can do. The greatest value a law has is its moral value. It is the silent pressure of the law on public opinion which gives it its greatest value. The punishment for the infringement of the law is not its only way of impressing itself on the people. It is the moral impact of a law that changes public sentiment, and to say that you cannot make men sober by law is as foolish

as to say you cannot keep cattle from destroying the wheat by building a fence between them and it, or to claim you cannot make a crooked twig grow straight by tying it straight. Humanity can do anything it wants to do. There is no limit to human achievement. Whoever declares that things cannot be done which are for the betterment of the race, insults the Creator of us all, who is not willing that any should perish, but that all should live and live abundantly.[127]

In a characteristic reversal, McClung refutes received wisdom that morality is beyond legislation, employing simple analogies from nature – the stray cow and the crooked branch – to recast human nature as almost infinitely malleable, with the state a benign parent training a child. This is a statement of remarkable confidence, not only in the possibility of creating a moral society by eradicating sin and error but also in the possibility of fully knowing God's will and of translating his plan of salvation for humanity into an earthly order of legal and social institutions. For McClung, sin was a defect to be remedied by good laws and by a social climate conducive to morality. An overemphasis on human sinfulness was, for her, a form of rebellion against God. Creating a neat rhetorical parallel, her conviction that society owed a duty to God to create the conditions for all to 'live abundantly' returns her, conceptually, to the redefinition with which she opened *In Times Like These*, when she argued against the complacent folding of hands often derived from the petition 'Thy will be done.' Repeating her earlier biblical assertion 'It is never God's will that any should perish,'[128] she affirmed that resignation and defeatism were as much to be combatted as social evils themselves.

In describing her idea of 'the Fair Deal,' Nellie McClung defined a land in which 'no prejudice is allowed to masquerade as a reason.'[129] As she set forward her understanding of what such a land would look like and how it might be brought into being, she was also engaged in a rhetorical undertaking to unmask prejudices masquerading as reasons, to revitalize the language in order to debunk the clichés that supported injustice, and to create a body of aphorisms and anecdotes to articulate fairer conceptions. Like the housewife cleaning out the dust-covered 'pigeon-holes and forgotten corners,'[130] she gave the language a full airing, replacing what was soiled or rhetorically malfunctioning with a fresh stock of expressions. With her gift for humour, parody, and anecdote, McClung demonstrated what a full national housecleaning might accomplish, and she inspired listeners and readers to take up their part in the work.

Conclusion

To move from the earnest, theologically orthodox social gospel of Agnes Machar to the spunky, theologically liberal social gospel of Nellie McClung is to travel a path fairly representative (if two such extraordinary women can ever be representative) of the shifts in emphasis and assumptions within the radical Christian community during the period 1875–1915. McClung was comfortably part of a secularizing world in which the practical application of Christian principles outweighed Machar's evangelical emphasis on doctrinal coherence and personal salvation. As Christians writing about social justice, however, they had much in common: both grounded their arguments in Scripture, outlining a faith and a commitment to reform in which the spiritual and the social were one. Their revulsion at suffering and their ethos as Christian disciples sharing a gospel of hope were a major part of their rhetorical appeal, and their self-positioning drew on the rhetoric of maternal feminism – of women's social service, self-sacrifice, purification of the nation – that sanctioned bold forays into the spheres of intellectual debate and political contestation.

The other four writers in this study positioned themselves quite differently in relation to maternal ideology, Christian discourse, and social values. In her colloquial, anecdotal columns, Flora MacDonald Denison embraced the ideal of social mothering to advocate a radical transformation in politics and culture; rejecting Christianity as barbaric and retrograde, she made the women's movement itself her source of spiritual conviction and emotive power, imagining herself a prophet of a new world order. Sara Jeannette Duncan and Kathleen Coleman, in contrast, were more wary of overtly ideological alignments and more strategically coy in the feminine and feminist postures they assumed.

Rejecting elements of the women's rights platform, they were yet boldly modern in their subject matter and rhetorical approach, by turns teasing, provocative, incisive, and frank and never less than intellectually agile. Duncan perfected an arch tone and ironical approach to puncture pieties on both sides of the Woman Question; she also argued seriously about culture and civic responsibility. Coleman scolded, reassured, instructed, and confided in almost equal measure, creating an atmosphere of maternal intimacy that drew readers' affection yet protected her privacy. Pauline Johnson used her poetry and stories for political advocacy, exploiting her exotic image as an Indian maiden to challenge Anglo-Canadians to live up to their national ideals. Though she made pointed criticisms of white complacency and injustice, her most consistent strategy was to stress the benefits to Anglo-Canadians of partnership with Native peoples. These women were not part of a single movement – not even of a loosely affiliated network – and their strategies of self-presentation were distinct, but all emerged from a culture that valued social commitment, and all developed a rhetoric based in part on powerful myths of womanhood. At a time when rapid social changes were calling into question the certainties of previous eras, they wrote with moral authority, intellectual acumen, and good sense, simultaneously challenging and reassuring their audiences.

This account has generally been told as a rousing tale of women triumphant: braving public disapprobation, breaking down social barriers, and supporting themselves and their causes through their wit and determination. Indeed, all these women understood themselves to be venturing where few of their countrywomen had been on behalf of causes larger than themselves, and all would have empathized with McClung's determination 'to leave something behind when I go; some small legacy of truth, some word that will shine in a dark place.'[1] Defending her activism to her brother, she called it 'the greatest adventure in the world.'[2]

That same sense of adventure is evident in the rousing words of all the writers addressed here. Only Duncan might have demurred at the idea of promoting a 'cause,' yet under cover of comic observation and biting satire, she goaded women to develop their moral and intellectual potential, assuring them provocatively, 'The day may come when women shall help to make the laws, but they will have to know a good deal more about law-making than at present.'[3] Coleman drew on the rhetoric of service to declare her purpose merely 'to answer questions truly as well as lies in one's power; to touch some one suffering heart, and relieve it of the too great burden of human sorrow,'[4] but the astonishing range of her answers established her as confessor, adviser, social reformer, and mother to her paper children, an oracle of sharp sense and compassionate morality during a period of social transition and theological disarray. The others openly declared themselves fighters. In one of her last poems, reputedly written just after she had received the diagnosis that her breast cancer was terminal,[5] Johnson swore to battle to the end: 'But though I fight alone, and fall, and die, / Talk terms of Peace? Not I.'[6] And in her advocacy for her 'dear Red brother of whatsoever tribe or Province,'[7] she was adamantly proud to tell some hard truths. Denison equated woman suffrage with the abolishment of all social evils: 'Is it worth while to assist in abolishing war? Is it worth while to assist in abolishing the white slave traffic? Then join some suffrage society and do your little or much towards the social betterment of the race.'[8] McClung, too, explicitly framed her advocacy in terms of 'the war that never ends'[9] – the war against prejudice, limitation, and despair. In answering the charge that 'didactic enthusiasm' stained the 'art' of her writing, she declared in her autobiography, 'I hope I have been a crusader.'[10] Machar chose as the epigraph for her industrial novel *Roland Graeme, Knight* the Tennysonian ideal 'To ride abroad, redressing human wrongs,'[11] a mission she herself embraced. All exhibited strongly felt purpose and a sense of exhilarating achievement.

There is also a darker side to their stories. Well before her death and increasingly so afterwards, Machar was seen as a quaint relic of Victorianism whose conviction and lofty ideals were out of keeping with the modern world. Dianne Hallman quotes the letter of a younger acquaintance of Machar, Elizabeth Shortt, one of the first women to graduate from the Royal Medical College at Queen's University in 1884, who found her an oddity in the 1890s: 'Miss Machar of course is all right as a literary light & a woman who really lives up to her preaching as far as I know & although she is a most ridiculous woman in appearance & and in some of her ideas she is in earnest.'[12] The vigour and seriousness with which Machar had engaged the major intellectual and social problems of her day were largely forgotten in the half-century following her death. Despite her early promise, Duncan never achieved through her fiction the readership or acclaim she had hoped for; as she turned towards increasingly sombre international themes, her reputation as a sparkling prose stylist declined, and the novel for which she had the highest hopes, *The Imperialist* (1904), received lukewarm reviews. Coleman ended a successful, if only marginally lucrative, career with a sense of bitterness and defeat when her employer at the *Mail and Empire* refused to increase her pay, forcing her to quit the paper to which she had given her most productive years. And though far from forgotten in her final days, Johnson died in poverty and far from home, having failed to produce the great work she had planned. The need to earn money kept a number of these writers from the sustained work they might otherwise have achieved.

For those with the highest hopes for the future, declining years brought the most severe disappointments. Denison seems to have lost faith in women within a few years of closing her *World* column. Retreating to Bon Echo, her nature resort in the highlands of Ontario, she devoted herself to preserving the memory of Walt Whitman and proclaiming the restorative effects of a life in nature. A 1917 issue of her newsletter *The Sunset of Bon Echo* describes the archetypal spoilt, vacuous, and pleasure-loving young woman who visited the resort looking for a husband. Denison asked doubtfully, 'Will she become wise and useful and helpful? Will she realize that it is best to be of service, or will she join that vast sisterhood of idle parasites, whose highest ambition is to rope in the man with the coin, and use and abuse the wealth earned by others?'[13] These were bitter words for one who had seen in the suffrage movement 'the greatest battle ever waged for human liberty in the world's history'[14] and who had prophesied hopefully that woman suffrage would end wars forever: 'Oh, what a veritable paradise we might have if – Think it over.'[15] Although she remained close friends with feminists such as Charlotte Perkins Gilman, who visited her at Bon Echo and wrote in *The Sunset* about its wholesome beauties,[16] Denison's faith in the gospel of sisterhood had suffered a severe blow when her heroine Emmeline Pankhurst defected from pacifism.

McClung, too, lost some of her optimism towards the end of her life. Writing in 1937 about the social changes she had witnessed, she recorded the endless hours of hopeful activity that now seemed to have been for nothing. 'I have been a temperance worker all my life,' she wrote. 'I have, like many other women, spoken, written, reasoned, entreated, studied charts and diagrams, made house-to-house canvasses, secured names on petitions, and worked to have bills amended in Parliament. Yet there is not much to show for all this expenditure of energy.'[17] In her autobiography, she was even more frank, confessing that 'while I will not give way to regret that I spent so many years working for the equality of women, I cannot refrain from saying that the sight of women lined up in front of the Government Liquor Stores fills me with a withering sense of disappointment.'[18] The modern age seemed, for McClung, to be one in which material advances had far outstripped human spiritual progress, and she foresaw a time of confusion and loss of purpose very different from the days in which she and her fighting sisters went 'singing up the hill,'[19] confident that they were ushering in a better world. She ended her life feeling that she had lost touch with the age she had once helped to shape.

Indeed, the collective impact of these writers on the twentieth century was far slighter than one might have expected while surveying the scene in the last decade of the nineteenth. Powerfully of its moment, their rhetoric was superseded by new discourses. The social gospel lost its urgency once the state began taking over most of the social service functions that the churches had performed; the women's movement splintered and lost momentum after the achievement of the federal franchise in 1918; women's columnists such as Duncan and Coleman were replaced, in the years following the First World War, by experts in the more narrowly focused fields of domestic science, housewares, fashion, and psychology; appeals to patriotism and the ideals of empire in the writing of Machar, Duncan, and Johnson were undermined with the advent of literary modernism. In an increasingly secular and specialized age that fetishized the new, their voices quickly came to seem outmoded.

Yet it would be wrong to underestimate their impact and that of others like them. In their day they were vivid, well-respected personalities of the sort that a prominent journalist, Hector Charlesworth, was proud to be associated with when he published his memoirs, mentioning Duncan admiringly and describing in some detail his friendships with Coleman and Johnson.[20] Historians of Canadian journalism have emphasized the key role of columnists such as Duncan, Coleman, and Denison in changing the face of the Canadian newspaper – softening it, personalizing it, and decisively broadening its appeal. The political advocacy of Johnson and McClung gave unprecedented dignity and ethical force to women's public self-presentations. All of these writers, though working in different registers and drawing on different rhetorical techniques, articulated the central conflicts of their age in effective ways and helped their audience to think about them productively. Through satire, exhortation, motherly advice, and polemic, they offered positive visions of the nation and bracing narratives of social revolution, expressing and shaping their culture's central concerns.

More generally, they made women publicly visible, putting their voices at the centre of debates in a way they had never been in the past and would not be for much of the following century. By making it possible for ordinary readers to think of consulting a woman for medical advice, theological explanation, political theory, or literary judgment, they significantly broadened the parameters of women's sphere and heightened the authority of women's viewpoints. For these reasons, their place in Canadian social and literary history deserves to be better known.

DURING THE YEARS THAT I WAS writing this monograph, I kept expecting that someone else, or dozens of others, would write a book of its kind; the persuasive, polemical, and autobiographical texts of turn-of-the-century prose writers, activists, and performers seemed such an obviously neglected and interesting subject, and the work of the relatively well-known Duncan, Johnson, and McClung, if not the others, seemed overdue for further study and reappraisal. As I chortled over Kit's spunky advice to the lovelorn in 'Woman's Kingdom' or marvelled at the intellectual maturity and confidence of twenty-four-year-old Duncan in her *Globe* columns or traced the development of McClung's compelling rhetoric during the Manitoba election campaign, I was surprised that so few scholars seemed to be interested in them. One cannot say of the Canadian literary critic what Duncan said of a biographer of Longfellow, that he 'has had a vast and voluminous quantity of material to select from, and apparently, to the dismayed perception of the reader, he has selected it all!'[21] For scholars, there remains a rich field from which to 'select.'

I want to end, then, by expressing hope that the next decade will see more work on early Canadian writers' voices, techniques, and world views. Even the few writers in this book who have received critical attention in the past remain promising subjects for further investigation. Despite Strong-Boag and Gerson's major study, Johnson's tremendously varied writings have only occasionally been read closely; there are few detailed analyses of her poems and stories and almost no work on her best-selling collection of Squamish tales *Legends of Vancouver* (1911). Biographical and critical attention to McClung by Mary Hallett and Marilyn Davis, Randi Warne, Strong-Boag, and Cecily Devereux, while valuable, has by no means said all there is to say about Canada's best-known feminist personality. Her journalism, especially the personal and occasional prose writings collected in *Leaves from Lantern*

Lane (1936) and *More Leaves from Lantern Lane* (1937), is an illuminating archive of McClung's views on aging, modernity, and the failure of feminism that has received almost no attention from critics.

The journalism and belletrist writings of Duncan, Coleman, Denison, and Machar are, unfortunately, even more obscure, with the result that their wit, social analysis, passion, invective, advice, calls to action, and portraits of contemporary society – often vivid, funny, surprising, and searing – are largely unknown and inaccessible to present-day critics. Because I have necessarily been selective in my analyses, the portrait of each writer that emerges in this study is incomplete and partial: I looked at only ten of Machar's more than one hundred periodical articles and at only the first ten years of Coleman's twenty-one-year-long career as a columnist. Much remains to be done to recover their learned and socially engaged prose writing. Similarly, more attention could well be paid to Duncan's literary views, social sketches, and satirical attacks in her newspaper writing, while Denison's social theories (in 'The Open Road to Democracy') and eco-feminist philosophy (in *The Sunset of Bon Echo*) deserve attention for their conscious iconoclasm and passion. Duncan's complex and subtle novels about Anglo-Indian society await further analysis as well.

New work on women writers in this period might look further into the pages of early Canadians newspapers and periodicals. Nick Mount has vividly explored the failure of such periodicals to provide a sufficiently creative and remunerative forum for their writers, who were frequently lured to more lucrative publishing positions south of the border. Despite their limitations, however, Canadian periodicals did prove a congenial venue for a number of women who found public recognition and a living – if not lavish – wage in the pages of the *Week*, the *Globe*, the Toronto *Empire*, the *Canadian Magazine*, and many more. 'Madge Merton' (Elmira Elliott Atkinson), who edited the women's page at *Saturday Night* and later wrote 'Madge Merton's Page' for the Toronto *Star*; Ethelwyn Wetherald, who took over 'Woman's World' at the *Globe* from Duncan and then became principal editor at the London *Advertizer*; and Faith Fenton (Alice Freeman) at the *Empire* and later the *Globe* all established public profiles of considerable renown by creating a distinct feminine style and persona. Prairie women journalists such as E. Cora Hind at the Winnipeg *Free Press* and Marion Francis Beynon at the *Grain Growers' Guide* combined an agrarian focus with feminist advocacy to establish outspoken personae as women of the people. Their contributions have been chronicled by scholars, including

Ramsay Cook, Carlotta Hacker, and Susan Jackel, but they merit more detailed attention; and there are many others about whom I know only a little, many of them mentioned in Marjory Lang's engaging study. The even more challenging task of investigating archival sources to establish the biographical and bibliographical facts of obscure writers remains vital and timely, as the essays in Helen Buss and Marlene Kadar's edited volume *Working in Women's Archives* (2001) indicate. Literary recovery work of the sort begun in MacMillan, McMullen, and Waterston's *Silenced Sextet* (1993) is also urgent.

Much of the criticism of the past fifteen years has been ideologically oriented, focusing on questions of race, class, and empire, and while the study of women's writing has benefited a great deal from such work, it has perhaps had the effect of preventing attention to other aspects of early Canadian culture. I hope that future criticism of early Canadian authors will take the form of a multifaceted, historically grounded inquiry that pays attention to details of language and considers the manifold relationships between writers, texts, their audiences, and the social and institutional contexts of literature. As far as possible, I hope that scholars will attempt to approach their material without preconceptions or aggressive agendas, and perhaps with generosity towards their subjects as well. Describing trends in literary criticism for *The Week*, Duncan argued that the best reviews exhibited humanity and justice: 'Altogether, criticism is becoming, to borrow a Howellsism, "a finer art" than it used to be. The critic is learning to walk humbly and to deal justly, in so far as the qualities of humanity and justice can be assimilated by human nature in the shape of a reviewer. He is less egotistical, less arrogant, less aggressive than of yore ... He resists, creditably often, the temptation of the clever sneer, and exerts himself instead to say the best he can without misleading.'[22] She was speaking about literary reviewing, but the same terms might be applied more broadly to criticism, which does not always remember to 'walk humbly and to deal justly,' still less to strive 'to say the best [one] can without misleading.' Much Canadian writing that deserves appreciative attention still awaits such analysis.

Notes

Introduction

1 Machar, 'New Ideal of Womanhood,' 661.
2 Ibid.
3 Wetherald, 'Some Canadian Literary Women,' 300.
4 Lunsford, 'On Reclaiming Rhetorica,' 6.
5 C.G. Holland, *William Dawson LeSueur*, 35.
6 O'Hagan, 'Some Canadian Women Writers,' 1053.
7 Lang, *Women Who Made the News*, 41.
8 McClung, *Stream Runs Fast*, 35.
9 Johnson papers, box 4, file 32.
10 Strong-Boag, Introduction, xiv.
11 Valverde, *Age of Light*, 34.
12 Ibid., 41.
13 Ibid., 34.
14 Ibid., 34–5; emphasis mine.
15 Henderson, *Settler Feminism*; see especially 12–16.
16 Forbes, *Challenging the Regional Stereotype*.
17 Ibid., 91.
18 Ibid., 94.
19 Ibid., 98.
20 Ibid., 99.
21 Valverde, *Age of Light*, 34–5.
22 Duncan, 'Other People and I,' 15 July 1885, 3. Here and elsewhere, I document individual column articles, when they lack differentiating titles, by date in the text or the notes, rather than in the bibliography.
23 Johnson, 'Strong Race Opinion,' 178.

24 Ibid.
25 Johnson may have had in mind Isabella Valancy Crawford's *Winona; or, the Foster-Sisters*, a prize-winning novel published serially in a Montreal paper, *The Favorite*, in 1873.
26 Johnson, 'Strong Race Opinion,' 180–1.
27 Ibid., 183.
28 Ibid.
29 Lang, *Women Who Made the News*, 31.
30 Denison, 'Under the Pines,' 14 August 1910, n.p.
31 Ibid., 13 February 1910, n.p.
32 Lang, *Women Who Made the News*, 46.
33 MacKay, 'Pauline Johnson,' 274.
34 Dubinsky, *Improper Advances*, 4.
35 Monture, '"Beneath the British Flag,"' 138.
36 Strong-Boag, Introduction, xx.
37 Valverde, '"When the Mother of the Race,"' 3.
38 Warsh, '"Oh, Lord,"' 70.
39 McClung scrapbooks, vol. 30.
40 Rutherford, *Victorian Authority*, 28.
41 Ibid., 77.
42 Strong-Boag and Gerson, *Paddling Her Own Canoe*, 112.
43 S.A. Cook, *'Through Sunshine and Shadow,'* 12.
44 Egan and Helms, 'Autobiography,' xv.
45 Dean, *Practising Femininity*, 9.
46 Strong-Boag and Gerson, *Paddling Her Own Canoe*, 4–5.
47 Gerson, *Purer Taste*, x.
48 Berger, *Sense of Power*, 99.
49 Valverde, *Age of Light*, 15.
50 Machar, 'Voices Crying in the Wilderness,' 170.
51 Ibid.
52 Kealey and Palmer, *Dreaming of What Might Be*, 57.
53 Machar, 'Voices Crying in the Wilderness,' 170.
54 Denison, 'Under the Pines,' 14 November 1909, n.p.
55 Duncan, 'Other People and I,' 1 July 1885, 3.
56 Machar, 'Woman's Work,' 295.
57 Quoted in Tausky, *Sara Jeannette Duncan: Selected Journalism*, 6.
58 Coleman, 'Woman's Kingdom,' 23 April 1892, 6.
59 Ibid., 15 December 1894, 5.
60 Machar, 'Views of Canadian Literature,' 391.
61 Denison, 'Under the Pines,' 13 February 1910, n.p.

62 Coleman, 'Woman's Kingdom,' 22 October 1892, 8.
63 Johnson papers, box 4, file 24.
64 L. Kealey, Introduction, 7–14.
65 Dean, *Practising Femininity*, 78.
66 Buss, *Mapping Our Selves*, 128–34.
67 Henderson, *Settler Feminism*, 13.
68 McClung, *In Times Like These*, 79.
69 Denison, 'Under the Pines,' 14 November 1909, n.p.
70 McClung, *In Times Like These*, 89.
71 McKillop, *Disciplined Intelligence*, 138.
72 R. Cook, *Regenerators*, 4.
73 Ibid., 24.
74 L. Kealey, Introduction, 5.
75 Ibid.
76 Allen, *Social Passion*, 16.
77 Ibid., 6.
78 McClung, *In Times Like These*, 10.

1. Agnes Maule Machar

1 Machar, 'Voices Crying in the Wilderness,' 169.
2 Ibid.
3 Ibid.
4 Ibid., 170.
5 Chenier, 'Agnes Maule Machar,' 13.
6 Wetherald, 'Some Canadian Literary Women,' 300.
7 Backhouse, *Petticoats and Prejudice*, 276.
8 Machar, 'Views of Canadian Literature,' 391; emphasis in original.
9 Machar, 'New Ideal,' 673.
10 Machar, 'Religion in Schools.'
11 Wetherald, 'Some Canadian Literary Women,' 300–1.
12 Guild, 'Canadian Celebrities,' 499.
13 Machar, 'Source of Moral Life,' 345.
14 Machar, 'Our Lady,' 234.
15 Quoted in Wetherald, 'Some Canadian Literary Women,' 300.
16 Gerson, Introduction, ix.
17 Guild, 'Canadian Celebrities,' 501.
18 *Ontario Public School History*, 258.
19 Lighthall, *Songs of the Great Dominion*, 458.
20 O'Hagan, 'Some Canadian Women Writers,' 1051.

21 R. Cook, *Regenerators*, 6.
22 Ibid., 188.
23 Ibid., 187.
24 Ibid., 191.
25 Ibid., 188.
26 Ibid., 6.
27 Ibid., 186.
28 McKillop, *Disciplined Intelligence*, 137.
29 Gerson, 'Three Writers,' 207.
30 Brouwer, '"Between-Age" Christianity,' 348.
31 Ibid.
32 Ibid., 357.
33 Ibid., 370.
34 Ibid., 356.
35 Hallman, 'Cultivating a Love of Canada,' 38.
36 Machar, 'Voices Crying in the Wilderness,' 169.
37 Ibid., 170.
38 Ibid.,
39 Ibid., 169.
40 Ibid., 170.
41 Ibid.
42 Machar, 'Unhealthy Conditions,' 566.
43 Trofimenkoff, 'One Hundred and Two Muffled Voices,' 213.
44 Machar, 'Unhealthy Conditions,' 566.
45 Ibid.
46 Ibid., 567.
47 Ibid.
48 Trofimenkoff, 'One Hundred and Two Muffled Voices,' 223.
49 Machar, 'Unhealthy Conditions,' 567–8.
50 Ibid., 569.
51 Machar, 'Our Lady,' 234.
52 Ibid.
53 Ibid.
54 Ibid., 235.
55 Machar, 'Creeds and Confessions,' 135.
56 Ibid.
57 Ibid., 144.
58 Ibid., 137.
59 Brouwer, '"Between-Age" Christianity,' 348.
60 Machar, 'Creeds and Confessions,' 135.

61 Ibid.
62 Ibid., 137.
63 Ibid., 136.
64 Ibid., 137.
65 Ibid.
66 Ibid., 139.
67 Ibid., 144.
68 Ibid., 143.
69 Ibid., 136.
70 Ibid., 146.
71 Ibid., 134.
72 Machar, *Roland Graeme*, 49.
73 Ibid.
74 Ibid., 50.
75 Ibid., 237
76 Ibid.
77 Ibid., 285.
78 Vipond, 'Blessed Are the Peacemakers,' 33.
79 Gerson, Introduction, xv.
80 Wetherald, 'Some Canadian Literary Women,' 300.
81 C.G. Holland, *William Dawson LeSueur*, 1.
82 Ibid., 4.
83 LeSueur, 'Prayer and Natural Law,' 212.
84 Machar, 'Divine Law of Prayer,' 145.
85 Ibid., 145.
86 Ibid.
87 Ibid., 144.
88 Ibid., 149.
89 Ibid., 147.
90 Ibid., 150.
91 Ibid., 153.
92 Ibid., 155.
93 Ibid.
94 Ibid., 151.
95 Ibid.
96 Ibid., 155.
97 Ibid., 152.
98 Ibid., 154.
99 Ibid.
100 Ibid., 146.

101 Machar, 'Source of Moral Life,' 344.
102 Ibid.
103 Ibid. 348.
104 Ibid., 347.
105 Ibid., 346.
106 Ibid.
107 Ibid., 345; emphasis in original.
108 Ibid.
109 Ibid., 350.
110 Ibid., 350–1.
111 MacCallum, 'Agnes Maule Machar,' 354.
112 Ibid.
113 Ibid., 356.
114 Daniells, 'Confederation,' 211.

2. Sara Jeannette Duncan

1 Duncan, 'Woman's World,' 1 November 1886, 6. Articles lacking individual titles are documented in the notes by date. Articles from *The Week* that do have distinctive titles are listed in the bibliography.
2 Charlesworth, *Candid Chronicles*, 89.
3 See, though, Goodwin, 'Early Journalism'; Tausky, *Sara Jeannette Duncan: Selected Journalism*; and Adams, 'Annotated Edition.'
4 Duncan, 'Saunterings,' 30 September 1886, 707.
5 Lang, *Women Who Made the News*, 31–6.
6 In calling for the vote, Duncan made it clear that the suffrage struggle concerned the sober duties of citizenship, rather than 'emancipation,' a feminist word she scorned. 'And now we ask the ballot,' she declared, 'not by way of emancipation, as its intelligent exercise would certainly add another burden to the rest that have been laid upon us by our own solicitation ... Women's request for the ballot ... is a simple declaration that the sex has reached the point of intelligence that will permit the useful exercise of a public spirit, and is desirous of accepting the duties and responsibilities and benefits that grow out of it' ('Other People and I,' 12 August 1885, 3).
7 Quoted in Lang, *Women Who Made the News*, 28.
8 For a fascinating study of Lewis, who wrote as Louis Lloyd for *The Week*, see Martin, *Lily Lewis*.
9 Lang, *Women Who Made the News*, 29.
10 Ibid., 57.

11 Quoted in Tausky, *Sara Jeannette Duncan: Selected Journalism*, 6.
12 Duncan, 'Woman's World,' 29 July 1886, 6.
13 Ibid.
14 Duncan, 'Other People and I,' 27 June 1885, 3.
15 Ibid.
16 Duncan, 'Woman's World,' 31 August 1886, 6.
17 Ibid.
18 Duncan, 'Woman's World,' 20 October 1886, 6.
19 Duncan, 'Other People and I,' 8 July 1885, 3.
20 Ibid., 15 July 1885, 3.
21 Duncan, 'Woman's World,' 13 July 1886, 10.
22 Ibid.
23 Ibid., 2 November 1886, 6.
24 Ibid.
25 Ibid.
26 Ibid.
27 Ibid.
28 Ibid., 30 September 1886, 6.
29 Ibid.
30 Ibid.
31 Ibid.
32 Ibid., 14 October 1886, 6.
33 Ibid.
34 Ibid.
35 Ibid.
36 Ibid.
37 Ibid.
38 Ibid., 23 August 1886, 4.
39 Fowler has identified the first woman as Alice McGillivray, who graduated
    from the Kingston Medical College in 1884 and became a professor there.
    According to Fowler, the other woman whom Duncan interviews is
    Augusta Stowe, daughter of Emily Howard Stowe, suffrage activist.
    Augusta graduated from the Toronto School of Medicine in 1883 and be-
    came demonstrator of anatomy, and later professor of pediatrics, at the
    Ontario Woman's Medical College, Toronto. She also ran her own private
    practice and worked at the Western Hospital. See Fowler, *Redney*, 44–5.
40 Duncan, 'Woman's World,' 23 August 1886, 4.
41 Ibid.
42 Ibid.
43 Tausky, *Sara Jeannette Duncan: Selected Journalism*, 2.

44 Tausky, *Sara Jeannette Duncan: Novelist of Empire*, 41.
45 Goodwin, *Early Journalism*, 93.
46 Ibid., 110.
47 Fowler, *Redney*, 94
48 Ibid., 14.
49 Dean, *Different Point of View*, 19–40.
50 Duncan, 'Woman's World,' 6 August 1886, 6.
51 Duncan, 'Saunterings,' 7 October 1886, 723–4.
52 Ibid., 724.
53 Ibid.
54 Ibid.
55 Duncan, 'The Maori,' 548.
56 Duncan, 'Wealth of Households,' 485.
57 Duncan, 'Society at the American Capital,' 589.
58 Duncan, 'Woman's World,' 12 July 1886, 4.
59 Duncan, 'Afternoon Tea,' 9 December 1886, 27.
60 Duncan, 'Society at the American Capital,' 589.
61 Duncan, 'Saunterings,' 21 October 1886, 756.
62 Duncan, 'Afternoon Tea,' 10 February 1887, 17.
63 Duncan, 'Study in Monochrome,' 180.
64 Duncan describes his entrance: 'About eleven, a tall figure came slowly and wearily up the aisle, a man of rather light colour, old, with masses of gray hair. I at once recognized Fred Douglass. His white wife was not with him, and nobody seemed to know him of his own black kindred. He pushed his way into an empty seat, a burly whitewasher, black as ebony, grumblingly rising to let him in. He sat through the service, his hands clasped on his stick, an old, bent, tired, pathetic figure. When the people sang he joined in the not unmusical refrain 'A-a-men!' and when the preacher's tones rose in crescendo higher than usual, his dull eye brightened and he seemed to listen. But he slept most of the time' (ibid.).
65 Ibid.
66 Ibid., 180–1.
67 Ibid., 181.
68 Duncan, 'W.D. Howells.'
69 Ibid.
70 Ibid.
71 Ibid.
72 Duncan, 'Woman Suffragists in Council.'
73 Ibid.
74 Ibid.

75 Duncan, 'Saunterings,' 30 September 1886, 707.

76 Ibid., 20 January 1887, 120.

77 Ibid., 13 January 1887, 111.

78 Ibid., 30 September 1886, 708.

79 Duncan, 'Woman's World,' 1 October 1886, 6.

80 Ibid.

81 Ibid.

82 Ibid.

83 Duncan, 'Woman Suffragists in Council,' 261.

84 Duncan, 'Other People and I,' 15 July 1885, 3.

85 Duncan, 'Extracts,' 463.

86 Ibid., 463–4.

87 Duncan, 'Other People and I,' 24 June 1885, 3.

88 Duncan, 'Extracts,' 463.

89 Ibid.

90 Ibid.

91 Ibid.

92 Cleverdon, *Woman Suffrage Movement*, 105–8.

93 Duncan, 'Other People and I,' 23 May 1885, 6.

94 Duncan, 'Extracts,' 463.

95 Duncan, 'Woman's World,' 15 March 1887, 6.

96 Duncan, 'Other People and I,' 5 August 1885, 3.

97 Ibid., 23 May 1885, 6.

98 Ibid., 12 August 1885, 3.

99 Duncan, 'Woman's World,' 1 March 1887, 6.

100 Duncan, 'Other People and I,' 5 August 1885, 3.

101 Ibid.

102 Duncan, 'Woman's World,' 15 October 1886, 6.

103 Ibid.

104 Duncan, 'Other People and I,' 17 June 1885, 3.

105 Ibid.

106 Ibid., 15 July 1885, 3.

107 Duncan, 'Woman's World,' 25 January 1887, 6.

108 Ibid., 13 January 1887, 6.

3. Pauline Johnson

1 Duncan, 'Woman's World,' 14 October 1886, 6.

2 Johnson, *Canadian Born*, v.

3 Quoted in Gray, *Flint and Feather*, 147.

4 Strong-Boag and Gerson, *Paddling Her Own Canoe*, 21–46.

5 Duncan, 'Woman's World,' 14 October 1886, 6.

6 Ibid.

7 Ibid.

8 Ibid.

9 Ibid.

10 York, '"Your Star,"' 11–15.

11 Gerson and Strong-Boag, *E. Pauline Johnson*, 38–9.

12 Johnson, '"Brant."'

13 Johnson papers, box 4, file 11.

14 Lyon, 'Pauline Johnson,' 139.

15 Keller, *Pauline*, 2.

16 Gray, *Flint and Feather*, 146

17 Ibid., 269.

18 Francis, *Imaginary Indian*, 117.

19 Ibid., 122–3.

20 Monture, '"Beneath the British Flag,"' 131.

21 Stong-Boag and Gerson, *Paddling Her Own Canoe*, 4.

22 Milz, '"Publica(c)tion,"' 134.

23 McRaye, *Pauline Johnson and Her Friends*, xii.

24 Lyon, 'Pauline Johnson,' 142.

25 Johnson papers, box 4, file 1.

26 Johnson, 'As Red Men Die.'

27 F.H. Holland, 'Indian Maid,' 7.

28 Johnson papers, box 4, file 11.

29 Daniells, 'Minor Poets,' 442.

30 Leighton, 'Performing Pauline Johnson,' 149.

31 Johnson, 'A Cry.'

32 Johnson, 'The Cattle Thief.'

33 Strong-Boag and Gerson, *Paddling Her Own Canoe*, 111–12.

34 Uncle Thomas, 'Impressions,' 6.

35 Johnson papers, box 4, file 11.

36 Ibid.

37 Mair, 'Pauline Johnson,' 282.

38 Johnson papers, box 4, file 24.

39 Johnson, 'Corn Husker.'

40 Van Steen, *Pauline Johnson*, 20–1.

41 Johnson papers, box 4, file 11.

42 Ibid., file 27.

43 Ibid., file 15.

44 Monture, '"Beneath the British Flag,"' 129.
45 Johnson papers, box 4, file 11.
46 Gray, *Flint and Feather*, 91.
47 Johnson papers, Box 4, File 1.
48 Ibid., file 3.
49 Strong-Boag and Gerson, *Paddling Her Own Canoe*, 115.
50 Johnson papers, box 4, file 11.
51 Ibid., file 15.
52 Ibid., file 14.
53 Ibid., file 3.
54 Ibid., file 14.
55 Ibid., file 11.
56 Mair, 'Pauline Johnson,' 281.
57 F.H. Holland, 'Indian Maid,' 7.
58 Milz, "Publica(c)tion,' 140.
59 Van Steen, *Pauline Johnson*, 15.
60 Strong-Boag and Gerson, *Paddling Her Own Canoe*, 186.
61 Ibid.,150.
62 Ibid., 149.
63 Ibid., 150.
64 Gray, *Flint and Feathers*, 91.
65 Duncan, 'Saunterings,' 21 October 1886, 757.
66 Johnson, 'My Mother,' 69.
67 Ibid.
68 Ibid., 71.
69 Ibid., 61.
70 Ibid., 60.
71 Johnson, 'Catharine,' 89.
72 Ibid., 91.
73 Ibid., 92.
74 Ibid., 94.
75 Ibid., 101.
76 Johnson, 'Strong Race Opinion,' 179.
77 Johnson, 'Red Girl's Reasoning,' 102.
78 Ibid., 105.
79 Ibid., 117.
80 Gerson and Strong-Boag, *E. Pauline Johnson*, 325.
81 Johnson, 'As It Was in the Beginning,' 147.
82 Ibid., 152.
83 Strong-Boag and Gerson, *Paddling Her Own Canoe*, 166.

84 Francis, *Imaginary Indian*, 119.
85 Ibid.
86 Ibid., 120.
87 Monture, '"Beneath the British Flag,"'131.
88 Johnson, 'A Pagan,' 213.
89 Ibid., 214.
90 Ibid., 215.
91 Johnson, 'We-hro's Sacrifice,' 222.
92 Ibid.
93 Ibid., 223.
94 Strong-Boag and Gerson, *Paddling Her Own Canoe*, 22.
95 Lyon, 'Pauline Johnson,' 144.
96 MacKay, 'Pauline Johnson,' 273.
97 Charlesworth, *Candid Chronicles*, 95.

4. Kit Coleman

1 Freeman, *Kit's Kingdom*, 18–23.
2 Lang, *Women Who Made the News*, 34.
3 Johnston, *Selling Themselves*, 36.
4 Charlesworth, *Candid Chronicles*, 95.
5 Ibid.
6 Coleman, 20 July 1895, 6. All dated references below are to Coleman's 'Woman's Kingdom' column in the Toronto *Mail* or *Mail and Empire*.
7 Ibid.
8 Lang, *Women Who Made the News*, 34.
9 Coleman, 1 August 1896, 24.
10 Coleman, 16 March 1895, 5.
11 Coleman, 8 December 1894, 6.
12 Lang, *Women Who Made the News*, 167.
13 Prentice et al., *Canadian Women*, 133.
14 Lang, *Women Who Made the News*, 133.
15 Coleman, 17 October 1891, n.p.
16 Coleman, 17 August 1895, 6.
17 Coleman, 9 July 1892, 8.
18 Coleman, 25 August 1894, 5.
19 Coleman, 21 March 1896, 5.
20 Coleman, 29 April 1893, 8.
21 Coleman, 20 April 1895, 5.
22 Coleman, 22 September 1894, 8.

23 Coleman, 30 April 1892, 8.
24 Fetherling, *Rise of Canadian Newspaper*, 70.
25 Rutherford, *Victorian Authority*, 132.
26 Ibid., 130.
27 Ibid., 132.
28 Freeman, *Kit's Kingdom*, 5.
29 Ibid., 11.
30 Ibid., 49.
31 Ibid., 71.
32 Ibid., 6.
33 Lang, *Women Who Made the News*, 31.
34 Charlesworth, *Candid Chronicles*, 94.
35 Freeman, *Kit's Kingdom*, 31.
36 Charlesworth, *Candid Chronicles*, 94.
37 Coleman, 18 October 1890, n.p.
38 Coleman, 20 August 1892, 8.
39 Coleman, 1 November 1890, 5.
40 Ibid.
41 Coleman, 9 July 1892, 8.
42 Coleman, 22 June 1895, 6.
43 Ibid.
44 Coleman, 27 July 1895, 6.
45 Coleman, 25 October 1890, 5.
46 Coleman, 22 December 1894, 6.
47 Coleman, 14 January 1893, n.p.
48 Coleman, 27 September 1890, 9.
49 Ibid.
50 Coleman, 30 January 1892, n.p.
51 Coleman, 22 October 1892, 8.
52 Coleman, 17 August 1895, 6.
53 Coleman, 23 May 1896, 5.
54 Roberts, 'Rocking the Cradle,' 38.
55 Denison, 'Under the Pines,' 6 February 1910, n.p.
56 Coleman, 11 August 1894, 5.
57 Coleman, 8 December 1894, 5.
58 Coleman, 18 March 1893, 8.
59 Coleman, 18 August 1894, 5.
60 Coleman, 1 September 1894, 5.
61 Coleman, 9 January 1897, 5.
62 Coleman, 5 January 1895, 5.

63 Coleman, 22 December 1894, 6.
64 Coleman, 13 April 1895, 5.
65 Coleman, 6 December 1890, n.p.
66 Coleman, 13 December 1890, 5.
67 Coleman, 7 November 1891, 5.
68 Coleman, 11 October 1890, n.p.
69 Coleman, 29 December 1894, 5.
70 Coleman, 14 August 1897, 4.
71 Coleman, 20 July 1895, 6.
72 Coleman, 5 July 1890, n.p.
73 Coleman, 11 August 1894, 5.
74 Ibid.
75 Coleman, 25 May 1895, 5.
76 Ibid.
77 Coleman, 30 June 1894, 5.
78 Coleman, 20 August 1892, 8.
79 Coleman, 3 September 1892, 6.
80 Coleman, 29 September 1894, 8.
81 Coleman, 28 February 1891, 5.
82 Ibid.
83 Coleman, 29 September 1894, 8.
84 Coleman, 25 July 1891, 11.
85 Coleman, 22 September 1894, 8.
86 Coleman, 26 January 1895, 5.
87 Coleman, 9 February 1895, 5.
88 Coleman, 9 February 1895, 5.
89 Coleman, 2 March 1895, 5.
90 Ibid.
91 Coleman, 21 March 1896, 5.
92 Coleman, 22 November 1890, n.p.
93 Coleman, 20 September 1890, 5.
94 Coleman, 15 November 1890, 5.
95 Coleman, 3 April 1897, 5.
96 Coleman, 8 December 1894, 6.
97 Coleman, 4 May 1895, 5.
98 Coleman, 29 October 1892, 8.
99 Coleman, 25 October 1890, 5.
100 Coleman, 27 December 1890, 5.
101 Coleman, 20 February 1892, 6.
102 McLaren, *Master Race,* 68–88; Valverde, *Age of Light,* 129–54.

103 Grant, *Profusion of Spires,* 213–18.
104 Coleman, 31 March 1894, 5.
105 Coleman, 25 October 1890, 5.
106 Coleman, 4 January 1896, 5.
107 Coleman, 10 August 1895, 6.
108 Coleman, 28 December 1895, 5.
109 Coleman, 22 June 1895, 6.
110 Coleman, 4 August 1894, 5.
111 Coleman, 6 June 1891, 11.
112 Coleman, 6 August 1892, 8.
113 Coleman, 5 January 1895, 5
114 Coleman, 13 May 1893, 8.
115 Coleman, 27 December 1890, 5.
116 Ibid.
117 Coleman, 20 August 1892, 5.
118 Ibid.
119 Coleman, 9 May 1891,11.
120 Ibid.
121 Coleman, 20 August 1892, 8.
122 Coleman, 30 May 1891, 11.
123 Coleman, 17 August 1895, 5.
124 Ibid.
125 Coleman, 20 August 1892, 8.
126 Coleman, 10 August 1895, 6.
127 Coleman, 11 August 1894, 5.
128 Coleman, 5 January 1895, 5
129 Coleman, 21 March 1896, 5.
130 Coleman, 6 August 1892, 8.
131 Coleman, 16 March 1895, 5.
132 Coleman, 26 October 1895, 5.
133 Coleman, 18 August 1894, 5.
134 Coleman, 1 November 1890, 5.
135 Coleman, 13 April 1895, 5.
136 Coleman, 22 November 1890, n.p.
137 Coleman, 10 October 1891, 11.
138 Coleman, 29 April 1893, 8.
139 Coleman, 13 May 1893, 8.
140 Coleman, 13 April 1895, 6.
141 Coleman, 27 July 1895, 6.
142 Coleman, 20 May 1897, 4.

143 Coleman, 4 February 1899, 4.
144 Ibid.
145 Coleman, 3 August 1895, 5.
146 Coleman, 5 June 1897, 4.
147 Coleman, 11 February 1899, 4.
148 Ibid.
149 Ibid.
150 Ibid.
151 Ibid.

5. Flora MacDonald Denison

1 Prentice et al., *Canadian Women*, 192.
2 Cleverdon, *Woman Suffrage Movement*, 29.
3 See R. Cook, *Regenerators*, 78–84, and McMullin, *Anatomy of a Seance*, 35–40.
4 Cleverdon, *Woman Suffrage Movement*, 16.
5 Denison, 'Under the Pines,' 10 October 1909, n.p. Denison's columns, available on microfilm at the Thomas Fisher Rare Book Library (University of Toronto), do not include page numbers.
6 Ibid., 17 October 1909.
7 Ibid., 28 November 1909.
8 The review quoted in Cleverdon, *Woman Suffrage Movement*, 32.
9 Denison, 'Under the Pines,' 7 November 1909.
10 Ibid., 12 September 1909.
11 Ibid., 3 July 1910.
12 Ibid.
13 Gorham, 'Flora MacDonald Denison,' 57.
14 Denison, 'Under the Pines,' 30 January 1910.
15 Ibid., 19 December 1909.
16 Ibid., 9 January 1910.
17 Ibid., 12 September 1909.
18 Gorham, 'Flora MacDonald Denison,' 47–54.
19 R. Cook, *Regenerators*, 79.
20 Gorham, 'Flora MacDonald Denison,' 66.
21 Ibid., 62.
22 Denison, 'Under the Pines,' 19 December 1909.
23 Cleverdon, *Woman Suffrage Movement*, 11.
24 Ibid., 16.
25 Ibid., 16.

26 Bacchi, *Liberation Deferred?* 31.
27 Gorham, 'Flora MacDonald Denison,' 62–5.
28 Denison, 'Under the Pines,' 26 December 1909.
29 Ibid., 3 October 1909.
30 Ibid.
31 Ibid.
32 Ibid.
33 Bacchi, *Liberation Deferred?* 104–6.
34 Denison, 'Under the Pines,' 14 November 1909.
35 Ibid., 23 January 1910.
36 Ibid., 13 February 1910.
37 Ibid., 12 September 1909.
38 Ibid.
39 Ibid.
40 Ibid.
41 Strong-Boag, 'Ever a Crusader,' 276.
42 Denison, 'Under the Pines,' 3 October 1909.
43 Ibid.
44 Ibid., 14 November 1909.
45 Ibid., 15 May 1910.
46 Ibid., 24 October 1909.
47 Ibid., 9 October 1910.
48 Ibid., 9 January 1910.
49 Ibid., 14 November 1909.
50 Ibid., 27 February 1910.
51 Ibid., 28 November 1909.
52 Ibid., 12 June 1910.
53 Ibid., 7 August 1910.
54 Ibid., 7 November 1909.
55 Ibid., 28 August 1910.
56 Ibid., 17 October 1909.
57 Ibid.
58 Ibid., 24 October 1909.
59 Ibid., 10 October 1909.
60 Ibid., 19 December 1909.
61 Dubinsky, *Improper Advances*, 104, 110–11.
62 Denison, 'Under the Pines,' 10 October 1909.
63 Ibid., 17 October 1909.
64 Ibid., 14 November 1909.
65 Ibid., 28 November 1909.

66 Ibid.
67 Ibid., 23 January 1910.
68 Ibid., 22 January 1911.
69 Ibid., 30 January 1910.
70 Ibid., 12 December 1909.
71 Ibid., 1 January 1911.
72 Ibid., 29 January 1911.
73 Ibid.
74 Ibid., 2 January 1910.
75 Ibid., 3 October 1909.
76 Ibid., 31 October 1909.
77 Ibid.
78 Ibid., 28 November 1909.
79 Ibid., 17 July 1910.
80 Ibid.
81 Ibid., 19 December 1909
82 Ibid., 2 January 1910.
83 Ibid., 26 December 1909.
84 Cleverdon, *Woman Suffrage Movement*, 4.
85 Ibid.
86 Bacchi, *Liberation Deferred?* 3.
87 Denison, 'Under the Pines,' 4 September 1910.
88 Ibid., 9 January 1910.
89 Ibid., 16 January 1910.
90 Ibid., 23 January 1910.
91 Quoted in Cleverdon, *Woman Suffrage Movement*, 33.
92 Denison, 'Under the Pines,' 27 March 1910.
93 Ibid., 27 November 1910.
94 Ibid., 15 May 1910.
95 Ibid.
96 Ibid., 24 April 1910.
97 Ibid., 3 April 1910.
98 Ibid., 15 May 1910.
99 Ibid., 4 September 1910.
100 Ibid., 15 May 1910.
101 Ibid., 12 June 1910.
102 Ibid., 18 December 1910.
103 Ibid., 28 August 1910.
104 Ibid., 18 December 1910.
105 Ibid., 6 February 1910.
106 Ibid., 31 October 1909.

107 Ibid., 4 September 1910.
108 Ibid., 5 March 1911.
109 Ibid., 19 February 1911.
110 Ibid., 11 September 1910.
111 Ibid.
112 Ibid., 9 October 1910.
113 Ibid., 12 June 1910.
114 Ibid., 3 April 1910.
115 Ibid., 27 February 1910.
116 Ibid., 12 June 1910.
117 Ibid., 27 February 1910.
118 Ibid., 18 December 1910.
119 Ibid., 21 November 1909.
120 Ibid., 27 February 1910.
121 Ibid., 12 June 1910.
122 Ibid., 18 September 1910.
123 Ibid., 18 December 1910.
124 Gorham, 'Flora MacDonald Denison,' 60–2.
125 Lacombe, '"Songs of the Open Road,"' 152.
126 Denison, *The Sunset of Bon Echo*, April-May 1916, 12.

6. Nellie McClung

1 'Thousands to Hear Mrs. McClung,' Winnipeg *Free Press*, 8 July 1914, McClung scrapbooks, vol. 35.
2 'A Great Tribute,' Winnipeg *Tribune*, n.d, ibid., vol. 35.
3 'Mrs. McClung's Manitoba Campaign,' unidentified clipping, 26 July 1914, ibid.
4 'Platform Nemesis' [my title], Hamilton *Herald*, 9 July 1914, ibid.
5 'A Campaign Incident,' unidentified, n.d., ibid.
6 'Mrs. Nellie McClung Conducting Whirlwind Campaign,' Brandon *News*, 23 June 1914, ibid.
7 McClung, *In Times Like These*, 34.
8 Ibid., 44.
9 Ibid., 4.
10 Strong-Boag, Introduction, vii.
11 Hancock, *No Small Legacy*, 81.
12 See especially Savage, *Our Nell*; Strong-Boag, Introduction; and Warne, *Literature as Pulpit*.
13 Hallett and Davis, *Firing the Heather*, 119–37.
14 Strong-Boag, Introduction.

15 Warne, *Literature as Pulpit*, 138.

16 Dean, *Practising Femininity*, 77–93.

17 Youmans, *Campaign Echoes*, x.

18 'Mrs. McClung's Manitoba Campaign,' unidentified, 26 July 1914, McClung scrapbooks, vol. 35; emphasis mine.

19 McClung, *Clearing in the West*, 281.

20 Ibid., 269.

21 Strong-Boag, 'Ever a Crusader,' 277.

22 'Thousands Crowd Massey Hall to Hear Mrs. Nellie McClung,' Toronto *Daily News*, n.d., McClung scrapbooks, vol. 36.

23 'Mrs. Nellie McClung,' unidentified, n.d., ibid.

24 'A Western Woman,' *Mail and Empire*, 9 November 1935, ibid., vol. 4.

25 'Thousands to Hear Mrs. McClung Fire the Final Volley,' Winnipeg *Free Press*, 8 July 1914, ibid., vol. 35.

26 Hallett and Davis, *Firing the Heather*, 128.

27 'Platform Nemesis' [my title], Hamilton *Herald*, 9 July 1914, McClung scrapbooks, vol. 35.

28 'Mrs. McClung's Manitoba Campaign,' unidentified, 26 July 1914, ibid.

29 'Manitoba Tories Worried over Lady Orator's Campaign,' Montreal *Herald*, 9 July 1914, ibid.

30 'Mrs. McClung Makes Spirited Address,' Killarney *Guide*, 25 June 1914, ibid.

31 'Red Apple' [my title], Chicago *Record-Herald*, n.d., , ibid., vol. 29.

32 'Growing Smiles in Canada,' Toronto *Globe*, 5 November 1910, ibid., vol. 30.

33 'Mrs. McClung at Zion Church,' Kenora *Examiner*, 27 March 1913, ibid., vol. 33.

34 'Social Responsibilities of Women,' *Canadian Thresherman and Farmer*, March 1913, ibid., vol. 35.

35 'Roblin Encounters Contrary Winds,' Toronto *Globe*, 6 July 1914, ibid.

36 'Mrs. McClung's Wonderful Reception by Crowded Walker Audience,' Winnipeg *Free Press*, 7 July 1914, ibid.

37 'Splendid Hearing for Mrs. McClung,' Winnipeg *Free Press*, 30 June 1914, ibid.

38 'In Beautiful Plains,' unidentified, 3 June 1914, ibid.

39 'Cannot Fool the Temperance People,' unidentified, n.d., ibid.

40 Richardson, 'Housekeeping in Canada,' unidentified, n.d., ibid.

41 'Thousands Crowd Massey Hall,' Toronto *Daily News*, n.d., ibid., vol. 36.

42 'Why Roblin Needs Huge War Chest,' Winnipeg *Free Press*, 12 June 1914, ibid., vol. 35.

43 'Says Roblin Govt. Has Improved the Local Option Law,' Brandon *Sun*, 3 July 1914, ibid.

44 'Mrs. McClung and the Recent Campaign,' Winnipeg *Tribune*, 20 July 1914, ibid.

45 'Canadian Leader Will Be Speaker,' unidentified, n.d., ibid., vol. 36.

46 'Noted Suffragette at Binscarth,' Binscarth *Express*, 23 April 1914, ibid., vol. 35.

47 Ibid.

48 'Our Women Folk,' *The Canadian Thresherman and Farmer*, March 1914, ibid.

49 'Social Responsibilities of Women,' *Canadian Thresherman and Farmer*, March 1913, ibid.

50 Ibid.

51 'Speakers on Woman Suffrage,' unidentified, n.d., ibid., vol. 33.

52 Ibid.

53 'White Ribboners in Winnipeg,' Cartwright *Review*, 11 June 1914, ibid., vol. 35.

54 Ibid.

55 Ibid.

56 Gertrude Richardson, 'Housekeeping in Canada,' unidentified, n.d., ibid.

57 'Why Roblin Needs Huge War Chest,' Winnipeg *Free Press*, 12 June 1914, ibid.

58 'There Was Silence' [my title], Cartwright *Review*, 11 June 1914, ibid.

59 'Big Turn Out at Carman Meeting,' unidentified, n.d., ibid.

60 'Hat Lifting' [my title], Winnipeg *Free Press*, 1 May 1914, ibid.

61 'Grain Growers to Hear Mrs. McClung,' unidentified, n.d., ibid.

62 'A Fit Place' [my title], Saskatoon *Star*, 10 July 1914, ibid.

63 '"New Chivalry"' Is Lecture Topic of Mrs. McClung,' Regina *Leader*, n.d., ibid., vol. 33.

64 McClung, *In Times Like These*, 48.

65 Ibid.

66 Ibid.

67 'Talks on Temperance,' Winnipeg *Free Press*, 5 May 1914, McClung scrapbooks, vol. 35.

68 Ibid.

69 Ibid.

70 'Heroine' [my title], Winnipeg *Free Press*, 11 July 1914, ibid.

71 'Mrs. McClung's Address,' Swan River *Star*, n.d., ibid.

72 'A Great Tribute,' Winnipeg *Tribune*, n.d., ibid.

73 'Invited Roblin Supporters but They Stayed Quiet,' unidentified, n.d., ibid.

74 'Strong Appeals for Women's Suffrage,' unidentified, n.d., ibid.

75 'Stirring Defence of Foreign Women,' unidentified, 3 August 1914, ibid.

76 McClung, *In Times Like These*, 11.

77 'Nellie L. McClung Works Hard for Mothers,' unidentified, n.d., McClung scrapbooks, vol. 35.

78 'Noted Suffragette at Binscarth,' Binscarth *Express*, 23 April 1914, ibid.

79 Ibid.

80 Ibid.

81 'Liberal Policy Good, Says Mrs. McClung,' Portage la Prairie *Graph*, 14 May 1914, ibid.

82 'Mrs. McClung's Meetings,' unidentified, n.d., ibid.

83 Hallett and Davis, *Firing the Heather*, 137.

84 'Mrs. Nellie McClung Conducting Whirlwind Campaign through Province,' Brandon *News*, 23 June 1914, McClung scrapbooks, vol. 35.

85 Ibid.

86 Ibid.

87 'Mrs. McClung's Manitoba Campaign,' unidentified, 26 July 1914, ibid.

88 McClung, *In Times Like These*, 41.

89 '"New Chivalry" Is Lecture Topic,' Regina *Leader*, n.d., McClung scrapbooks, vol. 33.

90 Ibid.

91 Ibid.

92 'White Ribboners in Winnipeg,' Cartwright *Review*, 11 June 1914, ibid., 35.

93 McClung, *In Times Like These*, 9.

94 Ibid.

95 Ibid.

96 Ibid.

97 Ibid., 18.

98 Ibid., 45.

99 Ibid., 46.

100 Ibid.

101 Ibid., 48.

102 Ibid., 47.

103 Ibid., 48.

104 Ibid., 71.

105 Ibid., 69.

106 Ibid., 75.

107 Ibid., 73.

108 Ibid., 74.

109 Ibid., 77.

110 Ibid., 78.

111 Ibid.

112 Ibid.

113 Ibid.
114 Ibid.
115 Ibid., 96.
116 Ibid.
117 Ibid., 97.
118 Ibid.
119 Ibid.
120 Ibid.
121 Ibid.
122 Ibid.
123 'Empire's Need Is Simpler Faith,' unidentified, n.d., McClung scrapbooks, vol. 36.
124 McClung, *In Times Like These*, 97.
125 Ibid., 100.
126 Ibid., 96.
127 Ibid., 105.
128 Ibid., 9.
129 Ibid., 97.
130 Ibid., 48.

Conclusion

1 McClung, *Stream Runs Fast*, 212.
2 Ibid., 216.
3 Duncan, 'Other People and I,' 1 July 1885, 3.
4 Coleman, 28 February 1891, 5.
5 Gerson and Strong-Boag, *E. Pauline Johnson*, 320.
6 Johnson, '"And He Said, Fight On,"' lines 5–6.
7 Johnson, *Canadian Born*, v.
8 Denison, 'Under the Pines,' April 1910, n.p.
9 McClung, *In Times Like These*, 7.
10 McClung, *Stream Runs Fast*, 69.
11 Machar, *Roland Graeme: Knight*, 1.
12 Shortt, qtd. in Hallman, 'Cultivating a Love,' 31.
13 Denison, *The Sunset of Bon Echo* 1, no. 4 (1917): 17.
14 Denison, 'Under the Pines,' 13 November 1910, n.p.
15 Ibid., 28 August 1910, n.p.
16 Denison, *The Sunset of Bon Echo* 1, no. 3 (Summer 1916): n.p.
17 McClung, *More Leaves from Lantern Lane*, 198.
18 McClung, *Stream Runs Fast*, 181.

19 Ibid.
20 Charlesworth, *Candid Chronicles*, 87–104.
21 Duncan, 'Longfellow.'
22 Duncan, 'Saunterings,' 4 November 1886, 781.

Bibliography

Allen, Richard. *The Social Passion: Religion and Social Reform in Canada, 1914–28*. Toronto: University of Toronto Press, 1971.

Adams, Catherine. 'An Annotated Edition of Sara Jeannette Duncan's Contributions to *The Week*.' MA research paper, Carleton University, 1980.

Bacchi, Carol Lee. *Liberation Deferred? The Ideas of the English-Canadian Suffragists, 1877–1918*. Toronto: University of Toronto Press, 1983.

Backhouse, Constance. *Petticoats and Prejudice: Women and Law in Nineteenth-Century Canada*. Toronto: Women's Press, 1995.

Berger, Carl. *The Sense of Power: Studies in the Ideas of Canadian Imperialism, 1867–1914*. Toronto: University of Toronto Press, 1970.

Booth, William. *In Darkest England and the Way Out*. London: London Headquarters of the Salvation Army, 1890.

Brouwer, Ruth Compton. 'The "Between-Age" Christianity of Agnes Machar.' *Canadian Historical Review* 65, no. 3 (1984): 347–70.

Buss, Helen M. *Mapping Our Selves: Canadian Women's Autobiography in English*. Montreal: McGill-Queen's University Press, 1993.

Buss, Helen M., and Marlene Kadar, eds. *Working in Women's Archives: Researching Women's Private Literature and Archival Documents*. Waterloo: Wilfrid Laurier University Press, 2001.

Butler, Judith. *Gender Trouble: Feminism and the Subversion of Identity*. New York: Routledge, 1990.

Charlesworth, Hector. *Candid Chronicles: Leaves from the Note Book of a Canadian Journalist*. Toronto: Macmillan, 1925.

Chenier, Nancy Miller. 'Agnes Maule Machar: Her Life, Her Social Concerns, and a Preliminary Bibliography of Her Writing.' MA research paper, Carleton University, 1977.

Christie, Nancy, and Michael Gauvreau. *A Full-Orbed Christianity: The Protestant Churches and Social Welfare in Canada, 1900–1940*. Montreal: McGill-Queen's University Press, 1996.

Cleverdon, Catherine. *The Woman Suffrage Movement in Canada*. 1950. Reprint, Toronto: University of Toronto Press, 1974.

Coleman, Daniel. *White Civility: The Literary Project of English Canada*. Toronto: University of Toronto Press, 2006.

Coleman, Kathleen Blake (Kit). 'Woman's Kingdom.' Toronto *Daily Mail*, 1890–5; Toronto *Mail and Empire*, 1895–9.

Cook, Ramsay. 'Francis Marion Beynon and the Crisis of Christian Reformism.' In *The West and the Nation: Essays in Honour of W.L. Morton*, ed. Carl Berger and Ramsay Cook. Toronto: McClelland and Stewart, 1976. 187–208.

– *The Regenerators: Social Criticism in Late Victorian English Canada*. Toronto: University of Toronto Press, 1985.

Cook, Sharon Anne. *'Through Sunshine and Shadow': The Woman's Christian Temperance Union, Evangelicalism, and Reform in Ontario, 1874–1930*. Montreal: McGill-Queen's University Press, 1995.

Crawford, Isabella Valancy. *Winona; or, The Foster-Sisters*. 1873. Ed. Len Early and Michael A. Peterman. Peterborough: Broadview Press, 2007.

Daniells, Roy. 'Confederation to the First World War.' In Klinck, *Literary History*, 205–21.

– 'Minor Poets, 1880–1920.' In Klinck, *Literary History*, 438–46.

Dean, Misao. *A Different Point of View: Sara Jeannette Duncan*. Montreal: McGill-Queen's University Press, 1991.

– *Practising Femininity: Domestic Realism and the Performance of Gender in Early Canadian Fiction*. Toronto: University of Toronto Press, 1998.

Denison, Flora MacDonald. Papers, scrapbooks, and correspondence. Thomas Fisher Rare Book Library, University of Toronto, Toronto.

– 'L'il Sue.' Unpublished manuscript, Denison papers.

– *Mary Melville: The Psychic*. Toronto: Austin, 1900.

– 'The Open Road towards Democracy.' Toronto Sunday *World*, 1911–13.

– *The Sunset of Bon Echo*. 1916–19.

– 'Under the Pines.' Toronto Sunday *World*, 1909–11.

– *War and Women*. Toronto: Canadian Suffrage Association, 1914.

Devereux, Cecily. *Growing a Race: Nellie L. McClung and the Fiction of Eugenic Feminism*. Montreal: McGill-Queen's University Press, 2005.

Dickens, Charles. *Little Dorrit*. 1855–7. Reprint, Boston: D. Estes, 1900.

Dubinsky, Karen. *Improper Advances: Rape and Heterosexual Conflict in Ontario, 1880–1929*. Chicago: University of Chicago Press, 1993.

Duncan, Sara Jeannette. 'Afternoon Tea.' *The Week*, 1886–8.

– *A Daughter of To-day*. 1894. Reprint, Ottawa: Tecumseh, 1988.

- 'Extracts from the "Woman's Journal," May 2, 2001.' *The Week,* 16 June 1887, 463–4.
- *The Imperialist.* 1904. Reprint, Toronto: McClelland and Stewart, 1990.
- 'Longfellow.' *The Week,* 17 June 1886, 463.
- 'The Maori.' *The Week,* 22 July 1886, 547–8.
- 'Other People and I.' Toronto *Globe,* 1886–7.
- 'Saunterings.' *The Week,* 1886–8.
- *A Social Departure: How Orthodocia and I Went round the World by Ourselves.* New York: D. Appleton, 1890.
- 'Society at the American Capital.' *The Week,* 12 August 1886, 589–90.
- 'A Study in Monochrome.' *The Week,* 18 February 1886, 180–1.
- 'W.D. Howells at Washington.' *The Week,* 22 April 1886, 327.
- 'The Wealth of Households.' *The Week,* 24 June 1886, 484–5.
- 'Woman Suffragists in Council.' *The Week,* 25 March 1886, 261.
- 'Woman's World.' Toronto *Globe,* 1886–7.

Egan, Susanna, and Gabriele Helms. 'Autobiography and Changing Identities: Introduction.' *Biography* 24, no. 1 (Winter 2001): ix–xx.

Ferguson, Ted. *Kit Coleman: Queen of Hearts.* Garden City, NY: Doubleday, 1978.

Fetherling, Douglas. *The Rise of the Canadian Newspaper.* Toronto: Oxford University Press, 1990.

Fiamengo, Janice. '"Baptized with tears and sighs": Sara Jeannette Duncan and the Rhetoric of Feminism.' In *ReCalling Early Canada: Reading the Political in Literary and Cultural Production,* Ed. Daniel Coleman. Edmonton: University of Alberta Press, 2005. 257–80.

Forbes, Ernest R. *Challenging the Regional Stereotype: Essays on the 20th Century Maritimes.* Fredericton: Acadiensis, 1989.

Fowler, Marian. *Redney: A Life of Sara Jeannette Duncan.* Toronto: Anansi, 1983.

Francis, Daniel. *The Imaginary Indian: The Image of the Indian in Canadian Culture.* Vancouver: Arsenal Pulp, 1993.

Freeman, Barbara M. *Kit's Kingdom: The Journalism of Kathleen Blake Coleman.* Ottawa: Carleton University Press, 1989.

George, Henry. *Progress and Poverty: An Inquiry into the Cause of Industrial Depression and of Increase of Want with Increase of Wealth: The Remedy.* 1879. Reprint, Garden City, NY: Doubleday, Page, 1906.

Gerson, Carole. Introduction. In Machar, *Roland Graeme, Knight,* vii–xxiv.
- *A Purer Taste: The Writing and Reading of Fiction in English in Nineteenth-Century Canada.* Toronto: University of Toronto Press, 1989.
- 'Three Writers of Victorian Canada: Rosanna Leprohon, James DeMille, Agnes Maule Machar.' In *Canadian Writers and Their Works,* vol. 1, ed. Robert Lecker et al. Downsview: ECW Press, 1983. 195–248.

Gerson, Carole, and Veronica Strong-Boag, eds. *E. Pauline Johnson, Tekahion-wake: Collected Poems and Selected Prose*. Toronto: University of Toronto Press, 2000.

Goodwin, Rae E. 'The Early Journalism of Sara Jeannette Duncan with a Chapter of Biography.' MA thesis, University of Toronto, 1964.

Gorham, Deborah. 'Flora MacDonald Denison: Canadian Feminist.' In L. Kealey, *A Not Unreasonable Claim*, 47–70.

Grant, John Webster. *A Profusion of Spires: Religion in Nineteenth-Century Ontario*. Toronto: University of Toronto Press, 1988.

Gray, Charlotte. *Flint and Feather: The Life and Times of E. Pauline Johnson, Tekahionwake*. Toronto: HarperCollins, 2002.

Green, Barbara. *Spectacular Confessions: Autobiography, Performative Activism, and the Sites of Suffrage, 1905–1938*. Houndmills: Macmillan, 1997.

Guild, Leman A. 'Canadian Celebrities, No. 73 – Agnes Maule Machar (Fidelis).' *Canadian Magazine*, October 1906, 499–501.

Hacker, Carlotta. *E. Cora Hind*. Don Mills: Fitzhenry & Whiteside, 1979.

Hallett, Mary, and Marilyn Davis. *Firing the Heather: The Life and Times of Nellie McClung*. Calgary: Fifth House, 1993.

Hallman, Dianne M. 'Cultivating a Love of Canada through History: Agnes Maule Machar, 1837–1927.' In *Creating Historical Memory: English-Canadian Women and the Work of History*, ed. Beverly Boutilier and Alison Prentice. Vancouver: UBC Press, 1997. 25–50.

Hancock, Carole. *No Small Legacy*. Kelowna: Northstone, 1996.

Henderson, Jennifer. *Settler Feminism and Race Making in Canada*. Toronto: University of Toronto Press, 2003.

Holland, Clifford G. *William Dawson LeSueur (1840–1917): A Canadian Man of Letters*. San Francisco: Mellen Research University Press, 1993.

Holland, F.H. 'The Indian Maid.' In 'Woman's World,' Toronto *Globe*, 26 October 1886, 7.

Howells, William Dean. *Their Wedding Journey*. 1871. Reprint, Boston: J.R. Osgood, 1872.

Jackel, Susan. '"First Days, Fighting Days": Prairie Presswomen and Suffrage Activism, 1906–1916.' In *First Days, Fighting Days: Women in Manitoba History*, ed. Mary Kinnear. Regina: Canadian Plains Research Centre, 1987. 53–75.

Johnson, E. Pauline. Papers, correspondence, and newspaper clippings. William Ready Division, McMaster University Library. Hamilton, Ontario.

– '"And He Said, Fight On."' 1913. In Gerson and Strong-Boag, *E. Pauline Johnson*, 164–5.

– 'As It Was in the Beginning.' 1899. In *The Moccasin Maker*, 144–56.

– 'As Red Men Die.' 1890. In Gerson and Strong-Boag, *E. Pauline Johnson*, 68–9.

- '"Brant," a Memorial Ode.' 1886. In Gerson and Strong-Boag, *E. Pauline Johnson*, 21–2.
- 'Brier.' 1893. In Gerson and Strong-Boag, *E. Pauline Johnson*, 91.
- *Canadian Born*. Toronto: Morang, 1903.
- 'Catharine of the "Crow's Nest."' 1910. In *The Moccasin Maker*, 86–101.
- 'The Cattle Thief.' 1894. In Gerson and Strong-Boag, *E. Pauline Johnson*, 97–9.
- 'The Corn Husker.' 1896. In Gerson and Strong-Boag, *E. Pauline Johnson*, 121.
- 'A Cry from an Indian Wife.' 1885. In Gerson and Strong-Boag, *E. Pauline Johnson*, 14–15.
- 'Give Us Barabbas.' 1899. In Gerson and Strong-Boag, *E. Pauline Johnson*, 129–30.
- *Legends of Vancouver*. 1911. Reprint, Vancouver: Douglas & McIntyre, 1997.
- *The Moccasin Maker*. 1913. Reprinted with introduction, annotation, and bibliography by A. LaVonne Brown Ruoff. Norman: University of Oklahoma Press, 1998.
- 'My Mother.' 1909. In *The Moccasin Maker*, 23–85.
- 'Ojistoh.' 1895. In Gerson and Strong-Boag, *E. Pauline Johnson*, 114–16.
- 'A Pagan in St. Paul's Cathedral.' 1906. In Gerson and Strong-Boag, *E. Pauline Johnson*, 213–15.
- 'A Prodigal.' 1902. In Gerson and Strong-Boag, *E. Pauline Johnson*, 137–8.
- 'A Red Girl's Reasoning.' 1893. In *The Moccasin Maker*, 102–26.
- 'The Re-interment of Red Jacket.' 1884. In Gerson and Strong-Boag, *E. Pauline Johnson*, 10–12.
- 'A Request.' 1886. In Gerson and Strong-Boag, *E. Pauline Johnson*, 22–3.
- 'Rondeau: Morrow-Land.' 1901. In Gerson and Strong-Boag, *E. Pauline Johnson*, 134.
- 'A Strong Race Opinion: On the Indian Girl in Modern Fiction.' 1892. In Gerson and Strong-Boag, *E. Pauline Johnson*, 177–83.
- 'We-hro's Sacrifice.' 1907. In Gerson and Strong-Boag, *E. Pauline Johnson*, 218–23.
Johnston, Russell. *Selling Themselves: The Emergence of Canadian Advertising*. Toronto: University of Toronto Press, 2001.
Kealey, Gregory S., and Bryan D. Palmer. *Dreaming of What Might Be: The Knights of Labor in Ontario, 1880–1900*. Cambridge: Cambridge University Press, 1982.
Kealey, Linda. Introduction. Kealey, *A Not Unreasonable Claim*, 1–14.
- ed. *A Not Unreasonable Claim: Women and Reform in Canada, 1880s–1920s*. Toronto: Women's Press, 1979.
Keller, Betty. *Pauline: A Biography of Pauline Johnson*. Vancouver: Douglas & McIntyre, 1981.

Klinck, Carl F., ed. *Literary History of Canada*. 2nd ed. Vol. 1, 1965. Reprint, Toronto: University of Toronto Press, 1976.

Lacombe, Michèle. '"Songs of the Open Road": Bon Echo, Urban Utopians and the Cult of Nature.' *Journal of Canadian Studies* 33, no. 2 (Summer 1998): 152–67.

Lang, Marjory. *Women Who Made the News: Female Journalists in Canada, 1880–1945*. Montreal: McGill-Queen's University Press, 1999.

Leighton, Mary Elizabeth. 'Performing Pauline Johnson: Representations of "the Indian Poetess" in the Periodical Press, 1892–95.' *Essays on Canadian Writing* 65 (Fall 1998): 141–64.

LeSueur, William Dawson. 'Prayer and Natural Law.' *Canadian Monthly and National Review*, March 1876, 211–21.

Lighthall, William D., ed. *Songs of the Great Dominion*. London: Walter Scott, 1889.

Lunsford, Andrea A. 'On Reclaiming Rhetorica.' In *Reclaiming Rhetorica: Women in the Rhetorical Tradition*, ed. Andrea A. Lunsford. Pittsburgh: University of Pittsburgh Press, 1995. 3–8.

Lyon, George W. 'Pauline Johnson: A Reconsideration.' *Studies in Canadian Literature* 15, no. 2 (1990): 136–59.

MacCallum, F.L. 'Agnes Maule Machar.' *Canadian Magazine*, March 1924, 354–6.

Machar, Agnes Maule. 'Birds and Bonnets.' *The Week*. 24 March 1887, 265–6.

– 'Compulsory Education.' *Rose-Belford's Canadian Monthly and National Review*, August 1881, 174–8.

– 'Creeds and Confessions.' *Canadian Monthly and National Review*, February 1876, 134–46.

– 'The Divine Law of Prayer.' *Canadian Monthly and National Review*, August 1876, 144–55.

– 'A Few Words on University Co-Education.' *Rose-Belford's Canadian Monthly and National Review*, March 1882, 313–19.

– *For King and Country: A Story of 1812*. Toronto: Adam, Stevenson, 1874.

– 'Higher Education for Women.' *Canadian Monthly and National Review*, February 1875, 144–57.

– *Marjorie's Canadian Winter: A Story of the Northern Lights*. Boston: Lothrop, 1893.

– 'Modern Theology and Modern Thought.' *Rose-Belford's Canadian Monthly and National Review*, March 1881, 297–304.

– 'The New Ideal of Womanhood.' *Rose-Belford's Canadian Monthly and National Review*, June 1879, 659–76.

– 'Our Lady of the Slums.' *The Week*, 13 March 1891, 234–5.

– 'Prayer for Daily Bread.' *Canadian Monthly and National Review,* May 1875, 415–525.
– 'Quebec to Ontario: A Plea for the Life of Riel, September, 1885.' 1885. In *Canadian Poetry: From the Beginnings through the First World War,* ed. Carole Gerson and Gwendolyn Davies. Toronto: McClelland and Stewart, 1994. 119–20.
– 'Religion in Schools: What Ought It to Be?' *The Week,* 18 October 1895, 1110.
– *Roland Graeme, Knight: A Novel of Our Time.* 1892. Reprint, Ottawa: Tecumseh, 1996.
– 'The Source of Moral Life.' *Rose-Belford's Canadian Monthly and National Review,* April 1880, 343–51.
– *Stories of the British Empire.* 2nd ed. Toronto: William Briggs, 1914.
– 'The Temperance Problem.' *Canadian Monthly and National Review,* April 1877, 369–78.
– 'Unhealthy Conditions of Women's Work in Factories.' *The Week,* 8 May 1896, 566–9.
– 'Views of Canadian Literature.' *The Week,* 23 March 1894, 391–2.
– 'Voices Crying in the Wilderness.' *The Week,* 13 February 1891, 169–70.
– 'Woman's Work.' *Rose-Belford's Canadian Monthly and National Review,* August 1878, 295–311.
MacKay, Isabel Ecclestone. 'Pauline Johnson: A Reminiscence.' *Canadian Magazine* 41, no. 3 (1913): 273–8.
MacMillan, Carrie, Lorraine McMullen, and Elizabeth Waterston. *Silenced Sextet: Six Nineteenth-Century Canadian Women Novelists.* Montreal: McGill-Queen's University Press, 1993.
Mair, Charles. 'Pauline Johnson: An Appreciation.' *Canadian Magazine* 41, no. 3 (1913): 281–3.
Martin, Peggy, ed. *Lily Lewis: Sketches of a Canadian Journalist.* Calgary: University of Calgary Press, 2006.
Mattingly, Carol. *Well-Tempered Women: Nineteenth-Century Temperance Rhetoric.* Carbondale: Southern Illinois University Press, 1998.
McClintock, Anne. *Imperial Leather: Race, Gender, and Sexuality in the Colonial Contest.* New York: Routledge, 1995.
McClung, Nellie L. Scrapbook collection. Provincial Archives of British Columbia, Victoria, British Columbia.
– *The Black-Creek Stopping House and Other Stories.* Toronto: Briggs, 1912.
– *Clearing in the West: My Own Story.* Toronto: Thomas Allen, 1935.
– *In Times Like These.* 1915. Reprint, Toronto: University of Toronto Press, 1972.
– *Leaves from Lantern Lane.* Toronto: Thomas Allen, 1936.
– *More Leaves from Lantern Lane.* Toronto: Thomas Allen, 1937.

- *The Second Chance*. Toronto: Briggs, 1910.
- *Sowing Seeds in Danny*. New York: Grosset & Dunlap, 1908.
- *The Stream Runs Fast: My Own Story*. Toronto: Thomas Allen, 1945.

McKillop, A.B. *A Disciplined Intelligence: Critical Inquiry and Canadian Thought in the Victorian Era*. Montreal: McGill-Queen's University Press, 1979.

McLaren, Angus. *Our Own Master Race: Eugenics in Canada, 1885–1945*. Toronto: McClelland and Stewart, 1990.

McMullin, Stan. *Anatomy of a Seance: A History of Spirit Communication in Central Canada*. Montreal and Kingston: McGill-Queen's University Press, 2004.

McRaye, Walter. *Pauline Johnson and Her Friends*. Toronto: Ryerson, 1947.

Milz, Sabine. "'Publica(c)tion': E. Pauline Johnson's Publishing Venues and Their Contemporary Significance.' *Studies in Canadian Literature* 29, no. 1 (2004): 127–45.

Mitchinson, Wendy. 'The WCTU: "For God, Home and Native Land": A Study in Nineteenth-Century Feminism.' In L. Kealey, *A Not Unreasonable Claim*, 151–67.

Montgomery, Lucy Maud. *Anne of Green Gables*. 1908. Reprint, Toronto: McClelland and Stewart, 1992.

Monture, Rick. '"Beneath the British Flag": Iroquois and Canadian Nationalism in the Work of Pauline Johnson and Duncan Campbell Scott.' *Essays on Canadian Writing* 75 (Winter 2002): 118–41.

Mount, Nick. *When Canadian Literature Moved to New York*. Toronto: University of Toronto Press, 2005.

O'Hagan, Thomas. 'Some Canadian Women Writers.' *The Week*, 25 September 1896, 1050–3.

The Ontario Public School History of England and Canada. Toronto: Macmillan Company, 1917.

Prentice, Alison, et al. *Canadian Women: A History*. Toronto: Harcourt, Brace, Jovanovich, 1988.

Roberts, Wayne. '"Rocking the Cradle for the World": The New Woman and Maternal Feminism, Toronto, 1877–1914.' In L. Kealey, *A Not Unreasonable Claim*, 15–45.

Rutherford, Paul. *A Victorian Authority: The Daily Press in Late Nineteenth-Century Canada*. Toronto: University of Toronto Press, 1982.

Savage, Candace. *Our Nell: A Scrapbook Biography of Nellie L. McClung*. Saskatoon: Western Producer Prairie Books, 1979.

Strong-Boag, Veronica. 'Ever a Crusader: Nellie McClung, First-Wave Feminist.' In *Rethinking Canada: The Promise of Women's History*, ed. Veronica Strong-Boag and Anita Clair Fellman. 3rd ed. Toronto: Oxford University Press, 1997. 271–84.

– Introduction. In McClung, *In Times Like These*. 1915. Reprint, Toronto: University of Toronto Press, 1972. vii–xxii.

Strong-Boag, Veronica, and Carole Gerson. *Paddling Her Own Canoe: The Times and Texts of Pauline Johnson (Tekahionwake)*. Toronto: University of Toronto Press, 2000.

Tausky, Thomas E. *Sara Jeannette Duncan: Novelist of Empire*. Port Credit: P.D. Meany, 1980.

– ed. *Sara Jeannette Duncan: Selected Journalism*. Ottawa: Tecumseh, 1978.

Trofimenkoff, Susan. 'One Hundred and Two Muffled Voices: Canada's Industrial Women in the 1880's.' In *Canada's Age of Industry, 1849–1896*, ed. Michael S. Cross and Gregory S. Kealey. Toronto: McClelland and Stewart, 1982. 212–29.

Uncle Thomas. 'Impressions.' Toronto *Globe*, 18 January 1892, 4–6.

Valverde, Mariana. *The Age of Light, Soap, and Water*. Toronto: McClelland and Stewart, 1991.

– '"When the Mother of the Race Is Free": Race, Reproduction, and Sexuality in First-Wave Feminism.' In *Gender Conflicts: New Essays in Women's History*, ed. Franca Iacovetta and Mariana Valverde. Toronto: University of Toronto Press, 1992. 3–26.

Van Steen, Marcus. *Pauline Johnson: Her Life and Work*. Toronto: Hodder and Stoughton, 1965.

Vipond, Mary. 'Blessed Are the Peacemakers: The Labour Question in Canadian Social Gospel Fiction.' *Journal of Canadian Studies* 10, no. 3 (August 1975): 32–43.

Warne, Randi R. *Literature as Pulpit: The Christian Social Activism of Nellie L. McClung*. Waterloo: Wilfrid Laurier University Press, 1993.

Warsh, Cheryl Krasnick. '"Oh, Lord, pour a cordial in her wounded heart': The Drinking Woman in Victorian and Edwardian Canada.' In *Drink in Canada: Historical Essays*, ed. Cheryl Krasnick Warsh. Montreal: McGill-Queen's University Press, 1993. 70–91.

Wetherald, A. Ethelwyn. 'Some Canadian Literary Women – II: Fidelis.' *The Week*, 5 April 1888, 300–1.

Williams, Andrea. 'Flora MacDonald Denison and the Rhetoric of the Early Women's Suffrage Movement in Canada.' In *The Changing Tradition: Women in the History of Rhetoric*, ed. Christine Mason Sutherland and Rebecca Sutcliffe. Calgary: University of Calgary Press, 1999. 173–82.

York, Lorraine. '"Your Star": Pauline Johnson and the Tensions of Celebrity Discourse.' *Canadian Poetry* 51 (Fall/Winter 2002): 8–17.

Youmans, Letitia. *Campaign Echoes: The Autobiography of Mrs. Letitia Youmans, the Pioneer of the White Ribbon Movement in Canada*. Toronto: Briggs, 1893.

Illustration Credits

Agnes Maule Machar. Courtesy of Queen's University Archives, Kingston Picture Collection, image V23 P-3.

Sara Jeannette Duncan. Courtesy of Library and Archives Canada, Johnston and Hoffman, image C-045447.

E. Pauline Johnson. Courtesy of BC Archives, image A-09684.

Kathleen Coleman. Courtesy of Library and Archives Canada, Marceau / Kathleen Blake Coleman fonds, image PA-164721.

Flora MacDonald Denison. Courtesy of Thomas Fisher Rare Book Library, University of Toronto, Denison papers, Ms. Collection 51, box 4, folder 48.

Nellie L. McClung. Courtesy of Glenbow Archives, image NA-1641-1.

Index